# Developing Graphics Frameworks
# with Java and OpenGL

# Developing Graphics Frameworks with Java and OpenGL

Lee Stemkoski

James Cona

CRC Press
Taylor & Francis Group
Boca Raton London New York

CRC Press is an imprint of the
Taylor & Francis Group, an **informa** business

First edition published 2022
by CRC Press
6000 Broken Sound Parkway NW, Suite 300, Boca Raton, FL 33487-2742

and by CRC Press
4 Park Square, Milton Park, Abingdon, Oxon, OX14 4RN

*CRC Press is an imprint of Taylor & Francis Group, LLC*

---

**Library of Congress Cataloging-in-Publication Data**

---

Names: Stemkoski, Lee, author. | Cona, James, author.
Title: Developing graphics frameworks with Java and OpenGL / Lee Stemkoski, James Cona.
Description: First edition. | Boca Raton, FL : CRC Press, 2022. | Includes bibliographical references and index.
Identifiers: LCCN 2021056181 | ISBN 9780367720834 (hbk) | ISBN 9780367720698 (pbk) | ISBN 9781003153375 (ebk)
Subjects: LCSH: OpenGL. | Java (Computer program language) | Computer graphics--Computer programs.
Classification: LCC T386.O64 S739 2022 | DDC 006.6--dc23/eng/20220104
LC record available at https://lccn.loc.gov/2021056181

---

ISBN: 978-0-367-72083-4 (hbk)
ISBN: 978-0-367-72069-8 (pbk)
ISBN: 978-1-003-15337-5 (ebk)

DOI: 10.1201/9781003153375

Typeset in Minion
by KnowledgeWorks Global Ltd.

# Contents

# About the Authors

**Lee Stemkoski** is a professor of mathematics and computer science. He earned his Ph.D. in mathematics from Dartmouth College in 2006 and has been teaching at the college level since. His specialties are computer graphics, video game development, and virtual and augmented reality programming.

**James Cona** is an up and coming software engineer who studied computer science at Adelphi University. Some of his specific interests include music, video game programming, 3D graphics, artificial intelligence, and clear and efficient software development in general.

# CHAPTER 1

# Introduction to Computer Graphics

The importance of computer graphics in modern society is illustrated by the great quantity and a variety of applications and their impact on our daily lives. Computer graphics can be two-dimensional (2D) or three-dimensional (3D), animated, and interactive. They are used in data visualization to identify patterns and relationships, and also in scientific visualization, enabling researchers to model, explore, and understand natural phenomena. Computer graphics are used for medical applications such as magnetic resonance imaging (MRI) and computed tomography (CT) scans, and architectural applications, such as creating blueprints or virtual models. They enable the creation of tools such as training simulators and software for computer-aided engineering and design. Many aspects of the entertainment industry make use of computer graphics to some extent: movies may use them for special effects, generating photorealistic characters, or rendering entire films, while video games are primarily interactive graphics-based experiences. Recent advances in computer graphics hardware and software have even helped virtual reality and augmented reality technology enter the consumer market.

The field of computer graphics is continuously advancing, finding new applications, and increasing in importance. For all these reasons, combined with the inherent appeal of working in a highly visual medium, the field of computer graphics is an exciting area to learn about, experiment with, and work in. In this book, you'll learn how to create a robust framework capable of rendering and animating interactive 3D scenes using modern graphics programming techniques.

Before diving into programming and code, you'll first need to learn about the core concepts and vocabulary in computer graphics. These ideas will be revisited repeatedly throughout this book, and so it may help to periodically review parts of this chapter to keep the overall process in mind. In the second half of this chapter, you'll learn how to install the necessary software and set up your development environment.

DOI: 10.1201/9781003153375-1

## 1.1 CORE CONCEPTS AND VOCABULARY

Our primary goal is to generate 2D images of 3D scenes; this process is called *rendering* the scene. Scenes may contain 2D and 3D objects, from simple geometric shapes such as boxes and spheres to complex models representing real-world or imaginary objects such as teapots or alien lifeforms. These objects may simply appear to be of a single color, or their appearance may be affected by *textures* (images applied to surfaces), light sources that result in *shading* (the darkness of an object not in direct light) and *shadows* (the silhouette of one object's shape on the surface of another object), or environmental properties such as fog. Scenes are rendered from the point of view of a virtual camera, whose relative position and orientation in the scene, together with its intrinsic properties such as angle of view and depth of field, determine which objects will be visible or partially obscured by other objects when the scene is rendered. A 3D scene containing multiple shaded objects and a virtual camera is illustrated in Figure 1.1. The region contained within the truncated pyramid shape outlined in white (called a *frustum*) indicates the space visible to the camera. In Figure 1.1, this region completely contains the red and green cubes, but contains only part of the blue sphere, and the yellow cylinder lies completely outside of this region. The results of rendering the scene in Figure 1.1 is shown in Figure 1.2.

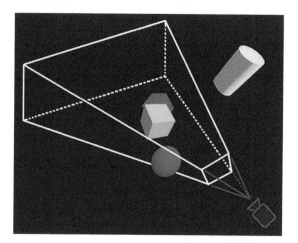

FIGURE 1.1   Three-dimensional scene with geometric objects, viewing region (white outline), and virtual camera (lower right).

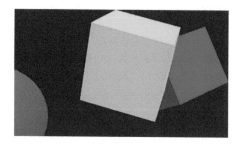

FIGURE 1.2   Results of rendering the scene from Figure 1.1.

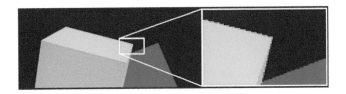

FIGURE 1.3    Zooming in on an image to illustrate individual pixels.

From a more technical, lower-level perspective, rendering a scene produces a *raster* – an array of pixels (picture elements) that will be displayed on a screen, arranged in a 2D grid. Pixels are typically extremely small; zooming in on an image can illustrate the presence of individual pixels, as shown in Figure 1.3.

On modern computer systems, pixels specify colors using triples of floating-point numbers between 0 and 1 to represent the amount of red, green, and blue light present in a color; a value of 0 represents no amount of that color is present, while a value of 1 represents that color is displayed at full (100%) intensity. These three colors are typically used since photoreceptors in the human eye take in those particular colors. The triple $(1, 0, 0)$ represents red, $(0, 1, 0)$ represents green, and $(0, 0, 1)$ represents blue. Black and white are represented by $(0, 0, 0)$ and $(1, 1, 1)$, respectively. Additional colors and their corresponding triples of values specifying the amounts of red, green, and blue (often called *RGB values*) are illustrated in Figure 1.4.

The quality of an image depends in part on its *resolution* (the number of pixels in the raster) and *precision* (the number of bits used for each pixel). As each bit has two possible values (0 or 1), the number of colors that can be expressed with N-bit precision is $2^N$. For example, early video game consoles with 8-bit graphics were able to display $2^8 = 256$ different colors. Monochrome displays could be said to have 1-bit graphics, while modern displays often feature "high color" (16-bit, 65,536 color) or "true color" (24-bit, more than 16 million colors) graphics. Figure 1.5 illustrates the same image rendered with high precision but different resolutions, while Figure 1.6 illustrates the same image rendered with high resolution but different precision levels.

In computer science, a *buffer* (or *data buffer*, or *buffer memory*) is a part of a computer's memory that serves as temporary storage for data while it is being moved from one location to another. Pixel data is stored in a region of memory called the *frame buffer*. A frame buffer

| | R | G | B | | | R | G | B |
|---|---|---|---|---|---|---|---|---|
| red | | 1 | 0 | 0 | black | | 0 | 0 | 0 |
| orange | | 1 | 0.5 | 0 | white | | 1 | 1 | 1 |
| yellow | | 1 | 1 | 0 | gray | | 0.5 | 0.5 | 0.5 |
| green | | 0 | 1 | 0 | brown | | 0.5 | 0.2 | 0 |
| blue | | 0 | 0 | 1 | pink | | 1 | 0.5 | 0.5 |
| violet | | 0.5 | 0 | 1 | cyan | | 0 | 1 | 1 |

FIGURE 1.4    Various colors and their corresponding (RGB) values.

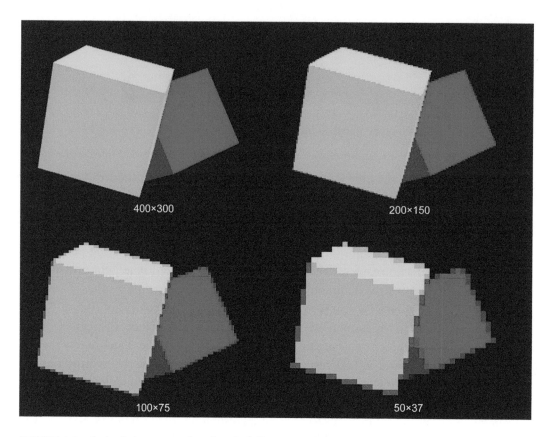

FIGURE 1.5   A single image rendered with different resolutions.

may contain multiple buffers that store different types of data for each pixel. At a minimum, the frame buffer must contain a *color buffer*, which stores RGB values. When rendering a 3D scene, the frame buffer must also contain a *depth buffer*, which stores distances from points on scene objects to the virtual camera. Depth values are used to determine whether the various points on each object are in front of or behind other objects (from the camera's perspective), and thus whether they will be visible when the scene is rendered. If one scene object obscures another and a transparency effect is desired, the renderer makes use of *alpha values*: floating-point numbers between 0 and 1 that specify how overlapping colors should be blended together; the value 0 indicates a fully transparent color, while the value 1 indicates a fully opaque color. Alpha values are also stored in the color buffer along with RGB color values; the combined data is often referred to as RGBA color values. Finally, frame buffers may contain a buffer called a *stencil buffer*, which may be used to store values used in generating advanced effects, such as shadows, reflections, or portal rendering.

   In addition to rendering 3D scenes, another goal in computer graphics is to create animated scenes. Animations consist of a sequence of images displayed in quick enough succession that the viewer interprets the objects in the images to be continuously moving or changing in appearance. Each image that is displayed is called a *frame*. The speed at which

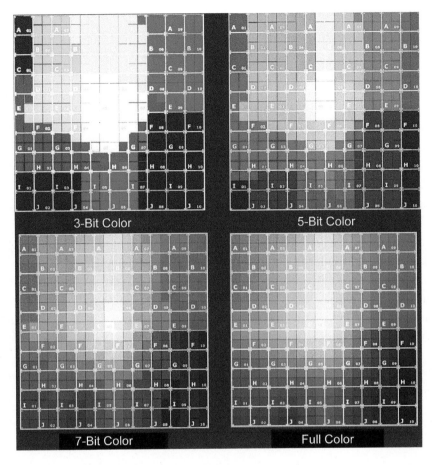

FIGURE 1.6    A single image rendered with different precisions.

these images appear is called the *frame rate* and is measured in *frames per second* (FPS). The standard frame rate for movies and television is 24 FPS. Computer monitors typically display graphics at 60 FPS. For virtual reality simulations, developers aim to attain 90 FPS, as lower frame rates may cause disorientation and other negative side effects in users. Since computer graphics must render these images in real-time, often in response to user inter-action, it is vital that computers be able to do so quickly.

In the early 1990s, computers relied on the *central processing unit* (CPU) circuitry to perform the calculations needed for graphics. As real-time 3D graphics became increas-ingly common in video game platforms (including arcades, gaming consoles, and per-sonal computers), there was increased demand for specialized hardware for rendering these graphics. This led to the development of the *graphics processing unit* (GPU), a term coined by the Sony Corporation that referred to the circuitry in their PlayStation video game console, released in 1994. The Sony GPU performed graphics-related computational tasks including managing a framebuffer, drawing polygons with textures, and shading and transparency effects. The term GPU was popularized by the Nvidia Corporation in 1999 with their release of the GeForce 256, a single-chip processor that performed geometric transformations and lighting calculations in addition to the rendering computations performed by earlier hardware implementations. Nvidia was the first company to produce a GPU capable of being programmed by developers: each geometric vertex could be processed by a short program, as could every rendered pixel, before the resulting image was displayed on screen. This processor, the GeForce 3, was introduced in 2001 and was also used in the XBox video game console. In general, GPUs feature a highly parallel structure that enables them to be more efficient than CPUs for rendering computer graphics. As computer technology advances, so does the quality of the graphics that can be rendered; modern systems are able to produce real-time photorealistic graphics at high resolutions.

Programs that are run by GPUs are called *shaders*, initially so named because they were used for shading effects, but now used to perform many different computations required in the rendering process. Just as there are many high-level programming languages (such as Java, Javascript, and Python) used to develop CPU-based applications, there are many shader programming languages. Each shader language implements an *application programming interface* (API), which defines a set of commands, functions, and protocols that can be used to interact with an external system – in this case, the GPU. Some APIs and their corresponding shader languages include:

- the DirectX API and High-Level Shading Language (HLSL), used on Microsoft platforms, including the XBox game console

- the Metal API and Metal Shading Language, which runs on modern Mac computers, iPhones, and iPads

- the OpenGL (Open Graphics Library) API and OpenGL Shading Language (GLSL), a cross-platform library

This book will focus on OpenGL, as it is the most widely adopted graphics API. As a cross-platform library, visual results will be consistent on any supported operating system. Furthermore, OpenGL can be used in concert with a variety of high-level languages using *bindings*: software libraries that bridge two programming languages, enabling functions from one language to be used in another. For example, some bindings to OpenGL include:

- JOGL (https://jogamp.org/jogl/www/) for Java

- WebGL (https://www.khronos.org/webgl/) for Javascript

- PyOpenGL (http://pyopengl.sourceforge.net/) for Python

The initial version of OpenGL was released by Silicon Graphics, Inc. (SGI) in 1992, and has been managed by the Khronos Group since 2006. The Khronos Group is a non-profit technology consortium, whose members include graphics card manufacturers and general technology companies. New versions of the OpenGL specification are released regularly to support new features and functions. In this book, you will learn about many of the

OpenGL functions that allow you to take advantage of the graphics capabilities of the GPU and render some truly impressive 3D scenes. The steps involved in this rendering process are described in detail in the sections that follow.

## 1.2 THE GRAPHICS PIPELINE

A *graphics pipeline* is an abstract model that describes a sequence of steps needed to render a 3D scene. Pipelining allows a computational task to be split into subtasks, each of which can be worked on in parallel, similar to an assembly line for manufacturing products in a factory, which increases overall efficiency. Graphics pipelines increase the efficiency of the rendering process, enabling images to be displayed at faster rates. Multiple pipeline models are possible; the one described in this section is commonly used for rendering real-time graphics using OpenGL, which consists of four stages (illustrated by Figure 1.7):

- *Application Stage:* initializing the window where rendered graphics will be displayed; sending data to the GPU.

- *Geometry Processing:* determining the position of each vertex of the geometric shapes to be rendered, implemented by a program called a vertex shader.

- *Rasterization:* determining which pixels correspond to the geometric shapes to be rendered.

- *Pixel Processing:* determining the color of each pixel in the rendered image, involving a program called a fragment shader.

Each of these stages are described in more detail in the sections that follow; the next chapter contains code that will begin to implement many of the processes described here.

### 1.2.1 Application Stage

The application stage primarily involves processes that run on the CPU. One of the first tasks is to create a window where the rendered graphics will be displayed. When working with OpenGL, this can be accomplished using a variety of programming languages. The window (or a canvas-like object within the window) must be initialized so that the graphics are read from the GPU frame buffer. In the case of animated or interactive applications, the main application contains a loop that re-renders the scene repeatedly, typically aiming for a rate of 60 FPS. Other processes that may be handled by the CPU include monitoring hardware for user input events, or running algorithms for tasks such as physics simulation and collision detection.

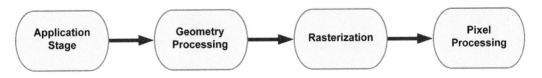

FIGURE 1.7 The graphics pipeline.

Another class of tasks performed by the application includes reading data required for the rendering process and sending it to the GPU. This data may include vertex attributes (which describe the appearance of the geometric shapes being rendered), images that will be applied to surfaces, and source code for the vertex shader and fragment shader programs (which will be used later on during the graphics pipeline). OpenGL describes the functions that can be used to transmit this data to the GPU; these functions are accessed through the bindings of the programming language used to write the application. Vertex attribute data is stored in GPU memory buffers called *vertex buffer objects* (VBOs), while images that will be used as textures are stored in *texture buffers*. It is important to note that this stored data is not initially assigned to any particular program variables; these associations are specified later. Finally, source code for the vertex shader and fragment shader programs needs to be sent to the GPU, compiled, and loaded. If needed, buffer data can be updated during the application's main loop, and additional data can be sent to shader programs as well.

Once the necessary data has been sent to the GPU, before rendering can take place, the application needs to specify the associations between attribute data stored in VBOs and attribute variables in the vertex shader program. A single geometric shape may have multiple attributes for each vertex (such as position and color), and the corresponding data is streamed from buffers to variables in the shader during the rendering process. It is also frequently necessary to work with many sets of such associations: there may be multiple geometric shapes (with data stored in different buffers) that are rendered by the same shader program, or each shape may be rendered by a different shader program. These sets of associations can be conveniently managed by using *vertex array objects* (VAOs), which store this information and can be activated and deactivated as needed during the rendering process.

## 1.2.2 Geometry Processing

In computer graphics, the shape of a geometric object is defined by a *mesh*: a collection of points that are grouped into lines or triangles, as illustrated in Figure 1.8.

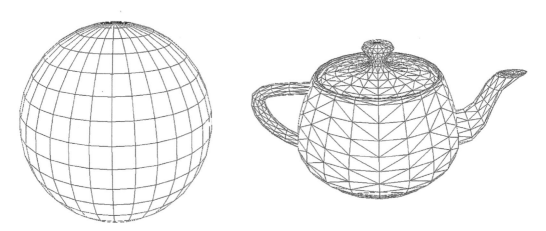

FIGURE 1.8   Wireframe meshes representing a sphere and a teapot.

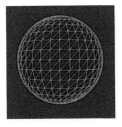  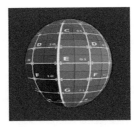 

FIGURE 1.9    Different renderings of a sphere: wireframe, vertex colors, texture, and with lighting effects.

In addition to the overall shape of an object, additional information may be required to describe how the object should be rendered. The properties or attributes that are specific to rendering each individual point are grouped together into a data structure called a *vertex*. At a minimum, a vertex must contain the 3D position of the corresponding point. Additional data contained by a vertex often includes:

- a color to be used when rendering the point

- *texture coordinates* (or *UV coordinates*), which indicate a point in an image that is mapped to the vertex

- *a normal vector*, which indicates the direction perpendicular to a surface, and are typically used in lighting calculations

Figure 1.9 illustrates different renderings of a sphere that make use of these attributes. Additional vertex attributes may be defined as needed.

During the geometry processing stage, the vertex shader is applied to each of the vertices; each attribute variable in the shader receives data from a buffer according to previously specified associations. The primary purpose of the vertex shader is to determine the final position of each point being rendered, which is typically calculated from a series of transformations:

- The collection of points defining the intrinsic shape of an object may be translated, rotated, and scaled so that the object appears to have a particular location, orientation, and size with respect to a virtual 3D world. This process is called *model transformation*; coordinates expressed from this frame of reference are said to be in *world space*.

- There may be a virtual camera with its own position and orientation in the virtual world. In order to render the world from the camera's point of view, the coordinates of each object in the world must be converted to a frame of reference relative to the camera itself. This process is called *view transformation*, and coordinates in this context are said to be in *view space* (or *camera space*, or *eye space*). The effect of the placement of the virtual camera on the rendered image is illustrated in Figure 1.10.

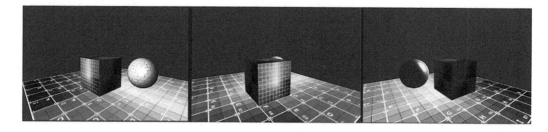

FIGURE 1.10    One scene rendered from multiple camera locations and angles.

- The set of points in the world considered to be visible, occupying either a box-shaped or frustum-shaped region, must be scaled to and aligned with the space rendered by OpenGL: a cube-shaped region consisting of all points whose coordinates are between −1 and 1. The position of each point returned by the vertex shader is assumed to be expressed in this frame of reference. Any points outside this region are automatically discarded or clipped from the scene; coordinates expressed at this stage are said to be in *clip space*. This task is accomplished with a *projection transformation*. More specifically, it is called *orthographic projection* or *perspective projection*, depending on whether the shape of the visible world region is a box or a frustum. A perspective projection is generally considered to produce more realistic images, as objects that are farther away from the virtual camera will require greater compression by the transformation and thus appear smaller when the scene is rendered. The differences between the two types of projections are illustrated in Figure 1.11.

In addition to these transformation calculations, the vertex shader may perform additional calculations and send additional information to the fragment shader as needed.

### 1.2.3 Rasterization

Once the final positions of each vertex have been specified by the vertex shader, the rasterization stage begins. The points themselves must first be grouped into the desired type of *geometric primitive*: points, lines, or triangles, which consist of sets of 1, 2, or 3 points. In the case of lines or triangles, additional information must be specified. For example, consider an array of points [A, B, C, D, E, F] to be grouped into lines. They could be grouped

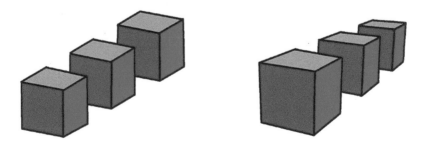

FIGURE 1.11    A series of cubes rendered with orthogonal projection (left) and perspective projection (right).

in disjoint pairs, as in (A, B), (C, D), (E, F), resulting in a set of disconnected line segments. Alternatively, they could be grouped in overlapping pairs, as in (A, B), (B, C), (C, D), (D, E), (E, F), resulting in a set of connected line segments (called a *line strip*). The type of geometric primitive and method for grouping points is specified using an OpenGL function parameter when the rendering process begins. The process of grouping points into geometric primitives is called *primitive assembly*.

Once the geometric primitives have been assembled, the next step is to determine which pixels correspond to the interior of each geometric primitive. Since pixels are discrete units, they will typically only approximate the continuous nature of a geometric shape, and a criterion must be given to clarify which pixels are in the interior. Three simple criteria could be:

- the entire pixel area is contained within the shape

- the center point of the pixel is contained within the shape

- any part of the pixel is contained within the shape

These effects of applying each of these criteria to a triangle is illustrated in Figure 1.12, where the original triangle appears outlined in blue, and pixels meeting the criteria are shaded gray.

For each pixel corresponding to the interior of a shape, a *fragment* is created: a collection of data used to determine the color of a single pixel in a rendered image. The data stored in a fragment always includes the *raster position*, also called *pixel coordinates*. When rendering a 3D scene, fragments will also store a *depth value*, which is needed when points on different geometric objects would overlap from the perspective of the viewer. When this happens, the associated fragments would correspond to the same pixel, and the depth value determines which fragment's data should be used when rendering this pixel.

Additional data may be assigned to each vertex, such as a color, and passed along from the vertex shader to the fragment shader. In this case, a new data field is added to each fragment. The value assigned to this field at each interior point is *interpolated* from the values at the vertices: calculated using a weighted average, depending on the distance from the interior point to each vertex. The closer an interior point is to a vertex, the greater the weight of that vertex's value when calculating the interpolated value. For example, if the

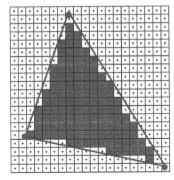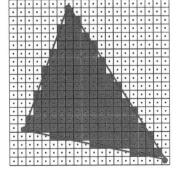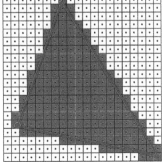

FIGURE 1.12   Different criteria for rasterizing a triangle.

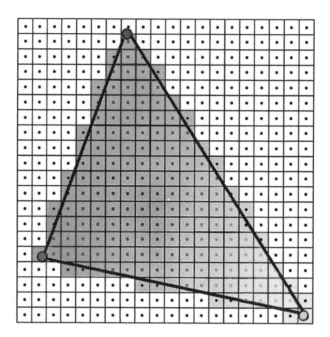

FIGURE 1.13    Interpolating color attributes.

vertices of a triangle are assigned the colors red, green, and blue, then each pixel corresponding to the interior of the triangle will be assigned a combination of these colors, as illustrated in Figure 1.13.

## 1.2.4  Pixel Processing

The primary purpose of this stage is to determine the final color of each pixel, storing this data in the color buffer within the frame buffer. During the first part of the pixel processing stage, a program called fragment shader is applied to each of the fragments to calculate their final color. This calculation may involve a variety of data stored in each fragment, in combination with data globally available during rendering, such as:

- a base color applied to the entire shape

- colors stored in each fragment (interpolated from vertex colors)

- textures (images applied to the surface of the shape, illustrated by Figure 1.14), where colors are sampled from locations specified by texture coordinates

- light sources, whose relative position and/or orientation may lighten or darken the color, depending on the direction the surface is facing at a point, specified by normal vectors

Some aspects of the pixel processing stage are automatically handled by the GPU. For example, the depth values stored in each fragment are used in this stage to resolve visibility issues in a 3D scene, determining which parts of objects are blocked from view by other objects. After the color of a fragment has been calculated, the fragment's depth value will

FIGURE 1.14    An image file (left) used as a texture for a 3D object (right).

be compared to the value currently stored in the depth buffer at the corresponding pixel coordinates. If the fragment's depth value is smaller than the depth buffer value, then the corresponding point is closer to the viewer than any that were previously processed, and the fragment's color will be used to overwrite the data currently stored in the color buffer at the corresponding pixel coordinates.

Transparency is also handled by the GPU, using the alpha values stored in the color of each fragment. The alpha value of a color is used to indicate how much of this color should be blended with another color. For example, when combining a color $C1$ with an alpha value of 0.6 with another color $C2$, the resulting color will be created by adding 60% of the value from each component of $C1$ to 40% of the value from each component of $C2$. Figure 1.15 illustrates a simple scene involving transparency.

FIGURE 1.15    Rendered scene with transparency.

However, rendering transparent objects has some complex subtleties. These calculations occur at the same time that depth values are being resolved, and so scenes involving transparency must render objects in a particular order: all opaque objects must be rendered first (in any order), followed by transparent objects ordered from the farthest to the closest with respect to the virtual camera. Not following this order may cause transparency effects to fail. For example, consider a scene, such as that in Figure 1.15, containing a single transparent object close to the camera and multiple opaque objects farther from the camera that appear behind the transparent object. Assume that, contrary to the previously described rendering order, the transparent object is rendered first, followed by the opaque objects in some unknown order. When the fragments of the opaque objects are processed, their depth value will be greater than the value stored in the depth buffer (corresponding to the closer transparent object), and so the opaque fragments' color data will automatically be discarded, rather than blended with the currently stored color. Even attempting to use the alpha value of the transparent object stored in the color buffer in this example does not resolve the underlying issue, because when the fragments of each opaque object are being rendered, it is not possible at this point to determine if they may have been occluded from view by another opaque fragment (only the closest depth value, corresponding to the transparent object, is stored), and thus it is unknown which opaque fragment's color values should be blended into the color buffer.

## 1.3 SETTING UP A DEVELOPMENT ENVIRONMENT

Most parts of the graphics pipeline discussed in the previous section – geometry processing, rasterization, and pixel processing – are handled by the GPU, and as mentioned previously, this book will use OpenGL for these tasks. For developing the application, there are many programming languages one could select from. This book will explain how to use Java to develop these applications, as well as a complete graphics framework to simplify the design and creation of interactive, animated, 3D scenes.

When beginning a large project, it is helpful to use an *integrated development environment* (IDE) to organize your code. One highly recommended IDE is IntelliJ because it includes features such as automatically compiling import statements for your classes, and automatic completion of functions, methods, and variable names as you type. You may use a different development environment if you wish, in which case you may skip ahead to Chapter 2.

To install IntelliJ, which was created by a software development company named JetBrains, use a web browser to navigate to the web page https://www.jetbrains.com/idea/. The current version of the website is illustrated in Figure 1.16; to proceed, click the download button.

Installation programs are available for Windows, Mac OS X, and a variety of other platforms. The freely available "Community Edition," illustrated in Figure 1.17, will be sufficient for developing the framework in this book.

IntelliJ is bundled with a *Java Development Kit* (JDK), which is the software used to compile and run Java code, so there is no need to install anything else.

FIGURE 1.16    Jetbrains homepage: https://www.jetbrains.com/idea/

To verify that everything has been installed correctly, it is traditional to write a "Hello, world!" program, which prints a message to a text console. To proceed, launch the IntelliJ software, and once it has opened (illustrated in Figure 1.18), select **New Project**.

By default, the JDK will be selected for you already. Click **Next** until a window appears where you can name the project. Name this project **Test** and click on **Finish**. After you do this, the IDE will perform background tasks to set up your environment. After a moment, the screen will display a folder hierarchy on the left, which includes the project and source files. Right-click on the **src** folder, highlight **New**, and click on **Java Class**, as shown in Figure 1.19.

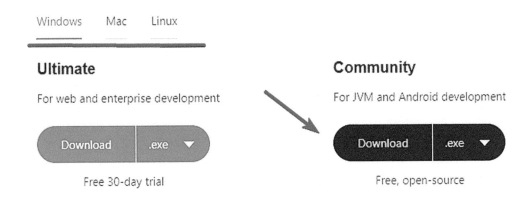

FIGURE 1.17    Jetbrains download page.

FIGURE 1.18    IntelliJ application start screen.

Name this class **HelloWorld**. (The corresponding file will automatically have the **.java** extension appended to the file.) Once this is done, you will see a file named HelloWorld. The file will contain a standard template code for a Java class. In this file, you only need to add a main method and a print statement. Add code so that the file appears as follows:

```java
public class HelloWorld
{
    public static void main(String[] args)
    {
        System.out.println("Hello World!");
    }
}
```

At this point you can compile and run the program. In the context menu, click **Build > Build Project**. After it finishes building, click **Run > Run "HelloWorld."** In the bottom area of the window, you will see a text console containing the output of your program, illustrated in Figure 1.20.

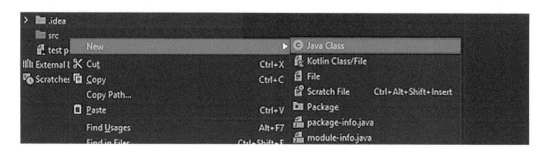

FIGURE 1.19    Creating a new Java class.

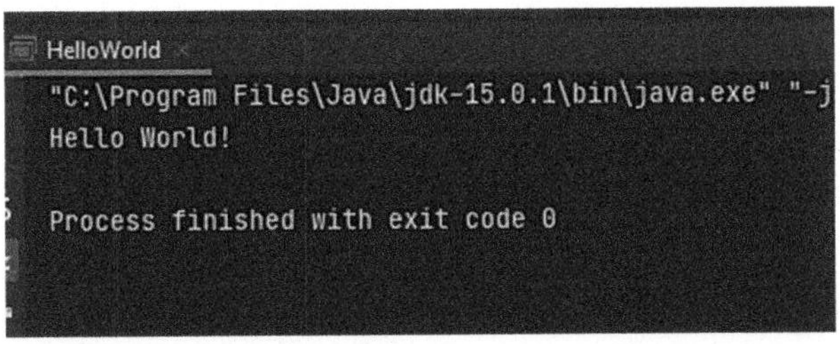

FIGURE 1.20   Running the HelloWorld program.

Once you see this output, you can be confident that IntelliJ has been installed and configured correctly.

## 1.4 SUMMARY AND NEXT STEPS

In this chapter, you learned about the core concepts and vocabulary used in computer graphics, including rendering, buffers, GPUs, and shaders. Then you learned about the four major stages in the graphics pipeline: the application stage, geometry processing, rasterization, and pixel processing; this section introduced additional terminology, including vertices, VBOs, VAOs, transformations, projections, fragments, and interpolation. Finally, you learned how to set up the Java development environment IntelliJ. In the next chapter, you will use Java to start implementing the graphics framework that will realize these theoretical principles.

# CHAPTER 2

# Introduction to LWJGL and OpenGL

In this chapter, you will learn how to create windows with the *Lightweight Java Game Library* (LWJGL) and how to draw graphics in these windows with OpenGL. You will start by rendering a point, followed by lines and triangles with a single color. Then you will draw multiple shapes with multiple colors, create a series of animations involving movement and color transitions, and implement interactive applications with keyboard-controlled movement.

## 2.1 CREATING WINDOWS WITH LWJGL

As indicated in the discussion of the graphics pipeline, the first step in rendering graphics is to develop an application where graphics will be displayed. This can be accomplished with a variety of programming languages; throughout this book, you will write windowed applications using Java and LWJGL, a popular Java game development library.

As you write code, it is important to keep several software engineering principles in mind, including organization, reusability, and extensibility. To support these principles, the software developed in this book uses an object-oriented design approach. To start, create a new project named **Java Graphics Framework**; throughout this book, it will be assumed that you are using IntelliJ, in which case you follow the same process described in Chapter 1 to create a new project. It is a standard while organizing project files to use a folder named **src** to store all source code, while other folders will be used for compiled class files or assets such as text and image files.

Within your project, you will also need to include the LWJGL libraries. This consists of a collection of classes stored in *Java Archive* files, also called JAR files, and indicated by the **.jar** extension. The necessary files can be downloaded from the code repository for this book. Alternatively, you may download the files directly from the LWJGL website: **http://lwjgl.org**. At the time of writing, the website enables you to download a customized collection of the JAR files you need as a ZIP file; you should select the native files for your operating system (Windows, MacOS, or Linux), the LWJGL core, the OpenGL components, and the STB components (which are used for working with image files in Chapter 5).

Once you have obtained the LWJGL JAR files, you need to add them to your project. Traditionally, they are added to a folder named **lib** (short for "libraries"). Navigate to your project folder, create a folder named **lib**, and copy all the JAR files into this new folder. After doing so, you will have to configure your development environment to recognize these files as dependencies, which enables you to write code using the classes stored in these files. The process will vary depending on your development environment. To do so with IntelliJ, in the menu bar, select **File** > **Project Structure**. In the window that appears, under the heading **Project Settings**, select **Modules**, and then click the + icon. Choose the option titled **JARs or Directories**. From the file browser window that appears next, navigate to and select the **lib** folder that you just created, and then click the OK button. This configures your project to use the code in this directory when compiling your applications.

In Java, a *package* is a directory containing classes that can be imported into applications; these will be used to further sort the code developed in this framework. First, create a new package named **core** by right-clicking the **src** folder, and selecting **New** > **Package**. Next, right click on the **core** package and create a new Java class called **Base**; this will be the class that initializes LWJGL and configures and displays the application window.

Anticipating that the applications created will eventually feature user interaction and animation, this class will be designed to handle the standard phases or "life cycle" of such an application:

- *Startup:* During this stage, objects are created, values are initialized, and any required external files are loaded.

- *The Main Loop:* This stage repeats continuously (typically 60 times per second) while the application is running, and consists of the following three substages:

  - *Process Input:* Check if the user has performed any action that sends data to the computer, such as pressing keys on a keyboard or clicking buttons on a mouse.

  - *Update:* Changing values of variables and objects.

  - *Render:* Create graphics that are displayed on the screen.

- *Shutdown:* This stage typically begins when the user performs an action indicating that the program should stop running (for example, by clicking a button to quit the application). This stage may involve tasks such as signaling the application to stop checking for user input and closing any windows that were created by the application.

These phases are illustrated by the flowchart in Figure 2.1.

The **Base** class will be designed to be extended by the various applications throughout this book. In accordance with the principle of modularization, processing user input will

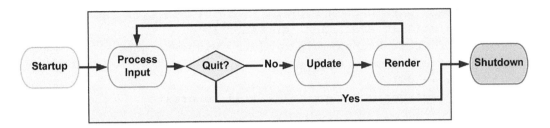

FIGURE 2.1    The phases of an interactive graphics-based application.

be handled by a separate class named **Input** that you will create later. In the **Base** Java class that you created, change the class definition to **public abstract class Base** and add the following code, which contains variables that are used when initializing the application window:

```
// window dimensions
private int windowWidth;
private int windowHeight;
// the window handle
private long window;
// is the main loop currently active?
private boolean running;
```

Afterwards, add the following code to define a set of methods, which will correspond to the different phases of the application life cycle. The code for the abstract methods will be supplied by classes extending the **Base** class, while the code for the remaining methods will be added later in this section.

```
public Base() { }
public void startup() { }
public abstract void initialize();
public abstract void update();
public void run(int windowWidth, int windowHeight) { }
public void shutdown() { }
```

To begin, in the **startup** method, insert the following code:

```
// initialize GLFW
boolean initSuccess = glfwInit();
if ( !initSuccess )
    throw new RuntimeException("Unable to initialize GLFW");

// create window and associated OpenGL context,
//   which stores framebuffer and other state information
glfwWindowHint(GLFW_CONTEXT_VERSION_MAJOR, 3);
glfwWindowHint(GLFW_CONTEXT_VERSION_MINOR, 2);
```

```
glfwWindowHint(GLFW_OPENGL_PROFILE, GLFW_OPENGL_CORE_PROFILE);
glfwWindowHint(GLFW_RESIZABLE, GL_FALSE);
window = glfwCreateWindow( windowWidth, windowHeight,
     "Graphics Window", 0, 0);
if ( window == 0 )
     throw new RuntimeException("Failed to create      the GLFW
window");

running = true;

// make all OpenGL function calls
//    apply to this context instance
glfwMakeContextCurrent(window);

// specify number of screen updates
//    to wait before swapping buffers.
// setting to 1 synchronizes application frame rate
//    with display refresh rate;
//    prevents visual "screen tearing" artifacts
glfwSwapInterval(1);
// detect current context and makes
//    OpenGL bindings available for use
GL.createCapabilities();
```

Next, inside the **run** method, insert the following code, which calls the methods corresponding to the phases of the application life cycle in the appropriate order:

```
this.windowWidth  = windowWidth;
this.windowHeight = windowHeight;

startup();

// application-specific startup code
initialize();

// main loop
while (running)
{
    // check for user interaction events
    glfwPollEvents();

    // check if window close icon is clicked
    if ( glfwWindowShouldClose(window) )
        running = false;

    // application-specific update code
    update();
```

```
    // swap the color buffers
    //  to display rendered graphics on screen
    glfwSwapBuffers(window);
}
```

```
shutdown();
```

Finally, inside the **shutdown** method, insert the following code:

```
// stop window monitoring for user input
glfwFreeCallbacks(window);
```

```
// close the window
glfwDestroyWindow(window);
```

```
// stop GLFW
glfwTerminate();
```

```
// stop error callback
glfwSetErrorCallback(null).free();
```

That concludes the code for the **Base** class for now; additional functionality will be added later to process user interaction. In addition to the comments throughout the code above, the following observations are noteworthy:

- The **windowWidth and windowHeight** parameters can be changed as desired. At present, if the screen size is set to non-square dimensions, this will cause the rendered image to appear stretched along one direction. This issue will be addressed in Chapter 4 when discussing aspect ratios.

- The title of the window is set within the function **glfwCreateWindow()** and can be changed as desired.

- A rendering technique called *double buffering* is used, which employs two image buffers. The pixel data from one buffer is displayed on screen while new data is being written into a second buffer. When the new image is ready, the application switches which buffer is displayed on screen and which buffer will be written to; this is accomplished in LWJGL with the functions **glfwSwapInterval()** and **glfwSwap-Buffers()**. The double buffering technique eliminates an unwanted visual artifact called *screen tearing*, in which the pixels from a partially updated buffer are displayed on screen, which happens when a single buffer is used and the rendering cycles are not synchronized with the display refresh rate.

- Starting in OpenGL version 3.2 (introduced in 2009), *deprecation* was introduced: older functions were gradually replaced by more efficient versions, and future versions may no longer contain or support the older functions. This led to *core* and *compatibility profiles*: core profiles are only guaranteed to implement functions present in the current version of the API, while compatibility profiles will additionally support many functions that may have been deprecated. Each hardware vendor decides which versions of OpenGL will be supported by each profile. In recent versions of Mac OS X (10.7 and later) at the time of writing, the core profile supported is 3.2, while the compatibility profile supported is 2.1. Since some of the OpenGL features (such as vertex array objects) that will be needed in constructing the graphics framework in this book were introduced in OpenGL Shading Language (GLSL) version 3.0, a core profile is specified for maximum cross-platform compatibility, using the function **glfwWindowHint()**

- The function **glfwWindowHint()**also allows you to configure the window properties.

- The **initialize** and **update** functions are meant to be implemented by the applications that extend this class.

- The **run** function contains all the phases of an interactive graphics-based application, as described previously; the corresponding code is indicated by comments beginning with **//**.

Next you are ready to test out the **Base** class and create a windowed application. First, in the **src** folder, create a new Java class named **Test_2_1**. Inside this newly created class, insert the following code:

```java
import core.Base;

public class Test_2_1 extends Base
{
    public void initialize()
    {
        System.out.println("Initializing program...");
    }

    public void update() { }

    // driver method
    public static void main(String[] args)
    {
        new Test_2_1().run();
    }
}
```

You can now build and run your program. A simple message is printed to the console during initialization. However, no print statements are present in the **update** function, as attempting to print text 60 times per second would cause extreme slowdown in any program. Run this program, and you should see a blank window appear on screen (as

FIGURE 2.2    The LWJGL window.

illustrated in Figure 2.2) and the text "**Initializing program...**" will appear in the terminal or console area. When you click on the button to close the window, the window should close, as expected.

## 2.2 DRAWING A POINT

Now that you can create a windowed application, the next goal is to render a single point on the screen. You will accomplish this by writing the simplest possible vertex shader and fragment shader, using OpenGL Shading Language. You will then learn how to compile and link the shaders to create a graphics processing unit (GPU) program. Finally, you will extend the framework begun in the previous section to use GPU programs to display graphics in the LWJGL application window.

### 2.2.1 OpenGL Shading Language

GLSL is a C-style language, as is Java. Similar to Java, there are "if statements" to process conditional statements, "for loops" to iterate a group of statements over a range of values, "while loops" to iterate a group of statements as long as a given condition is true, and functions that take a set of inputs and perform some computations (and optionally return an output value). Like Java, variables in GLSL must be declared with an assigned type, the end of each statement must be indicated with a semicolon, statements are grouped using braces, comments are preceded by "//", and functions must specify the types of their input parameters and return value. The details of the differences in Java and GLSL syntax will be illustrated and indicated as the features are introduced in the examples throughout this book.

The basic data types in GLSL are boolean, integer, and floating point values, indicated by **bool**, **int**, and **float**, respectively. GLSL also has vector data types, which are often used to store values indicating positions, colors, and texture coordinates. Vectors may have two, three, or four components, indicated by **vec2**, **vec3**, and **vec4** (for vectors consisting of floats). As a C-like language, GLSL provides arrays and *structs*: user-defined data types. To facilitate graphics-related computations, GLSL also features matrix data types, which often store transformations (translation, rotation, scaling, and projections), and sampler data types, which represent textures; these will be introduced in later chapters.

The components of a vector data type can be accessed in multiple ways. For example, once a **vec4** named **v** has been initialized, its components can be accessed using array notation (**v[0]**, **v[1]**, **v[2]**, **v[3]** ), or using dot notation with any of the following three systems: ( **v.x, v.y, v.z, v.w** ) or ( **v.r, v.g, v.b, v.a** ) or ( **v.s, v.t, v.p, v.q** ). While all these systems are interchangeable, programmers typically choose a system related to the context for increased readability: (x, y, z, w) are used for positions, (r, g, b, a) are used for colors (red, green, blue, alpha), and (s, t, p, q) are used for texture coordinates.

Every shader must contain a function named **main**, similar to the C programming language. No values are returned (which is indicated by the keyword **void**) and there are no parameters required by the main function, thus every shader has the general following structure:

```
void main()
{
    // code statements here
}
```

In the description of the graphics pipeline from the previous chapter, it was mentioned that a vertex shader will receive data about the geometric shapes being rendered via buffers. At this point, you may be wondering how vertex attribute data is sent from buffers to a vertex shader if the **main** function takes no parameters. In general, data is passed in and out of shaders via variables that are declared with certain *type qualifiers*: additional keywords that modify the properties of a variable. For example, many programming languages have a qualifier to indicate that the value of a variable will remain constant; in GLSL, this is indicated by the keyword **const**. Additionally, when working with shaders, the keyword **in** indicates that the value of a variable will be supplied by the previous stage of the graphics pipeline, while the keyword **out** indicates that a value will be passed along to the next stage of the graphics pipeline. More specifically, in the context of a vertex shader, **in** indicates that values will be supplied from a buffer, while **out** indicates that values will be passed to the fragment shader. In the context of a fragment shader, **in** indicates that values will be supplied from the vertex shader (interpolated during the rasterization stage), while **out** indicates values will be stored in one of the various buffers (color, depth, or stencil).

There are two particular **out** variables that are required when writing shader code for a GPU program. First, recall that the ultimate goal of the vertex shader is to calculate the position of a point. OpenGL uses the built-in variable **gl_Position** to store this value;

a value must be assigned to this variable by the vertex shader. Second, recall that the ultimate goal of the fragment shader is to calculate the color of a pixel. Early versions of OpenGL used a built-in variable called **gl_FragColor** to store this value and each fragment shader was required to assign a value to this variable. Later versions of OpenGL require fragment shader code to explicitly declare an **out** variable for this purpose. Finally, it should be mentioned that both of these variables are **vec4** type variables. For storing color data, this makes sense as red, green, blue, and alpha (transparency) values are required. For storing position data, this is less intuitive, as a position in three-dimensional space can be specified using only $x$, $y$, and $z$ coordinates. By including a fourth coordinate (commonly called $w$ and set to the value 1), this makes it possible for geometric transformations (such as translation, rotation, scaling, and projection) to be represented by and calculated using a single matrix, which will be discussed in detail in Chapter 3.

As indicated at the beginning of this section, the current goal is to write a vertex shader and a fragment shader that will render a single point on the screen. The code presented here will avoid the use of buffers and exclusively use built-in variables. (You do not need to create any new files or enter any code at this time.) The vertex shader will consist of the following code:

```
void main()
{
    gl_Position = vec4(0.0, 0.0, 0.0, 1.0);
}
```

In early versions of OpenGL, the simplest possible fragment shader could have consisted of the following code:

```
void main()
{
    gl_FragColor = vec4(1.0, 1.0, 0.0, 1.0);
}
```

For more modern versions of OpenGL, where you need to declare a variable for the output color, you can use the following code for the fragment shader:

```
out vec4 fragColor;
void main()
{
    fragColor = vec4(1.0, 1.0, 0.0, 1.0);
}
```

Taken together, the vertex shader and the fragment shader produce a program that renders a single point in the center of the screen, colored yellow. If desired, these values can be altered within certain bounds. The $x$, $y$, and $z$ components of the position vector may be changed to any value between –1.0 and 1.0 and the point will remain visible; any values outside this range place the point outside of the region rendered by OpenGL and will result in an empty image being rendered. Changing the z coordinate (within this range) will have no visible effect at this time, since no perspective transformations are being applied. Similarly, the r, g, and b components of the color vector may be changed as desired, although dark colors may be difficult to distinguish on the default black background color. It should also be noted that the number types **int** and **float** may not be interchangeable; in certain circumstances, entering 1 rather than 1.0 may cause shader compilation errors.

## 2.2.2 Compiling GPU Programs

Now that you have learned the basics about writing shader code, the next step is to learn how to compile and link the vertex and fragment shaders to create a GPU program. To continue with the goal of creating a reusable framework, you will create a utility class that will perform these tasks. In this section and those that follow, many of the functions from OpenGL will be introduced and described in the following style:

**functionName(** *parameter1, parameter2, … * **)**
  Description of function and parameters.

Many of these functions will have syntax identical to that presented in the official OpenGL reference pages maintained by the Khronos Group at https://www.khronos.org/registry/OpenGL-Refpages/.

The first step toward compiling GPU programs involves the individual shaders. Shader objects must be created to store shader source code, the source code must be sent to these objects, and then the shaders must be compiled. These tasks are accomplished using the following three functions:

**glCreateShader(** *shaderType* **)**
  Creates an empty shader object, which is used to store the source code of a shader and returns a value by which it can be referenced. The type of shader (such as a vertex shader or a fragment shader) is specified with the *shaderType* parameter, whose value will be an OpenGL constant such as GL_VERTEX_SHADER or GL_FRAGMENT_SHADER.

**glShaderSource(** *shaderRef, shaderCode* **)**
  Stores the source code in the string parameter *shaderCode* in the shader object referenced by the parameter *shaderRef*.

**glCompileShader(** *shaderRef* **)**
  Compiles the source code stored in the shader object referenced by the parameter *shaderRef*.

Since mistakes may be made when writing shader code, compiling a shader may or may not succeed. Unlike application compilation errors, which are typically automatically displayed to the programmer, shader compilation errors need to be checked for specifically.

This process is typically handled in multiple steps: checking if compilation was successful, and if not, retrieving the error message, and deleting the shader object to free up memory. This is handled with the following functions:

**glGetShaderiv(** *shaderRef, shaderInfo* **)**
Returns information from the shader referenced by the parameter *shaderRef*. The type of information retrieved is specified with the *shaderInfo* parameter, whose value will be an OpenGL constant such as GL_SHADER_TYPE (to determine the type of shader) or GL_COMPILE_STATUS (to determine if compilation was successful).

**glGetShaderInfoLog(** *shaderRef* **)**
Returns information about the compilation process (such as errors and warnings) from the shader referenced by the parameter *shaderRef*.

**glDeleteShader(** *shaderRef* **)**
Frees the memory used by the shader referenced by the parameter *shaderRef*, and makes the reference available for future shaders that are created.

With an understanding of these functions, coding in Java can begin. LWJGL provides access to the needed functions and constants via the OpenGL package. To begin, you will create a class containing static methods to load text files containing shader code, and then use the previously mentioned OpenGL functions to create shader objects, upload shader code, and compile shader programs. In the **core** package, create a new Java class named **OpenGLUtils** containing the following code:

```
package core;

import static org.lwjgl.opengl.GL40.*;
import java.nio.file.Files;
import java.nio.file.Paths;

public class OpenGLUtils
{
    public static int initFromFiles(
            String vertexShaderFileName,
            String fragmentShaderFileName )
    {
        return initProgram(
                readFile(vertexShaderFileName),
                readFile(fragmentShaderFileName) );
    }

    public static String readFile(String fileName)
    {
        String text = "";
        try
```

```java
        {
            text = new String(
                Files.readAllBytes(Paths.get(fileName)));
        }
        catch (Exception ex)
        {
            ex.printStackTrace();
        }
        return text;
    }


    // array used to store debug codes
    static int[] status = new int[1];

    public static int initShader(String shaderCode,
        int shaderType)
    {
        // specify specific OpenGL version
        shaderCode = "#version 330 \n" + shaderCode;

        // create empty shader object and return reference value
        int shaderRef = glCreateShader(shaderType);

        // stores the source code in the shader
        glShaderSource(shaderRef, shaderCode);

        // compiles source code stored in the shader object
        glCompileShader(shaderRef);

        // query whether shader compile was successful
        glGetShaderiv(shaderRef, GL_COMPILE_STATUS, status);
        if (status[0] == GL_FALSE)
    {
            // retrieve error message
            String errorMessage = glGetShaderInfoLog(shaderRef);
            // free memory used to store shader program
            glDeleteShader(shaderRef);
            // halt program and print error message
            throw new RuntimeException(errorMessage);
        }

        // compilation was successful;
        // return shader reference value
        return shaderRef;
    }
}
```

Next, a program object must be created and the compiled shaders must be attached and linked together. These tasks require the use of the following OpenGL functions:

**glCreateProgram( )**
> Creates an empty program object, to which shader objects can be attached, and returns a value by which it can be referenced.

**glAttachShader(** *programRef, shaderRef* **)**
> Attaches a shader object specified by the parameter *shaderRef* to the program object specified by the parameter *programRef*.

**glLinkProgram(** *programRef* **)**
> Links the vertex and fragment shaders previously attached to the program object specified by the parameter *programRef*. Among other things, this process verifies that any variables used to send data from the vertex shader to the fragment shader are declared in both shaders consistently.

As was the case with checking for shader compilation errors, program linking errors need to be checked manually. This process is completely analogous, and uses the following functions:

**glGetProgramiv(** *programRef, programInfo* **)**
> Returns information from the program referenced by the parameter *programRef*. The type of information retrieved is specified with the *programInfo* parameter, whose value will be an OpenGL constant such as GL_LINK_STATUS (to determine if linking was successful).

**glGetProgramInfoLog(** *programRef* **)**
> Returns information about the linking process (such as errors and warnings) from the program referenced by the parameter *programRef*.

**glDeleteProgram(** *programRef* **)**
> Frees the memory used by the program referenced by the parameter *programRef*, and makes the reference available for future programs that are created.

Next, return to the **OpenGLUtils** file, and add the following method:

```
public static int initProgram(
    String vertexShaderCode, String fragmentShaderCode)
{

    int vertexShaderRef   = initShader(vertexShaderCode,
  GL_VERTEX_SHADER);
    int fragmentShaderRef = initShader(fragmentShaderCode,
      GL_FRAGMENT_SHADER);
```

```
        // create empty program object and store reference to it
        int programRef = glCreateProgram();

        // attach previously compiled shader programs
        glAttachShader(programRef, vertexShaderRef);
        glAttachShader(programRef, fragmentShaderRef);

        // link vertex shader to fragment shader
        glLinkProgram(programRef);

        // query whether program link was successful
        glGetProgramiv(programRef, GL_LINK_STATUS, status);
        if (status[0] == GL_FALSE)
        {
          // retrieve error message
             String errorMessage =
                  glGetProgramInfoLog(programRef);
             // free memory used to store program
             glDeleteProgram(programRef);
             // halt application and print error message
             throw new RuntimeException(errorMessage);
        }

        // linking was successful;
        // return program reference value
        return programRef;
}
```

There is one additional OpenGL function that can be useful when debugging to determine what version of OpenGL/GLSL your computer supports:

**glGetString(** *name* **)**

    Returns a string describing some aspect of the currently active OpenGL implementation, specified by the parameter *name*, whose value is one of the OpenGL constants: GL_VENDOR, GL_RENDERER, GL_VERSION, or GL_SHADING_VERSION.

In the **OpenGLUtils** class, add the following method:

```
public static void checkVersion()
{
     System.out.println("Vendor: " +
        glGetString(GL_VENDOR) );
     System.out.println("Renderer: " +
        glGetString(GL_RENDERER) );
     System.out.println("OpenGL version supported: " +
        glGetString(GL_VERSION) );
}
```

In the **Base** class, after the line **GL.createCapabilities()**, add the following code:

```
OpenGLUtils.checkVersion();
System.out.println("LWJGL version: " + Version.getVersion() );
```

In the next section, you will learn how to use the methods from the **OpenGLUtils** class to compile shader code in an application.

## 2.2.3  Rendering in the Application

Next, you will create another application (once again, extending the **Base** class), that contains the shader code previously discussed and uses the functions from the **OpenGLUtils** class to compile the shaders and create the program. In the application itself, there are a few more tasks that must be performed that also require OpenGL functions.

As mentioned in the discussion of the graphics pipeline in the previous chapter, *vertex array objects* (VAOs) will be used to manage vertex related data stored in vertex buffers. Even though this first example does not use any buffers, many implementations of OpenGL require a VAO to be created and bound in order for the application to work correctly. The two functions you will need are as follows:

**glGenVertexArrays(** *vaoCount* **)**
> Returns a set of available VAO references. The number of references returned is specified by the integer parameter *vaoCount*.

**glBindVertexArray(** *vaoRef* **)**
> Binds a VAO referenced by the parameter *vaoRef*, after first creating the object if no such object currently exists. Unbinds any VAO that was previously bound.

Next, in order to specify the program to be used when rendering, and to start the rendering process, you will need to use the following two functions:

**glUseProgram(** *programRef* **)**
> Specifies that the program to be used during the rendering process is the one referenced by the parameter *programRef*.

**glDrawArrays(** *drawMode, firstIndex, indexCount* **)**
> Renders geometric primitives (points, lines, or triangles) using the program previously specified by glUseProgram. The program's vertex shader uses data from arrays stored in enabled vertex buffers, beginning at the array index specified by the parameter *firstIndex*. The total number of array elements used is specified by the parameter *indexCount*. The type of geometric primitive rendered and the way in which the vertices are grouped is specified by the parameter *drawMode*, whose value is an OpenGL constant such as GL_POINTS, GL_LINES, GL_LINE_LOOP, GL_TRIANGLES, or GL_TRIANGLE_FAN.

Finally, an aesthetic consideration: depending on your computer display, it may be difficult to observe a single point, which is rendered as a single pixel by default. To make this point easier to see, you can use the following function to increase the size of the rendered point.

**glPointSize(** *size* **)**

Specifies that points should be rendered with diameter (in pixels) equal to the integer parameter *size*. (If not specified, the default value is 1).

Before you create the next application, you must create the fragment shader and vertex shader files to store the shader code used in the application. In the **src** folder, create a new text file (not a Java class!) named **Test_2_2.frag**, containing the following code:

```
out vec4 fragColor;
void main()
{
    fragColor = vec4(1.0, 1.0, 0.0, 1.0);
}
```

Next, create a text file named **Test_2_2.vert** containing the following code:

```
void main()
{
    gl_Position = vec4(0.0, 0.0, 0.0, 1.0);
}
```

You are now prepared to write the application. In the **src** folder, create a new Java class named **Test_2_2** with the following code. In particular, observe that the path to the vertex and fragment shader files previously created is specified relative to the project root directory. This assumes that in your development environment, your project has been configured so that the project root directory is also the root directory for the project resource files (which may include text files, image files, etc.). This may be accomplished in IntelliJ by right-clicking the project root folder, selecting **Mark Directory As**, and then selecting **Resources Root**.

```
import static org.lwjgl.opengl.GL40.*;
import core.*;

public class Test_2_2 extends Base
{
    public int programRef;

    public void initialize()
    {
        // load code, send to GPU, and compile;
        //    store program reference
        programRef = OpenGLUtils.initFromFiles(
            "./src/Test_2_2.vert", "./src/Test_2_2.frag" );
```

```
        // set up vertex array object
        int vaoRef = glGenVertexArrays();
        glBindVertexArray(vaoRef);

        // render settings (optional)

        // set point width and height
        glPointSize(10);
    }

    public void update()
    {
        // select program to use when rendering
        glUseProgram( programRef );

        // render geometric objects using selected program
        glDrawArrays(GL_POINTS, 0, 1);
    }

    // driver method
    public static void main(String[] args)
    {
        new Test_2_2().run();
    }
}
```

In this program, the size of the rendered point is set to be 10 pixels in diameter. When you run this program, a window should appear similar to Figure 2.3.

Once you have successfully run this program and viewed the rendered point, you should experiment with changing the shader code. As mentioned previously, experiment with changing the $x$, $y$, and $z$ components of the position vector, or the $r$, $g$, and $b$ components

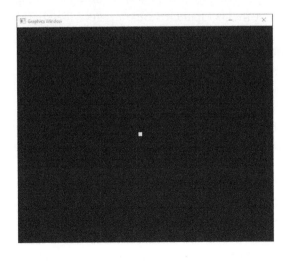

FIGURE 2.3   Rendering a single point.

of the color vector. Try changing the point size specified in the main application. You may even want to purposefully introduce errors in the shader code to learn what error messages are displayed in each case. Some common errors include:

- not including a semicolon at the end of a statement

- using an **int** instead of a **float**

- assigning the wrong data type to a variable (such as assigning a **vec3** to the **vec4** type variable **gl_Position**)

- using the wrong number of values in a vector

Try introducing each of the errors into your shader code one at a time and familiarize yourself with the corresponding error messages. Once you are finished experimenting with the code, the next topic you will learn about is using vertex buffers to draw two-dimensional shapes.

## 2.3 DRAWING SHAPES

Every vertex shader that you write (with the single exception of the one-point example from the previous section) will use arrays of data stored in vertex buffers. Multiple points are needed to specify the shape of any two-dimensional or three-dimensional object. In what follows, you will learn about the OpenGL functions that enable applications to work with vertex buffers, create a reusable class to perform these tasks, and then write a series of applications that use this class to create one or more shapes with one or more colors.

### 2.3.1 Using Vertex Buffers

Most of the tasks involving vertex buffers take place when an application is initialized, and so it may be helpful to review the discussion of the application stage in the graphics pipeline from the previous chapter. In brief, the relevant steps in this stage are creating buffers, storing data in buffers, and specifying associations between vertex buffers and shader variables. These tasks are handled by the six OpenGL functions described in this section, starting with:

**glGenBuffers(** *bufferCount* **)**
> Returns a set of available vertex buffer references. The number of references returned is specified by the integer parameter *bufferCount*.

Note that in contrast to the OpenGL functions glCreateShader and glCreateProgram, the function glGenBuffers does not actually create an object; this is handled by the next function.

**glBindBuffer(** *bindTarget, bufferRef* **)**
> Creates a buffer object referenced by the parameter *bufferRef* if no such object exists. The buffer object is bound to the target specified by the parameter *bindTarget*, whose value is an OpenGL constant such as GL_ARRAY_BUFFER (for vertex attributes) or GL_TEXTURE_BUFFER (for texture data).

Binding a buffer to a target is a necessary precursor for much of what happens next. The OpenGL functions that follow – those that relate to a buffer in some way – do not contain a parameter that directly references a buffer. Instead, some functions (such as **glBufferData**, discussed next) include a parameter like *bindTarget* and thus affect whichever buffer is currently bound to *bindTarget*. In other cases, the function may only be applicable to a particular type of buffer, in which case *bindTarget* is implicit and thus not included. For example, functions that only apply to vertex attribute data (such as **glVertexAttribPointer**, discussed later) only affect vertex buffers, and thus automatically affect the buffer bound to GL_ARRAY_BUFFER.

> **glBufferData(** *bindTarget, bufferData, bufferUsage* **)**
> Allocates storage for the buffer object currently bound to the target specified by the parameter *bindTarget*, and stores the information from the parameter *bufferData*. (Any data that may have been previously stored in the associated buffer is deleted.) The parameter *bufferUsage* indicates how the data will most likely be accessed, and this information may be used by the GL implementation to improve performance. The value of *bufferUsage* is an OpenGL constant such as GL_STATIC_DRAW (which indicates the buffer contents will be modified once), or GL_DYNAMIC_DRAW (which indicates the buffer contents will be modified many times).

In order to set up an association between a vertex buffer and a shader variable, the reference to the shader variable in a given program must be obtained. This can be accomplished by using the following function:

> **glGetAttribLocation(** *programRef, variableName* **)**
> Returns a value used to reference an attribute variable (indicated by the type qualifier **in**) with name indicated by the parameter *variableName* and declared in the vertex shader of the program referenced by the parameter *programRef*. If the variable is not declared or not used in the specified program, the value −1 is returned.

Once the reference for an attribute variable has been obtained and the corresponding vertex buffer is bound, the association between the buffer and variable can be established using the function presented next:

> **glVertexAttribPointer(** *variableRef, size, baseType, normalize, stride, offset* **)**
> Specifies that the attribute variable indicated by the parameter *variableRef* will receive data from the array stored in the vertex buffer currently bound to GL_ARRAY_BUFFER. The basic data type is specified by the parameter *baseType*, whose value is an OpenGL constant such as GL_INT or GL_FLOAT. The number of components per attribute is specified by the parameter *size*, which is the integer 1, 2, 3, or 4 depending on if the attribute is a basic data type or a vector with 2, 3, or 4 components, respectively. The flexibility offered by the last three parameters

will not be needed in this book, but in brief: the parameter *normalize* is a Boolean value that specifies if vector attributes should be rescaled to have length 1, while the parameters *stride* and *offset* are used to specify how this attribute's data should be read from the associated buffer (it is possible to pack and interleave data for multiple attributes into a single buffer, which can be useful in reducing total calls to the GPU).

So, for example, if the shader variable has type **int**, then you would use the parameters *size*=1 and *baseType*=GL_INT, while if the shader variable has type **vec3** (a vector containing three **float** values), then you would use the parameters *size*=3 and *baseType*=GL_FLOAT. (The final three parameters will not be covered in this book, and they will always be assigned their default values of *normalize*=False, *stride*=0, and *offset*=None.)

Even after an association has been specified, the corresponding buffer will not be accessed during rendering unless explicitly enabled with the following function:

**glEnableVertexAttribArray(** *variableRef* **)**
> Specifies that the values in the vertex buffer bound to the shader variable referenced by the parameter *variableRef* will be accessed and used during the rendering process.

Finally, as a reminder, VAOs will be used to manage the vertex-related data specified by these functions. While a VAO is bound, it stores information including the associations between vertex buffers and attribute variables in a program, how data is arranged within each buffer, and which associations have been enabled.

## 2.3.2 An Attribute Class

With the previously described OpenGL functions, you are now ready to create a Java class to manage attribute data and related tasks. The information managed by the class will include the type of data (**float**, **vec2**, **vec3**, or **vec4**), an array containing the data, and the reference of the vertex buffer where the data is stored. The two main tasks handled by the class will be storing the array of data in a vertex buffer and associating the vertex buffer to a shader variable in a given program; each of these tasks will be implemented with a method. To begin, in the **core** package, create a new Java class file named **Attribute** with the following code:

```
package core;
import static org.lwjgl.opengl.GL40.*;

public class Attribute
{
    // type of elements in data array:
    // int | float | vec2 | vec3 | vec4
    private String dataType;
```

```java
// array of data to be stored in buffer
public float[] dataArray;

// store results of generating buffers
private int[] resultArray = new int[1];

// reference of available buffer from GPU
private int bufferRef;

public Attribute(String dataType, float[] dataArray)
{
    this.dataType = dataType;
    this.dataArray = dataArray;
    // returns a single buffer reference
    bufferRef = glGenBuffers();
    // upload data immediately
    uploadData();
}

// store this data in a GPU buffer
public void uploadData()
{
    // select buffer used by the following functions
    glBindBuffer(GL_ARRAY_BUFFER, bufferRef);

    // store data in currently bound buffer
    glBufferData(GL_ARRAY_BUFFER, dataArray,
      GL_STATIC_DRAW);
}

// associate variable in program with this buffer
public void associateVariable(int programRef,
    String variableName)
{
    // get reference for program variable with given name
    int variableRef = glGetAttribLocation(programRef,
        variableName);

    // if program does not reference variable, exit
    if (variableRef == -1)
        return;

    // select buffer used by the following functions
    glBindBuffer(GL_ARRAY_BUFFER, bufferRef);

    // specify how data will be read
    //    from the currently bound buffer
    //     into the specified variable
```

```
            if ( dataType.equals("int") )
                glVertexAttribPointer(variableRef, 1, GL_INT,
                    false, 0, 0);
            else if ( dataType.equals("float") )
                glVertexAttribPointer(variableRef, 1, GL_FLOAT,
                    false, 0, 0);
            else if ( dataType.equals("vec2") )
                glVertexAttribPointer(variableRef, 2, GL_FLOAT,
                    false, 0, 0);
            else if ( dataType.equals("vec3") )
                glVertexAttribPointer(variableRef, 3, GL_FLOAT,
                    false, 0, 0);
            else if ( dataType.equals("vec4") )
                glVertexAttribPointer(variableRef, 4, GL_FLOAT,
                    false, 0, 0);
            else
                throw new RuntimeException(
                    " Attribute " + variableName +
                    " has unknown type " + dataType );

            // indicate that data will be streamed
    //   to this variable from a buffer
            glEnableVertexAttribArray(variableRef);
        }
}
```

In addition to the comments throughout the code above, note the following design considerations:

- The code from the **uploadData** function could have been part of the class initialization. However, this functionality is separated in case the values in the variable **data** need to be changed and the corresponding buffer updated later, in which case the function can be called again.

- This class does not store the name of the variable or the reference to the program that will access the buffer, because in practice there may be more than one program that does so, and the variables in each program may have different names.

- It may not appear that the information from **glVertexAttribPointer** – in particular, the associations between vertex buffers and program variables – is being stored anywhere. However, this information is in fact stored by whichever VAO was bound prior to these function calls.

## 2.3.3 Hexagons, Triangles, and Squares

In this section, you will create an application that draws outlined shapes, which require arrays of point data. Considering aesthetics once again: since you will be rendering lines with the following program, you may wish to increase their width to make them easier to see (the default line width is a single pixel). This can be accomplished with the following function:

**glLineWidth**( *width* )
>Specifies that lines should be rendered with width (in pixels) equal to the integer parameter *width*. (If not specified, the default value is 1.) Some OpenGL implementations only support lines of width 1, in which case attempting to set the width to a value larger than 1 will cause an error.

With this knowledge, you are now ready to create applications that render one or more shapes. This next application renders an outlined hexagon. First you need to write the shader programs, which as before are contained in text files in the **src** folder. First, create a copy of **Test_2_2.frag** and name it **Test_2_3.frag**; the code in this file does not need to be changed. Second, create a new text file named **Test_2_3.vert**. Inside this file, insert the following code:

```
in vec3 position;
void main()
{
    gl_Position = vec4(position.x, position.y, position.z, 1.0);
}
```

Now you are prepared to create the application itself. Create a new Java class named **Test_2_3** with the following code:

```
import static org.lwjgl.opengl.GL40.*;
import core.*;

public class Test_2_3 extends Base
{
    public int programRef;

    public void initialize()
    {
        // load code, send to GPU, and compile;
        //    store program reference
        programRef = OpenGLUtils.initFromFiles(
                "./src/Test_2_3.vert",
                "./src/Test_2_3.frag" );

        // render settings (optional)

        // set line width
        glLineWidth(4);
```

```java
    // setup vertex array object
        int vaoRef = glGenVertexArrays();
        glBindVertexArray(vaoRef);

        float[] positionData = {
                0.8f,   0.0f, 0.0f,
                0.4f,   0.6f, 0.0f,
               -0.4f,   0.6f, 0.0f,
               -0.8f,   0.0f, 0.0f,
               -0.4f, -0.6f, 0.0f,
                0.4f, -0.6f, 0.0f  };
        Attribute positionAttribute = new Attribute(
            "vec3", positionData );
        positionAttribute.associateVariable(
            programRef, "position" );
    }

    public void update()
    {
        // select program to use when rendering
        glUseProgram( programRef );

        // render geometric objects using selected program
        glDrawArrays(GL_LINE_LOOP, 0, 6);
    }

    // driver method
    public static void main(String[] args)
    {
        new Test_2_3().run();
    }
}
```

There are many similarities between this application and the previous application (the file **Test_2_2**, which rendered a single point): the fragment shader code is identical (pixels are colored yellow), and both use the functions **initializeProgram**, **glUseProgram**, and **glDrawArrays**. The major differences are:

- The vertex shader declares a **vec3** variable named **position** with the type qualifier **in**. This indicates that **position** is an attribute variable, and thus it will receive data from a vertex buffer.

- The vertex attribute is set up and configured with three lines of code, corresponding to the following tasks: create an array of position data, create an Attribute object (which also stores data in a buffer), and set up the association with the attribute variable **position**.

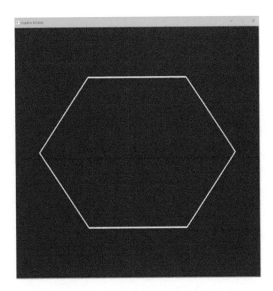

FIGURE 2.4   Rendering six points with GL_LINE_LOOP.

- A VAO is created to store information related to the vertex buffer. The VAO reference is not stored in a class variable, because there is only one set of associations to manage and so the VAO remains bound the entire time. (When there are multiple sets of associations to manage, the VAO references will be stored in class variables so that they can be bound in the **update** function when needed.)

- The **glDrawArrays** function parameter GL_LINE_LOOP indicates that lines will be rendered from each point to the next, and the last point will also be connected to the first

When you run this program, a window should appear similar to that shown in Figure 2.4.

This is an opportune time to experiment with draw mode parameters. Two additional line rendering configurations are possible. If you want to draw a line segment from each point to the next but not connect the last point to the first, this is accomplished with the parameter GL_LINE_STRIP. Alternatively, if you want to draw a series of disconnected line segments, then you would use GL_LINES, which connects each point with an even index in the array to the following point in the array. If the array of points is denoted by [A, B, C, D, E, F], then GL_LINES groups the points into the disjoint pairs (A, B), (C, D), (E, F) and draws a line segment for each pair. (If the number of points to render was odd, then the last point would be ignored in this case.) These cases are illustrated in Figure 2.5; note that A represents the rightmost point and the points in the array are listed in counterclockwise order.

It is also possible to render two-dimensional shapes with filled-in triangles. As is the case with rending lines, there are multiple parameters that result in different groupings of points. The most basic is GL_TRIANGLES, which groups points into disjoint triples, analogous to how GL_LINES groups points into disjoint pairs; continuing the previous notation,

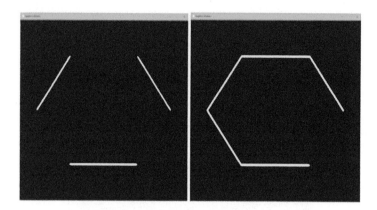

FIGURE 2.5    Rendering six points with GL_LINES(Left) and GL_LINE_STRIP(Right).

the groups are (A, B, C) and (D, E, F). Also useful in this example is GL_TRIANGLE_FAN, which draws a series of connected triangles where all triangles share the initial point in the array, and each triangle shares an edge with the next, resulting in a fan-like arrangement. For this example, the groups are (A, B, C), (A, C, D), (A, D, E), and (A, E, F), which results in a filled-in hexagon (and would similarly fill any polygon where the points are specified in order around the circumference). These cases are illustrated in Figure 2.6.

Now that you have seen how to use a single buffer in an application, you will next render two different shapes (a triangle and a square), whose vertex positions are stored in two separate buffers with different sizes. No new concepts or functions are required, and there are no changes to the shader code from the previous example. The main difference is that the **glDrawArrays** function will need to be called twice (once to render each shape), and prior to each call, the correct buffer needs to be associated to the attribute variable **position**. This will require two VAOs to be created and bound when needed (before associating variables and before drawing shapes), and therefore the VAO references will

FIGURE 2.6    Rendering six points with GL_TRIANGLES and GL_TRIANGLE_FAN.

be stored in variables with class-level scope. To proceed, create a new Java class named **Test_2_4** with the following code:

```java
import static org.lwjgl.opengl.GL40.*;

import core.*;

public class Test_2_4 extends Base
{
    public int programRef, vaoTri, vaoSquare;

    public void initialize()
    {
        // load code, send to GPU, and compile;
        // store program reference
        programRef = OpenGLUtils.initFromFiles(
                "./src/Test_2_3.vert",
                "./src/Test_2_3.frag" );

        // render settings (optional)

        // set line width
        glLineWidth(4);

        // setup vertex array object: triangle
        vaoTri = glGenVertexArrays();
        glBindVertexArray(vaoTri);

        float[] positionDataTri = {
                -0.5f, 0.8f, 0.0f,
                -0.2f, 0.2f, 0.0f,
                -0.8f, 0.2f, 0.0f  };
        Attribute positionAttributeTri =
    new Attribute( "vec3", positionDataTri );
        positionAttributeTri.associateVariable(
            programRef, "position" );

        // setup vertex array object: square
        vaoSquare = glGenVertexArrays();
        glBindVertexArray(vaoSquare);

        float[] positionDataSquare = {
                0.8f, 0.8f, 0.0f,
                0.8f, 0.2f, 0.0f,
                0.2f, 0.2f, 0.0f,
                0.2f, 0.8f, 0.0f  };
        Attribute positionAttributeSquare =
    new Attribute( "vec3", positionDataSquare );
```

```
            positionAttributeSquare.associateVariable(
                programRef, "position" );
        }

        public void update()
        {
            // using same program to render both shapes
            glUseProgram( programRef );

            // draw the triangle
            glBindVertexArray( vaoTri );
            glDrawArrays( GL_LINE_LOOP,  0,  3 );

            // draw the square
            glBindVertexArray( vaoSquare );
            glDrawArrays( GL_LINE_LOOP,  0,  4 );
        }

        // driver method
        public static void main(String[] args)
        {
            new Test_2_4().run();
        }
    }
```

The result of running this application is illustrated in Figure 2.7.

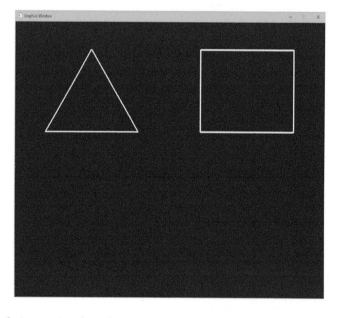

FIGURE 2.7    Rendering a triangle and a square.

Now that you have learned how to work with multiple buffers, you may want to use them for purposes other than positions. For example, as previously mentioned, buffers can be used to store vertex colors. Since attribute data is passed into the vertex shader, but the color data needs to be used in the fragment shader, this requires you to pass data from the vertex shader to the fragment shader, which is the topic of the next section.

### 2.3.4 Passing Data between Shaders

In this section, you will create an application that renders six points (once again, arranged in a hexagonal pattern) in six different colors. This requires data (in particular, the color data) to be sent from the vertex shader to the fragment shader. Recall from the introductory explanation of OpenGL Shading Language that *type qualifiers* are keywords that modify the properties of a variable, and in particular:

- In a vertex shader, the keyword **in** indicates that values will be supplied from a buffer, while the keyword **out** indicates that values will be passed to the fragment shader.

- In a fragment shader, the keyword **in** indicates that values will be supplied from the vertex shader, after having been interpolated during the rasterization stage.

This application described will use the shaders that follow. First, create a new text file named **Test_2_5.vert** containing the vertex shader code:

```
in vec3 position;
in vec3 vertexColor;
out vec3 color;
void main()
{
    gl_Position = vec4(position.x, position.y, position.z, 1.0);
    color = vertexColor;
}
```

Note the presence of two **in** variables; this is because there are two vertex attributes, **position** and **vertexColor**. The data arrays for each of these attributes will be stored in a separate buffer and associated to the corresponding variable. The arrays should contain the same number of elements; the length of the arrays is the number of vertices. For a given vertex, the same array index will be used to retrieve data from each of the attribute arrays. For example, the vertex that uses the value from index N in the position data array will also use the value from index N in the vertex color data array.

In addition, the vertex shader contains an **out** variable, **color**, which will be used to transmit the data to the fragment shader; a value must be assigned to this (and in general, any **out** variable) within the vertex shader. In this case, the value in **vertexColor** just "passes through" to the variable **color**; no computations are performed on this value.

Next, create a new text file named **Test_2_5.frag** containing the fragment shader code:

```
in vec3 color;
out vec4 fragColor;
void main()
{
    fragColor = vec4(color.r, color.g, color.b, 1.0);
}
```

Note here the presence of an **in** variable, which must have the same name as the corresponding **out** variable from the vertex shader. (Checking for pairs of **out**/**in** variables with consistent names between the vertex and fragment shaders is one of the tasks performed when a program is linked.) The components of the vector are accessed using the (r, g, b) naming system for readability, as they correspond to color data in this context.

With an understanding of these new shaders, you are ready to create the application. It uses separate **Attribute** objects to manage the attribute data, but only one VAO needs to be created since these vertex buffers are associated with different variables in the program. To proceed, create a new Java class named **Test_2_5** containing the following code:

```
import static org.lwjgl.opengl.GL40.*;
import core.*;

public class Test_2_5 extends Base
{
    public int programRef, vaoRef;

    public void initialize()
    {
        // load code, send to GPU, and compile;
        //     store program reference
        programRef = OpenGLUtils.initFromFiles(
                "./src/Test_2_5.vert",
                "./src/Test_2_5.frag" );

        // render settings (optional)

        // set line width
        glPointSize(10);
        glLineWidth(4);

        // setup vertex array object
        vaoRef = glGenVertexArrays();
        glBindVertexArray(vaoRef);
```

```
        float[] positionData = {
                0.8f,   0.0f, 0.0f,
                0.4f,   0.6f, 0.0f,
               -0.4f,   0.6f, 0.0f,
               -0.8f,   0.0f, 0.0f,
               -0.4f,  -0.6f, 0.0f,
                0.4f,  -0.6f, 0.0f  };
        Attribute positionAttribute = new Attribute(
            "vec3", positionData );
        positionAttribute.associateVariable(
            programRef, "position" );

        float[] colorData = {
                1.0f, 0.0f, 0.0f,
                1.0f, 0.5f, 0.0f,
                1.0f, 1.0f, 0.0f,
                0.0f, 1.0f, 0.0f,
                0.0f, 0.0f, 1.0f,
                0.5f, 0.0f, 1.0f  };
        Attribute colorAttribute = new Attribute(
            "vec3", colorData );
        colorAttribute.associateVariable(
            programRef, "vertexColor" );
    }

    public void update()
    {
        glUseProgram( programRef );

        // draw the object
        glBindVertexArray( vaoRef );
        glDrawArrays( GL_POINTS,  0,  6 );
    }

    // driver method
    public static void main(String[] args)
    {
        new Test_2_5().run();
    }
}
```

The result of running this application is illustrated in Figure 2.8.

Recall from the previous chapter that during the graphics pipeline, between the geometry processing stage (which involves the vertex shader) and the pixel processing stage (which involves the fragment shader) is the rasterization stage. At this point, the programs are sufficiently complex to illustrate the interpolation of vertex attributes that occurs during this stage.

FIGURE 2.8    Rendering six points with vertex colors, using GL_POINTS.

During the rasterization stage, points are grouped into *geometric primitives*: points, lines, or triangles, depending on the draw mode specified. Then the GPU determines which pixels correspond to the space occupied by each geometric primitive. For each of these pixels, the GPU generates a fragment, which stores the data needed to determine the final color of each pixel. Any vertex data passed from the vertex shader via an **out** variable will be interpolated for each of these fragments; a weighted average of the vertex values is automatically calculated, depending on the distances from the interior point to the original vertices. It is this interpolated value that is sent to the corresponding **in** variable in the fragment shader.

For a numerical example of interpolation, suppose a line segment is to be drawn between a point *P1* with color *C1* = [1, 0, 0] (red) and a point *P2* with color *C2* = [0, 0, 1] (blue). All points along the segment will be colored according to some combination of the values in *C1* and *C2*; points closer to *P1* will have colors closer to *C1* (more red) while points closer to *P2* will have colors closer to *C2* (more blue). For example, the point on the segment exactly halfway between *P1* and *P2* will be colored 0.5 * *C1* + 0.5 * *C2* = [0.5, 0, 0.5], a shade of purple. For another example, a point that is a 25% of the distance along the segment from *P1* to *P2* will be colored 0.75 * *C1* + 0.25 * *C2* = [0.75, 0, 0.25], a reddish-purple. Similarly, colors of points within a triangle are weighted averages of the colors of its three vertices; the color of an interior point depends on the distance from the interior point to each of these three vertices. To see examples of color interpolation within lines and triangles, you can run the previous program but changing the *drawMode* parameter of **glDrawArrays** to either GL_LINE_LOOP or GL_TRIANGLE_FAN; the results are illustrated in Figure 2.9.

Many times, you may want to draw a shape that is a single color. This is technically possible using the previous shaders: if your shape has N vertices, you could create an array that contains the same color N times. However, there is a much less redundant approach to accomplish this task using *uniform variables*, which are introduced in the next section.

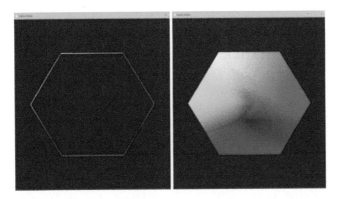

FIGURE 2.9 Rendering six points with vertex colors, using GL_LINE_LOOP and GL_TRIANGLE_FAN.

## 2.4 WORKING WITH UNIFORM DATA

There are many scenarios in computer graphics where you may want to repeatedly use the same information in shader programming. For example, you may want to translate all the vertices that define a shape by the same amount, or you may want to draw all the pixels corresponding to a shape with the same color. The most flexible and efficient way to accomplish such tasks is by using *uniform variables*: global variables that can be accessed by both the vertex shader and the fragment shader, and whose values are constant while each shape is being drawn (but can be changed between draw function calls).

### 2.4.1 Introduction to Uniforms

Uniform shader variables, declared with the type qualifier **uniform**, provide a mechanism to send data directly from variables in a CPU application to variables in a GPU program. In contrast to attribute data, uniform data is not stored in GPU buffers and is not managed with VAOs. Similar to attribute data, a reference to the location of the uniform variable must be obtained before data may be sent to it. This is accomplished with the following OpenGL function:

**glGetUniformLocation(** *programRef, variableName* **)**
>   Returns a value used to reference a uniform variable (indicated by the type qualifier **uniform**) with name indicated by the parameter *variableName* and declared in the program referenced by the parameter *programRef*. If the variable is not declared or not used in the specified program, the value –1 is returned.

The other OpenGL functions required to work with uniforms are used to store data in uniform variables. However, unlike the function **glVertexAttribPointer** that specified the data type with its parameters *baseType* and *size*, specifying different types of uniform data is handled by different functions. The notation {*a* | *b* | *c* | ...} used below (similar to that used in the official OpenGL documentation provided by the Khronos group) indicates that one of the values *a*, *b*, *c*, ... in the set should be each chosen to specify the name of a function. In other words, the notation below indicates that the possible function names are **glUniform1f**, **glUniform2f**, **glUniform3f**, **glUniform4f**, **glUniform1i**, **glUniform2i**, **glUniform3i**, and **glUniform4i**.

> **glUniform{ 1 | 2 | 3 | 4 }{ f | i }(** *variableRef, value1, …* **)**
>
> Specify the value of the uniform variable referenced by the parameter *variableRef* in the currently bound program. The number chosen in the function name refers to the number of values sent, while the letter (**f** or **i**) refers to the data type (float or integer).
>
> For example, to specify a single integer value, the form of the function you need to use is **glUniform1i( variableRef, value1 )**, while to specify the values for a **vec3** (a vector consisting of three floats), you would instead use **glUniform3f( variableRef, value1, value2, value3 )**. The boolean values **true** and **false** correspond to the integers 1 and 0, respectively, and **glUniform1i** is used to transmit this data.

## 2.4.2 A Uniform Class

Just as you previously created an **Attribute** class to simplify working with attributes, in this section you will create a **Uniform** class to simplify working with uniforms, using the two OpenGL functions discussed in the previous section. Each Uniform object will store a value and the name of the value type. One of the tasks of each Uniform object will be to locate the reference to the shader variable that will receive the value stored in the object. The variable reference will be stored in the Uniform object, since it is not stored by a VAO, as was the case when working with attributes. The other task will be to send the value in the Uniform object to the associated shader variable. This will need to be done repeatedly, as there will typically be multiple geometric objects, each using different values in the uniform variables, which need to be sent to the shader program before the corresponding geometric object is rendered.

Since vectors are a commonly used data type in OpenGL, you will create a corresponding **Vector** class before creating the **Uniform** class. Since this class will later have additional mathematical features added, you will store this (and eventually, other math-related classes) in a new package. Inside the **src** folder, create a new package called **math**. Inside this new package, create a new Java class named **Vector** with the following code:

```
package math;

public class Vector
{
    public double[] values;

    // initialize zero vector with given size
    public Vector(int size)
    {
        values = new double[size];
    }
```

```
    // initialize with given values
    public Vector(double... v)
    {
        values = new double[v.length];
        for (int i = 0; i < v.length; i++)
            values[i] = v[i];
    }

    public String toString()
    {
      String s = "[";
      for (int i = 0; i < values.length; i++)
            s += String.format("%6.2f", values[i]);
        s += "]";
        return s;
    }
}
```

The **Uniform** class will be a generic class that takes a type parameter **T**, corresponding to the type of data being stored. The GLSL types **int** and **bool** correspond to the Java class **Integer**; the GLSL type **float** corresponds to the Java class **Float**; the GLSL types **vec2**, **vec3**, and **vec4** correspond to the Java class **Vector** that was just created. In the **core** package, create a new Java class named **Uniform** with the following code:

```
package core;

import static org.lwjgl.opengl.GL40.*;
import java.util.Arrays;
import math.Vector;

// variable types: Integer | Float | Vector
public class Uniform<T>
{
    // store name of GLSL type:
    // int | bool | float | vec2 | vec3 | vec4
    private String dataType;

    // data to be sent to uniform variable
    public T data;

    // store results of generating buffers
    private int[] resultArray = new int[1];

    // reference for variable location in program
    private int variableRef;
```

```java
public Uniform(String dataType, T data)
{
    this.dataType = dataType;
    this.data = data;
}


// get and store reference for program variable with name
public void locateVariable(int programRef,
    String variableName)
{

    variableRef = glGetUniformLocation(programRef,
        variableName);
}


// store data in uniform variable previously located
public void uploadData()
{
    // if program does not reference variable, exit
    if (variableRef == -1)
        return;

    if (dataType.equals("int"))
        glUniform1i(variableRef, (Integer)data);
    else if (dataType.equals("bool"))
        glUniform1i(variableRef, (Integer)data);
    else if (dataType.equals("float"))
        glUniform1f(variableRef, (Float)data);
    else if (dataType.equals("vec2"))
    {
        Vector v = (Vector)data;
        glUniform2f(variableRef,
            (float)v.values[0],
            (float)v.values[1]);
    }
    else if (dataType.equals("vec3"))
    {
        Vector v = (Vector)data;
        glUniform3f(variableRef,
            (float)v.values[0],
            (float)v.values[1],
            (float)v.values[2]);
    }
    else if (dataType.equals("vec4"))
    {
        Vector v = (Vector)data;
        glUniform4f(variableRef,
```

```
              (float)v.values[0],
              (float)v.values[1],
              (float)v.values[2],
              (float)v.values[3]);
        }
    }
}
```

### 2.4.3 Applications and Animations

In this section, you will use the **Uniform** class to help render an image containing two triangles with the same shape, but in different locations and with different colors. The code to accomplish this includes the following features:

- a single vertex buffer, used to store the positions of the vertices of a triangle (centered at the origin)
- a single GPU program containing two uniform variables:
  - one used by the vertex shader to translate the position of the triangle vertices
  - one used by the fragment shader to specify the color of each pixel in the triangle
- two **Uniform** objects (one to store the position, one to store the color) for each triangle

To continue, in the **src** folder, create a text file named **Test_2_6.vert** containing the following vertex shader code:

```
in vec3 position;
uniform vec3 translation;
void main()
{
  vec3 pos = position + translation;
  gl_Position = vec4(pos.x, pos.y, pos.z, 1.0);
}
```

Then create a text file named **Test_2_6.frag**, containing the following fragment shader code:

```
uniform vec3 baseColor;
out vec4 fragColor;
void main()
{
  fragColor = vec4(baseColor.r, baseColor.g,
        baseColor.b, 1.0);
}
```

Finally, create a new Java class named **Test_2_6** with the following code:

```java
import static org.lwjgl.opengl.GL40.*;
import core.*;
import math.Vector;

public class Test_2_6 extends Base
{
    public int programRef, vaoRef;
    public Uniform<Vector> translation1, translation2,
            baseColor1, baseColor2;

    public void initialize()
    {
        // load code, send to GPU, and compile;
        //    store program reference
        programRef = OpenGLUtils.initFromFiles(
                "./src/Test_2_6.vert",
                "./src/Test_2_6.frag" );

        // setup vertex array object
        vaoRef = glGenVertexArrays();
        glBindVertexArray(vaoRef);

        float[] positionData = {
                0.0f,  0.2f, 0.0f,
                0.2f, -0.2f, 0.0f,
               -0.2f, -0.2f, 0.0f  };
        Attribute positionAttribute = new Attribute(
            "vec3", positionData );
        positionAttribute.associateVariable(
            programRef, "position" );

        // set up uniforms
        translation1 = new Uniform<Vector>(
          "vec3", new Vector(-0.5f, 0.0f, 0.0f) );
        translation1.locateVariable(programRef, "translation");

        translation2 = new Uniform<Vector>(
          "vec3", new Vector(0.5f, 0.0f, 0.0f) );
        translation2.locateVariable(programRef, "translation");

        baseColor1 = new Uniform<Vector>(
          "vec3", new Vector(1.0f, 0.0f, 0.0f) );
        baseColor1.locateVariable(programRef, "baseColor");
```

```
        baseColor2 = new Uniform<Vector>(
            "vec3", new Vector(0.0f, 0.0f, 1.0f) );
        baseColor2.locateVariable(programRef, "baseColor");
    }

    public void update()
    {
        glUseProgram( programRef );
        glBindVertexArray( vaoRef );

        // draw the first triangle
        translation1.uploadData();
        baseColor1.uploadData();
        glDrawArrays( GL_TRIANGLES, 0, 3 );

        // draw the second triangle
        translation2.uploadData();
        baseColor2.uploadData();
        glDrawArrays( GL_TRIANGLES, 0, 3 );
    }

    // driver method
    public static void main(String[] args)
    {
        new Test_2_6().run();
    }
}
```

The result of running this application is illustrated in Figure 2.10.

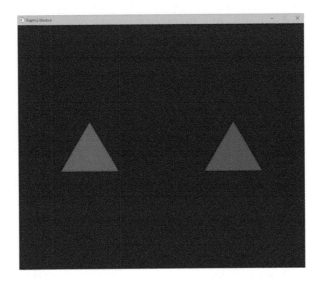

FIGURE 2.10   Two similar triangles rendered using uniform variables.

Next, you will create animated effects by continuously changing the values stored in uniform variables.

In the previous application code examples, you may have wondered why the **glDraw-Arrays** function was called within the **update** function – since the objects being drawn were not changing, the result was that the same image was rendered 60 times per second. In those examples, the rendering code technically could have been placed in the **initialize** function instead without affecting the resulting image (although it would have been rendered only once). The goal was to adhere to the "life cycle" structure of an application discussed at the beginning of this chapter, which becomes strictly necessary at this point. Starting in this section, the appearance of the objects will change over time, and thus the image must be rendered repeatedly.

Since geometric shapes will appear in different positions in subsequent renders, it is important to refresh the drawing area, resetting all the pixels in the color buffer to some default color. If this step is not performed, then in each animation frame the rendered shapes will be drawn superimposed on the previous frame, resulting in a smeared appearance. To specify the color used when clearing (which effectively becomes the background color), and to actually perform the clearing process, the following two OpenGL functions will be used:

**glClearColor(** *red, green, blue, alpha* **)**
> Specify the color used when clearing the color buffer; the color components are specified by the parameters *red, green, blue,* and *alpha*. Each of these parameters is a float between 0 and 1; the default values are all 0.

**glClear(** *mask* **)**
> Reset the contents of the buffer(s) indicated by the parameter *mask* to their default values. The value of mask can be one of the OpenGL constants such as GL_COLOR_BUFFER_BIT (to clear the color buffer), GL_DEPTH_BUFFER_BIT (to clear the depth buffer), GL_STENCIL_BUFFER_BIT (to clear the stencil buffer), or any combination of the constants, combined with the bitwise or operator "|."

In the next application, you will draw a triangle that continuously moves to the right, and once it moves completely past the right edge of the screen, it will reappear on the left side. (This behavior is sometimes called a *wrap-around effect*, popularized by various 1980s arcade games.) The same shader code will be used as before, and **Uniform** objects will be created for the triangle. The **Uniform** corresponding to the translation variable will have its value changed (the first component, representing the x-coordinate, will be incremented) during the **update** function, prior to clearing the color buffer and rendering the triangle. The wrap-around effect is accomplished by checking if the translation x-coordinate is greater than a certain positive value, and if so, setting it to a certain negative value (these values depending on the size of the triangle).

Create a new Java class named **Test_2_7** with the following code:

```java
import static org.lwjgl.glfw.GLFW.*;
import static org.lwjgl.opengl.GL40.*;

import core.*;

import math.Vector;

public class Test_2_7 extends Base
{
    public int programRef, vaoRef;
    // must declare uniform class type here
    //    for update function to work
    public Uniform<Vector> translation, baseColor;

    public void initialize()
    {
        // load code, send to GPU, and compile;
        //    store program reference
        programRef = OpenGLUtils.initFromFiles(
                "./src/Test_2_6.vert",
                "./src/Test_2_6.frag" );

        // specify color used when clearing the screen
        glClearColor(0.0f, 0.0f, 0.0f, 1.0f);

        // setup vertex array object
        vaoRef = glGenVertexArrays();
        glBindVertexArray(vaoRef);

        float[] positionData = {
                0.0f,   0.2f, 0.0f,
                0.2f, -0.2f, 0.0f,
               -0.2f, -0.2f, 0.0f  };
        Attribute positionAttribute = new Attribute(
            "vec3", positionData );
        positionAttribute.associateVariable(
            programRef, "position" );

        // set up uniforms
        translation = new Uniform<Vector>(
          "vec3", new Vector(-0.5f, 0.0f, 0.0f) );
        translation.locateVariable( programRef, "translation" );

        baseColor = new Uniform<Vector>(
          "vec3", new Vector(1.0f, 0.0f, 0.0f) );
        baseColor.locateVariable( programRef, "baseColor" );

    }
```

```java
public void update()
{

    // update data

    // increase x coordinate of translation
    translation.data.values[0] += 0.01f;

    // if triangle passes off-screen on the right,
    //   change translation so it reappears on the left
    if (translation.data.values[0] > 1.2f)
        translation.data.values[0] = -1.2f;

    // render scene

    // reset color buffer with specified color
    glClear(GL_COLOR_BUFFER_BIT);

    glUseProgram( programRef );
    glBindVertexArray( vaoRef );
    translation.uploadData();
    baseColor.uploadData();
    glDrawArrays( GL_TRIANGLES, 0, 3 );

}

// driver method
public static void main(String[] args)
{
    new Test_2_7().run();
}
}
```

It can be difficult to convey an animation with a series of static images, but to this end, Figure 2.11 shows a series of images captured with short time intervals between them.

FIGURE 2.11    Frames from an animation of a triangle moving to the right.

In the previous application, the movement of the triangle was specified relative to whatever its current position was (it continuously moved to the right of its starting position). The next application will feature time-based movement: the position will be calculated from equations expressed in terms of a time variable.

Since keeping track of time will be useful in many applications, you will begin by adding related functionality to the **Base** class. The variable **time** will keep track of the number of seconds the application has been running, which will be used to calculate time-based movement. The variable **deltaTime** will keep track of the number of seconds that have elapsed during the previous iteration of the run loop (typically 1/60, or approximately 0.017 seconds), which will be useful for future applications. Open the **Base** class from the **core** package, and add the following global variables to the class:

```
// number of seconds application has been running
public float time;

// seconds since last iteration of run loop
public float deltaTime;

// store time data from last iteration of run loop
private long previousTime;
private long currentTime;
```

In the **startup** method, add the following lines of code after the line where the **running** variable is set to true:

```
time = 0;
deltaTime = 1/60f;
currentTime = System.currentTimeMillis();
previousTime = System.currentTimeMillis();
```

Then, in the **run** function, directly after the statement **glfwPollEvents()** add the following code:

```
// recalculate time variables
currentTime = System.currentTimeMillis();
deltaTime = (currentTime - previousTime) / 1000f;
time += deltaTime;
previousTime = currentTime;
```

In the next application, a triangle will move along a circular path. This is most easily accomplished by using the trigonometric functions sine (sin) and cosine (cos), both of which smoothly oscillate between the values −1 and 1. Positions $(x, y)$ along a circular path can be expressed with the equations

$$x = \cos(t), \quad y = \sin(t)$$

In your application, the variable $t$ will be the total elapsed time. This particular circular path is centered at the origin and has radius 1; for a path centered at $(a, b)$ with radius $r$, you can use the equations

$$x = r * \cos(t) + a, \quad y = r * \sin(t) + b$$

To keep the entire triangle visible as it moves along this path, you will need to use a radius value less than 1.

The code for this application is nearly identical to the previous application, and so to begin, in the main folder, make a new Java class named **Test_2_8**, and copy the code from the class **Test_2_7** into this new class. In the class **Test_2_8**, delete the code between the comments "**update data**" and "**render scene**," and in its place, add the following code:

```
translation.data.values[0] = (float)(0.75 * Math.cos(time));
translation.data.values[1] = (float)(0.75 * Math.sin(time));
```

With these additions, the code for this application is complete.

When you run this application, you will see a triangle moving in a circular path around the origin, in a counterclockwise direction. The **sin** and **cos** functions have a *period* of $2\pi$ units, meaning that they repeat their pattern of values during each interval of this length, and thus the triangle will complete a complete revolution around the origin every $2\pi$ (approximately 6.283) seconds. As before, part of this animation is illustrated with a sequence of images, which are displayed in Figure 2.12.

In the final example of this section, instead of an animation based on changing position, you will create an animation where the triangle color shifts back and forth between red and black. This will be accomplished by changing the value of the red component of the color variable. As before, you will use a sine function to generate oscillating values. Since the components that specify color components range between 0 and 1, while a sine function ranges between –1 and 1, the output values from the sine function will have to be modified. Since the function $f(t) = \sin(t)$ ranges from –1 to 1, the function $f(t) = \sin(t) + 1$ shifts the output values to the range 0 to 2. Next, you must scale the size of the range; the function $f(t) = (\sin(t) + 1) / 2$ ranges from 0 to 1. Further adjustments are also possible: for example, given a constant $c$, the function $\sin(c * t)$ will traverse its range of output values $c$ times faster than $\sin(t)$. The final version of the equation you will use is $f(t) = (\sin(3*t) + 1) / 2$.

FIGURE 2.12   Frames from an animation of a triangle moving along a circular path.

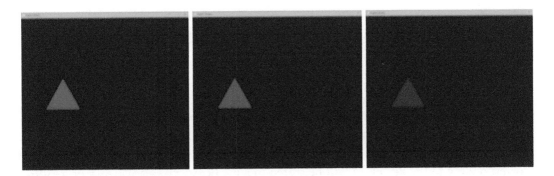

FIGURE 2.13   Frames from an animation of a triangle shifting color.

To create this example, create a new Java class named **Test_2_9** and copy the code from the class **Test_2_8**. As before, delete the code between the comments "**update data**" and "**render scene**," and in its place, add the following code:

```
// change colors
baseColor.data.values[0] =
    (float)((Math.sin(3*(time)) + 1) / 2);
```

Running this application, you should see the color of the triangle shifting between red and black every few seconds. This animation is illustrated with a sequence of images, which are displayed in Figure 2.13.

If desired, you could even make the triangle's color shift along a greater range of colors by also modifying the green and blue components of the color variable. In this case, the sine waves will also need to be shifted, so that each component reaches its peak value at different times. Mathematically, this can be accomplished by adding values to the $t$ variable within the sine function. This can be accomplished, for example, by replacing the code added above with the following:

```
baseColor.data.values[0] =
    (float)((Math.sin(time) + 1) / 2);
baseColor.data.values[1] =
    (float)((Math.sin(time + 2.1) + 1) / 2);
baseColor.data.values[2] =
    (float)((Math.sin((time + 4.2) + 1) / 2));
```

Feel free to experiment with and combine these different animations to see what you can produce!

## 2.5 ADDING INTERACTIVITY

In this section, you will add the ability for the user to interact with an application using the keyboard. The first step will be to create a new class, which will be named **Input**, and before creating a graphics-based application, you will test it with a text-based application.

After establishing that keyboard input works as expected, you will then use this functionality into a graphics-based application, where the user can move a triangle around the screen using the arrow keys.

## 2.5.1 Keyboard Input with LWJGL

The LWJGL library provides support for working with user input events, such as interaction with the keyboard. In particular, the LWJGL function **glfwSetKeyCallback** specifies code that will run when the user presses or releases a key; in this case, a value corresponding to the key event will be stored in a list (**keyPressedQueue** or **keyReleasedQueue**) in the **Input** class.

An event or action is said to be *discrete* if it happens once at an isolated point in time, or *continuous* if it continues happening during an interval of time. The keyboard events previously described are discrete, but many applications also feature continuous actions (such as moving an object on screen) that occur for the entire period during which a key is pressed down. Unfortunately, there seems to be no standard vocabulary for these standard discrete and continuous states; for example, a "key down" state sometimes refers to the discrete event when a key is initially pressed, and sometimes refers to the continuous state of a key after the initial press and before the key is released. Here, **keyDownList** and **keyUpList** will store names of keys corresponding to the discrete press and release events, while **keyPressedList** will store names of keys in the continuous state between these discrete events. For readability, the contents of each list can be queried using functions you will create in the **Input** class. The contents of these lists will be updated in the **Input** class **update** method, based on what has been stored in the **keyPressedQueue** and **keyReleasedQueue** since the last update. In particular, keys that are designated as down or up should only remain so for a single iteration of the main application loop, and so the contents of the corresponding lists must be cleared before processing the data in the queue variables.

To proceed, in the **core** package, create a new Java class file named **Input** with the following code:

```java
package core;

import java.util.ArrayList;
import static org.lwjgl.glfw.GLFW.*;

public class Input
{
    public boolean quit;

    public ArrayList<Integer> keyPressQueue;
    public ArrayList<Integer> keyReleaseQueue;

    public ArrayList<Integer> keyDownList;
    public ArrayList<Integer> keyPressedList;
    public ArrayList<Integer> keyUpList;
```

```java
// requires listening window reference
public Input(long window)
{
    quit = false;

    keyPressQueue   = new ArrayList<Integer>();
    keyReleaseQueue = new ArrayList<Integer>();

    keyDownList    = new ArrayList<Integer>();
    keyPressedList = new ArrayList<Integer>();
    keyUpList      = new ArrayList<Integer>();

    // specify code to run when key is pressed or released
    glfwSetKeyCallback(window,
        (window_, key, scancode, action, mods) ->
        {
            if ( action == GLFW_PRESS )
                keyPressQueue.add(key);

            if ( action == GLFW_RELEASE )
                keyReleaseQueue.add(key);
        }
    );
}

public void update()
{
    // reset discrete key states
    keyDownList.clear();
    keyUpList.clear();

    // process queued press/release events;
    // add to or remove from corresponding lists
    for (Integer key : keyPressQueue)
    {
        keyDownList.add(key);
        keyPressedList.add(key);
    }
    for (Integer key : keyReleaseQueue)
    {
        keyUpList.add(key);
        keyPressedList.remove(key);
    }

    // finished processing queues; clear contents
    keyPressQueue.clear();
    keyReleaseQueue.clear();
}
```

```java
    public boolean isKeyDown(Integer key)
    {
        return keyDownList.contains(key);
    }

    public boolean isKeyPressed(Integer key)
    {
        return keyPressedList.contains(key);
    }

    public boolean isKeyUp(Integer key)
    {
        return keyUpList.contains(key);
    }
}
```

Once this class is complete, in the **Base** class, add the following class variable:

```java
// handle user input events
public Input input;
```

Also add the following line of code right before the time variables are initialized:

```java
input = new Input(window);
```

Finally, in the **run** method, after the time variables are updated, add the following code:

```java
// process input
input.update();
```

As previously indicated, you will now create a text-based application to verify that these modifications work as expected, and to illustrate how the class will be used in practice. Create a new Java class named **Test_2_10** containing the following code:

```java
import static org.lwjgl.glfw.GLFW.*;
import core.*;

public class Test_2_10 extends Base
{

    public void initialize()
    {
        System.out.println("Initializing...");
    }
```

```
public void update()
{
    // typical usage
    if (input.isKeyDown(GLFW_KEY_SPACE))
        System.out.println( "space key" );
    if (input.isKeyPressed(GLFW_KEY_RIGHT))
        System.out.println( "right arrow key" );
    if (input.isKeyUp(GLFW_KEY_A))
        System.out.println( "letter 'A' key" );

}

// driver method
public static void main(String[] args)
{
    new Test_2_10().run();
}
}
```

When you run this program, pressing the space bar key should cause a single message to appear each time it is pressed, regardless of how long it is held down. In contrast, pressing the right arrow key should cause a series of messages to continue to appear until the key is released. A complete list of the constants corresponding to the keyboard keys can be found in the documentation at https://www.glfw.org/.

## 2.5.2 Incorporating with Graphics Programs

Now that the framework is able to process discrete and continuous keyboard input, you will create the graphics-based application described earlier, that enables the user to move a triangle using the arrow keys. As this application is similar to many of the animation examples previously discussed, begin by making a new class named **Test_2_11**, and in this class, copy the code from the class **Test_2_7**. In this new file, add the following variable right under the declaration of the uniform variable:

```
public float speed = 0.5f;
```

The **speed** variable specifies how quickly the triangle will move across the screen. Recalling that the horizontal or x-axis values displayed on screen range from −1 to 1, a speed of 0.5 indicates that the triangle will move all the way across the screen in 4 seconds.

Next, in the **update** function, delete the code between the comments "**update data**" and "**render scene**," and in its place, add the following code:

```
float distance = speed * deltaTime;
if (input.isKeyPressed(GLFW_KEY_LEFT))
    translation.data.values[0] -= distance;
if (input.isKeyPressed(GLFW_KEY_RIGHT))
```

```
      translation.data.values[0]  += distance;
if (input.isKeyPressed(GLFW_KEY_DOWN))
      translation.data.values[1]  -= distance;
if (input.isKeyPressed(GLFW_KEY_UP))
      translation.data.values[1]  += distance;
```

Note that this segment of code begins by calculating how far the triangle should be moved across the screen (the distance travelled), taking into account the elapsed time since the previous render, which is stored in the variable **deltaTime** that you added to the **Base** class earlier in the chapter. The calculation itself is based on the physics formula *speed = distance / time*, which is equivalent to *distance = speed * time*. Also note that a sequence of **if** statements are used, rather than **if-else** statements, which allows the user to press multiple keys simultaneously and move in diagonal directions, or even press keys indicating opposite directions, whose effects will cancel each other out. You may have noticed that translations of the z component (the forward/backward direction) were not included; this is because such a movement will not change the appearance of the shape on screen, since perspective transformations have not yet been introduced into the framework.

Once you have finished adding this code, run the application and try pressing the arrow keys to move the triangle around the screen. Congratulations on creating your first interactive GPU-based graphics program!

## 2.6 SUMMARY AND NEXT STEPS

In this chapter, you learned how to create animations and interactive applications. Each of these examples involved polygon shapes (the z coordinate of each point was always set to zero), and the movement was limited to translations (of the x and y coordinates). A natural next goal is to transform these shapes in more advanced ways, such as combining rotations with translations. Perspective transformations also need to be introduced so that translations in the z-direction and rotations around the *x*-axis and *y*-axis of the scene will appear as expected. In the next chapter, you will learn the mathematical foundations required to create these transformations, and in the process, create truly three-dimensional scenes.

# CHAPTER 3

# Matrix Algebra and Transformations

In this chapter, you will learn about some mathematical objects – vectors and matrices – that are essential to rendering three-dimensional (3D) scenes. After learning some theoretical background, you will apply this knowledge to create a **Matrix** class that will be fundamental in manipulating the position and orientation of geometric objects. Finally, you will learn how to incorporate matrix objects into the rendering of an interactive 3D scene.

## 3.1 INTRODUCTION TO VECTORS AND MATRICES

When creating animated and interactive graphics applications, you will frequently want to transform sets of points defining the shape of geometric objects. You may want to translate the object to a new position, rotate the object to a new orientation, or scale the object to a new size. Additionally, you will want to project the viewable region of the scene into the space that is rendered by OpenGL. This will frequently be a perspective projection, where objects appear smaller the further away they are from the virtual camera. These ideas were first introduced in Chapter 1, in the discussion of the graphics pipeline and geometry processing; these calculations take place in a vertex shader. In Chapter 2, you learned how to work with points (using the vector data types **vec3** and **vec4**), and you implemented a transformation (two-dimensional translation). In this chapter, you will learn about a data structure called a *matrix* – a rectangular or two-dimensional array of numbers – that is capable of representing all of the different types of transformations you will need in 3D graphics. For these matrix-based transformations, you will learn how to:

- apply a transformation to a point
- combine multiple transformations into a single transformation
- create a matrix corresponding to a given description of a transformation

DOI: 10.1201/9781003153375-3

### 3.1.1 Vector Definitions and Operations

In Chapter 2, you worked with vector data types, such as **vec3**, which are data structures whose components are floating-point numbers. In this section, you will learn about vectors from a mathematical point of view. For simplicity, the topics in this section will be introduced in a two-dimensional context. In Section 3.1.3, you will learn how each of the concepts is generalized to higher-dimensional settings.

A *coordinate system* is defined by an origin point and the orientation and scale of a set of coordinate axes. A *point* $P = (x, y)$ refers to a location in space, specified relative to a coordinate system. A point is typically drawn as a dot, as illustrated by Figure 3.1. Note that in the diagram, the axes are oriented so that the *x*-axis is pointing to the right, and the *y*-axis is pointing upward; the direction of the arrow represents the direction in which the values increase. The orientation of the coordinate axes is somewhat arbitrary, although having the *x*-axis point to the right is a standard choice. In most two-dimensional mathematics diagrams, as well as OpenGL, the *y*-axis points upward. However, in many two-dimensional computer graphics applications, the origin is placed in the top-left corner of the screen or drawing area, and the *y*-axis points downward. It is always important to know the orientation of the coordinate system you are working in!

A *vector* $v = \langle m, n \rangle$ refers to a *displacement* – an amount of change in each coordinate – and is typically drawn as an arrow pointing along the direction of displacement, as illustrated by Figure 3.2. The point where the arrow begins is called the *initial point* or *tail*; the point where the arrow ends is called the *terminal point* or *head*, and indicates the result when the displacement has been applied to the initial point. The distance between

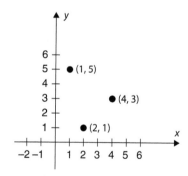

FIGURE 3.1   A collection of points.

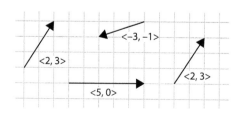

FIGURE 3.2   A collection of vectors.

the initial and terminal points of the vector is called its *length* or *magnitude*, and can be calculated from the components of the vector. Vectors are not associated to any particular location in space; the same vector may exist at different locations. A vector whose initial point is located at the origin (when a coordinate system is specified) is said to be in *standard position*.

To further emphasize the difference between location and displacement, consider navigating in a city whose roads are arranged as lines in a grid. If you were to ask someone to meet you at the intersection of 42nd Street and 5th Avenue, this refers to a particular location, and corresponds to a point. If you were to ask someone to travel five blocks North and three blocks East from their current position, this refers to a displacement (a change in their position), and corresponds to a vector.

Each of these mathematical objects – points and vectors – are represented by a list of numbers, but as explained above, they have different geometric interpretations. In this book, notation will be used to quickly distinguish these objects. When referring to vectors, bold lowercase letters will be used for variables, and angle brackets will be used when listing components, as in $v = \langle 1, 4 \rangle$. In contrast, when referring to points, regular (that is, non-bold) uppercase letters will be used for variables, and standard parentheses will be used when listing components, as in $P = (3, 2)$. Individual numbers (that are not part of a point or vector) are often called *scalars* in this context (to clearly distinguish them from points and vectors), and will be represented with regular lowercase letters, as in $x = 5$. Additionally, subscripted variables will sometimes be used when writing the components of a point or vector, and these subscripts may be letters or numbers, as in $P = (p_x, p_y)$ or $P = (p_1, p_2)$ for points, and $v = \langle v_x, v_y \rangle$ or $v = \langle v_1, v_2 \rangle$ for vectors.

While many algebraic operations can be defined on combinations of points and vectors, those with a geometric interpretation will be most significant in what follows. The first such operation is vector addition, which combines two vectors $v = \langle v_1, v_2 \rangle$ and $w = \langle w_1, w_2 \rangle$ and produces a new vector according to the formula

$$v + w = \langle v_1, v_2 \rangle + \langle w_1, w_2 \rangle = \langle v_1 + w_1, v_2 + w_2 \rangle$$

For example, $\langle 2, 5 \rangle + \langle 4, -2 \rangle = \langle 6, 3 \rangle$. Geometrically, this corresponds to displacement along the vector $v$, followed by displacement along the vector $w$; this can be visualized by aligning the terminal point of $v$ with the initial point of $w$. The result is a new vector $u = v + w$ that shares the initial point of $v$ and the terminal point of $w$, as illustrated in Figure 3.3.

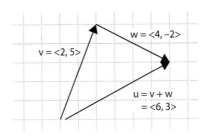

FIGURE 3.3   Vector addition.

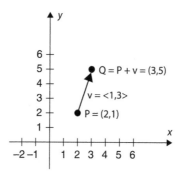

FIGURE 3.4   Adding a vector to a point.

There is also a geometric interpretation for adding a vector $v$ to a point $P$ with the same algebraic formula; this corresponds to translating a point to a new location, which yields a new point. Align the vector $v$ so its initial point is at location $P$, and the result is the point $Q$ located at the terminal point of $v$; this is expressed by the equation $P+v=Q$. For example, $(2, 2)+\langle 1, 3\rangle =(3, 5)$, as illustrated in Figure 3.4.

The sum of two points does not have any clear geometric interpretation, but the difference of two points does. Rearranging the equation $P+v=Q$ yields the equation $v=Q-P$, which can be thought of as calculating the displacement vector between two points by subtracting their coordinates.

The component wise product of two points or two vectors does not have any clear geometric interpretation. However, multiplying a vector $v$ by a scalar $c$ does. This operation is called *scalar multiplication*, and is defined by

$$c\cdot v=c\cdot\langle v_1, v_2\rangle=\langle c\cdot v_1, c\cdot v_2\rangle$$

For example, $2\cdot\langle 3, 2\rangle=\langle 6, 4\rangle$. Geometrically, this corresponds to scaling the vector; the length of $v$ is multiplied by a factor of $|c|$ (the absolute value of $c$), and the direction is reversed when $c<0$. Figure 3.5 illustrates scaling a vector $v$ by various amounts.

The operations of vector addition and scalar multiplication will be particularly important in what follows. Along these lines, consider the vectors $i=\langle 1, 0\rangle$ and $j=\langle 0, 1\rangle$. Any other

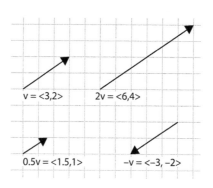

FIGURE 3.5   Scalar multiplication.

vector $v = \langle x, y \rangle$ can be written in terms of $i$ and $j$ using vector multiplication and scalar multiplication in exactly one way, as follows:

$$v = \langle x, y \rangle = \langle x, 0 \rangle + \langle 0, y \rangle = x \cdot \langle 1, 0 \rangle + y \cdot \langle 0, 1 \rangle = x \cdot i + y \cdot j$$

Any set of vectors with these properties is called a *basis*. There are many sets of basis vectors, but since $i$ and $j$ are in a sense the simplest such vectors, they are called the *standard basis* (for two-dimensional space).

## 3.1.2 Linear Transformations and Matrices

The main goal of this chapter is to design and create functions that transform sets of points or vectors in certain geometric ways. These are often called vector functions, to distinguish them from functions that have scalar valued input and output. They may also be called transformations to emphasize their geometric interpretation. These functions may be written as $F\big( (p_1, p_2) \big) = (q_1, q_2)$, or $F(\langle v_1, v_2 \rangle) = \langle w_1, w_2 \rangle$, or occasionally vectors will be written in column form, as in:

$$F\left( \begin{bmatrix} v_1 \\ v_2 \end{bmatrix} \right) = \begin{bmatrix} w_1 \\ w_2 \end{bmatrix}$$

The latter of these three expressions is most commonly used in a traditional mathematical presentation, but the alternative expressions are often used for writing mathematics within sentences.

Vector functions with differing levels of complexity are easy to write. As simple examples, one may consider the *zero function*, where the output is always the zero vector:

$$F(\langle v_1, v_2 \rangle) = \langle 0, 0 \rangle$$

There is also the *identity function*, where the output is always equal to the input:

$$F(\langle v_1, v_2 \rangle) = \langle v_1, v_2 \rangle$$

At the other extreme, one could invent all manner of arbitrary complicated expressions, such as:

$$F(\langle v_1, v_2 \rangle) = \left\langle v_1 - 3 \cdot cos(3v_2), (v_1)^7 + ln(|v_2|) + \pi \right\rangle$$

Most of which lack any geometrical significance whatsoever.

The key is to find a relatively simple class of vector functions which can perform the types of geometric transformations described at the beginning of this chapter. It will be particularly helpful to choose to work with vector functions that can be simplified in some useful way. One such set of functions are *linear functions* or *linear transformations*, which are functions $F$ that satisfy the following two equations relating to scalar multiplication and vector addition: for any scalar $c$ and vectors $v$ and $w$,

$$F(c \cdot v) = c \cdot F(v)$$

$$F(v + w) = F(v) + F(w)$$

One advantage to working with such functions involves the standard basis vectors $i$ and $j$: if $F$ is a linear function and the values of $F(i)$ and $F(j)$ are known, then it is possible to calculate the value of $F(v)$ for any vector $v$, even when a general formula for the function $F$ is not given. For example, assume that $F$ is a linear function, $F(i) = \langle 1, 2 \rangle$, and $F(j) = \langle 3, 1 \rangle$. Then by using the equations that linear functions satisfy, the value of $F(\langle 4, 5 \rangle)$ can be calculated as follows:

$$F(\langle 4, 5 \rangle) = F(\langle 4, 0 \rangle + \langle 0, 5 \rangle)$$

$$= F(\langle 4, 0 \rangle) + F(\langle 0, 5 \rangle)$$

$$= F(4 \cdot \langle 1, 0 \rangle) + F(5 \cdot \langle 0, 1 \rangle)$$

$$= 4 \cdot F(\langle 1, 0 \rangle) + 5 \cdot F(\langle 0, 1 \rangle)$$

$$= 4 \cdot F(i) + 5 \cdot F(j)$$

$$= 4 \cdot \langle 1, 2 \rangle + 5 \cdot \langle 3, 1 \rangle$$

$$= \langle 4, 8 \rangle + \langle 15, 5 \rangle$$

$$= \langle 19, 13 \rangle$$

In a similar way, the general formula for $F(\langle x, y \rangle)$ for this example can be calculated:

$$F(\langle x, y \rangle) = F(\langle x, 0 \rangle + \langle 0, y \rangle)$$

$$= F(\langle x, 0 \rangle) + F(\langle 0, y \rangle)$$

$$= F(x \cdot \langle 1, 0 \rangle) + F(y \cdot \langle 0, 1 \rangle)$$

$$= x \cdot F(\langle 1, 0 \rangle) + y \cdot F(\langle 0, 1 \rangle)$$

$$= x \cdot F(i) + y \cdot F(j)$$

$$= x \cdot \langle 1, 2 \rangle + y \cdot \langle 3, 1 \rangle$$

$$= \langle x, 2x \rangle + \langle 3y, y \rangle$$

$$= \langle x + 3y, 2x + y \rangle$$

In fact, the same line of reasoning establishes the most general case: if $F$ is a linear function, where $F(i) = \langle a, c \rangle$ and $F(j) = \langle b, d \rangle$, then the formula for the function $F$ is $F(\langle x, y \rangle) = \langle a \cdot x + b \cdot y, c \cdot x + d \cdot y \rangle$, since:

$$F(\langle x, y \rangle) = F(\langle x, 0 \rangle + \langle 0, y \rangle)$$

$$= F(\langle x, 0 \rangle) + F(\langle 0, y \rangle)$$

$$= F(x \cdot \langle 1, 0 \rangle) + F(y \cdot \langle 0, 1 \rangle)$$

$$= x \cdot F(\langle 1, 0 \rangle) + y \cdot F(\langle 0, 1 \rangle)$$

$$= x \cdot F(i) + y \cdot F(j)$$

$$= x \cdot \langle a, c \rangle + y \cdot \langle b, d \rangle$$

$$= \langle a \cdot x, c \cdot x \rangle + \langle b \cdot y, d \cdot y \rangle$$

$$= \langle a \cdot x + b \cdot y, c \cdot x + d \cdot y \rangle$$

In addition to these useful algebraic properties, it is possible to visualize the geometric effect of a linear function on the entire space. To begin, consider a unit square consisting of the points $\langle u, v \rangle = u \cdot i + v \cdot j$, where $0 \le u \le 1$ and $0 \le v \le 1$, the dot-shaded square labeled as $S$ on the left side of Figure 3.6. Assume $F$ is a linear function with $F(i) = m$ and $F(j) = n$. Then, the set of points in $S$ is transformed to the set of points that can be written as:

$$F(u \cdot i + v \cdot j) = u \cdot F(i) + v \cdot F\langle j \rangle = u \cdot m + v \cdot n$$

This area is indicated by the dot-shaded parallelogram labeled as $T$ on the right side of Figure 3.6. Similarly, the function $F$ transforms each square region on the left of Figure 3.6 into a parallelogram shaped region on the right of Figure 3.6.

The formula for a linear function $F$ can be written in column form as

$$F\left( \begin{bmatrix} x \\ y \end{bmatrix} \right) = \begin{bmatrix} a \cdot x + b \cdot y \\ c \cdot x + d \cdot y \end{bmatrix}$$

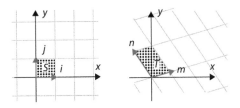

FIGURE 3.6 The geometric effects of a linear transformation.

It is useful to think of the vector $\langle x, y \rangle$ as being operated on by the set of numbers $a$, $b$, $c$, $d$, which naturally leads us to a particular mathematical notation: these numbers can be grouped into a rectangular array of numbers called a *matrix*, typically enclosed within square brackets, and the function $F$ can be rewritten as:

$$F\left(\begin{bmatrix} x \\ y \end{bmatrix}\right) = \begin{bmatrix} a & b \\ c & d \end{bmatrix} \begin{bmatrix} x \\ y \end{bmatrix}$$

In accordance with this notation, the *product* of a matrix and a vector is defined by the equation

$$\begin{bmatrix} a & b \\ c & d \end{bmatrix} \begin{bmatrix} x \\ y \end{bmatrix} = \begin{bmatrix} a \cdot x + b \cdot y \\ c \cdot x + d \cdot y \end{bmatrix}$$

For example, consider the linear function

$$F\left(\begin{bmatrix} x \\ y \end{bmatrix}\right) = \begin{bmatrix} 2 & 3 \\ 4 & 1 \end{bmatrix} \begin{bmatrix} x \\ y \end{bmatrix}$$

Then, $F(\langle 5, 6 \rangle)$ can be calculated as follows:

$$F\left(\begin{bmatrix} 5 \\ 6 \end{bmatrix}\right) = \begin{bmatrix} 2 & 3 \\ 4 & 1 \end{bmatrix} \begin{bmatrix} 5 \\ 6 \end{bmatrix} = \begin{bmatrix} 2 \cdot 5 + 3 \cdot 6 \\ 4 \cdot 5 + 1 \cdot 6 \end{bmatrix} = \begin{bmatrix} 28 \\ 26 \end{bmatrix}$$

Similarly, to calculate $F(\langle -3, 1 \rangle)$:

$$F\left(\begin{bmatrix} -3 \\ 1 \end{bmatrix}\right) = \begin{bmatrix} 2 & 3 \\ 4 & 1 \end{bmatrix} \begin{bmatrix} -3 \\ 1 \end{bmatrix} = \begin{bmatrix} 2 \cdot (-3) + 3 \cdot 1 \\ 4 \cdot (-3) + 1 \cdot 1 \end{bmatrix} = \begin{bmatrix} -3 \\ -11 \end{bmatrix}$$

Once again, it will be helpful to use notation to distinguish between matrices and other types of mathematical objects (scalars, points, and vectors). When referring to a matrix, bold uppercase letters will be used for variables, and square brackets will be used to enclose the grid of numbers or variables. This notation can be used to briefly summarize the previous observation: if $F$ is a linear function, then $F$ can be written in the form $F(v) = A \cdot v$ for some matrix $A$. Conversely, one can also show that if $F$ is a vector function defined by matrix multiplication, that is, if $F(v) = A \cdot v$, then $F$ also satisfies the equations that define a linear function; this can be verified by straightforward algebraic calculations. Therefore, these two descriptions of vector functions – those that are linear and those defined by matrix multiplication – are equivalent; they define precisely the same set of functions.

Two of the vector functions previously mentioned can both be represented using matrix multiplication: the zero function can be written as

$$F\left(\begin{bmatrix} x \\ y \end{bmatrix}\right) = \begin{bmatrix} 0 & 0 \\ 0 & 0 \end{bmatrix}\begin{bmatrix} x \\ y \end{bmatrix} = \begin{bmatrix} 0 \cdot x + 0 \cdot y \\ 0 \cdot x + 0 \cdot y \end{bmatrix} = \begin{bmatrix} 0 \\ 0 \end{bmatrix}$$

while the identity function can be written as

$$F\left(\begin{bmatrix} x \\ y \end{bmatrix}\right) = \begin{bmatrix} 1 & 0 \\ 0 & 1 \end{bmatrix}\begin{bmatrix} x \\ y \end{bmatrix} = \begin{bmatrix} 1 \cdot x + 0 \cdot y \\ 0 \cdot x + 1 \cdot y \end{bmatrix} = \begin{bmatrix} x \\ y \end{bmatrix}$$

The matrix in the definition of the identity function is called the *identity matrix*, and appears in a variety of contexts, as you will see.

When introducing notation for vectors, it was indicated that subscripted variables will sometimes be used for the components of a vector. When working with a matrix, *double* subscripted variables will sometimes be used for its components; the subscripts will indicate the position (row and column) of the component in the matrix. For example, the variable $a_{12}$ will refer to the entry in row 1 and column 2 of the matrix $A$, and in general, $a_{mn}$ will refer to the entry in row $m$ and column $n$ of the matrix $A$. The contents of the entire matrix $A$ can be written as:

$$A = \begin{bmatrix} a_{11} & a_{12} \\ a_{21} & a_{22} \end{bmatrix}$$

At this point, you know how to apply a linear function (written in matrix notation) to a point or a vector. In many contexts (and in computer graphics in particular), you will want to apply multiple functions to a set of points. Given two functions $F$ and $G$, a new function $H$ can be created by defining $H(v) = F(G(v))$; the function $H$ is called the *composition of* $F$ and $G$. As it turns out, if $F$ and $G$ are linear functions, then $H$ will be a linear function as well. This can be verified by checking that the two linearity equations hold for $H$, making use of the fact that the linearity equations are true for the functions $F$ and $G$ by assumption. The derivation relating to vector addition is as follows:

$$H(v+w) = F\big(G(v+w)\big)$$
$$= F\big(G(v)+G(w)\big)$$
$$= F\big(G(v)\big) + F\big(G(w)\big)$$
$$= H(v) + H(w)$$

The derivation relating to scalar multiplication is as follows:

$$H(c \cdot v) = F(G(c \cdot v))$$
$$= F(c \cdot G(v))$$
$$= c \cdot F(G(v))$$
$$= c \cdot H(v)$$

The reason this is significant is that given two linear functions – each of which can be represented by a matrix, as previously observed – their composition can be represented by a *single* matrix, since the composition is also a linear function. By repeatedly applying this reasoning, it follows that the composition of *any number* of linear functions can be represented by a *single* matrix. This immediately leads to the question: how can the matrix corresponding to the composition be calculated? Algebraically, given two transformations $F(v) = A \cdot v$ and $G(v) = B \cdot v$, the goal is to find a matrix $C$ such that the transformation $H(v) = C \cdot v$ is equal to $F(G(v)) = A \cdot (B \cdot v)$ for all vectors $v$. In this case, one writes $C = A \cdot B$. This operation is referred to as *matrix multiplication*, and $C$ is called the *product* of the matrices $A$ and $B$.

The formula for matrix multiplication may be deduced by computing both sides of the equation $C \cdot v = A \cdot (B \cdot v)$ and equating the coefficients of $x$ and $y$ on either side of the equation. Expanding $C \cdot v$ yields:

$$C \cdot v = \begin{bmatrix} c_{11} & c_{12} \\ c_{21} & c_{22} \end{bmatrix} \begin{bmatrix} x \\ y \end{bmatrix} = \begin{bmatrix} c_{11} \cdot x + c_{12} \cdot y \\ c_{21} \cdot x + c_{22} \cdot y \end{bmatrix}$$

Similarly, expanding $A \cdot (B \cdot v)$ yields:

$$A \cdot (B \cdot v) = \begin{bmatrix} a_{11} & a_{12} \\ a_{21} & a_{22} \end{bmatrix} \left( \begin{bmatrix} b_{11} & b_{12} \\ b_{21} & b_{22} \end{bmatrix} \cdot \begin{bmatrix} x \\ y \end{bmatrix} \right)$$

$$= \begin{bmatrix} a_{11} & a_{12} \\ a_{21} & a_{22} \end{bmatrix} \cdot \begin{bmatrix} b_{11} \cdot x + b_{12} \cdot y \\ b_{21} \cdot x + b_{22} \cdot y \end{bmatrix}$$

$$= \begin{bmatrix} a_{11}(b_{11} \cdot x + b_{12} \cdot y) + a_{12}(b_{21} \cdot x + b_{22} \cdot y) \\ a_{21}(b_{11} \cdot x + b_{12} \cdot y) + a_{22}(b_{21} \cdot x + b_{22} \cdot y) \end{bmatrix}$$

$$= \begin{bmatrix} (a_{11} \cdot b_{11} + a_{12} \cdot b_{21}) \cdot x + (a_{11} \cdot b_{12} + a_{12} \cdot b_{22}) \cdot y \\ (a_{21} \cdot b_{11} + a_{22} \cdot b_{21}) \cdot x + (a_{21} \cdot b_{12} + a_{22} \cdot b_{22}) \cdot y \end{bmatrix}$$

Thus, matrix multiplication $C = A \cdot B$ is defined as:

$$\begin{bmatrix} c_{11} & c_{12} \\ c_{21} & c_{22} \end{bmatrix} = \begin{bmatrix} (a_{11} \cdot b_{11} + a_{12} \cdot b_{21}) + (a_{11} \cdot b_{12} + a_{12} \cdot b_{22}) \\ (a_{21} \cdot b_{11} + a_{22} \cdot b_{21}) + (a_{21} \cdot b_{12} + a_{22} \cdot b_{22}) \end{bmatrix}$$

This formula can be written more simply using a vector operation called the *dot product*. Given vectors $v = \langle v_1, v_2 \rangle$ and $w = \langle w_1, w_2 \rangle$, the dot product $d = v \cdot w$ is a (scalar) number, defined by:

$$d = v \cdot w = \langle v_1, v_2 \rangle \cdot \langle w_1, w_2 \rangle = v_1 \cdot w_1 + v_2 \cdot w_2$$

As an example of a dot product calculation, consider:

$$\langle 3, 4 \rangle \cdot \langle 7, 5 \rangle = 3 \cdot 7 + 4 \cdot 5 = 41$$

To restate the definition of matrix multiplication: partition the matrix $A$ into row vectors and the matrix $B$ into column vectors. The entry $c_{mn}$ of the product matrix $C = A \cdot B$ is equal to the dot product of row vector $m$ from matrix $A$ (denoted by $a_m$) and column vector $n$ from matrix $B$ (denoted by $b_n$), as illustrated in the following formula, where partitions are indicated by dashed lines.

$$A \cdot B = \begin{bmatrix} a_{11} & a_{12} \\ \hline a_{21} & a_{22} \end{bmatrix} \cdot \begin{bmatrix} b_{11} & b_{12} \\ b_{21} & b_{22} \end{bmatrix}$$

$$= \begin{bmatrix} a_1 \\ \hline a_2 \end{bmatrix} \cdot \begin{bmatrix} b_1 & b_2 \end{bmatrix}$$

$$= \begin{bmatrix} a_1 \cdot b_1 & a_1 \cdot b_2 \\ a_2 \cdot b_1 & a_2 \cdot b_2 \end{bmatrix}$$

$$= \begin{bmatrix} c_{11} & c_{12} \\ c_{21} & c_{22} \end{bmatrix}$$

As an example of a matrix multiplication computation, consider:

$$\begin{bmatrix} 2 & 3 \\ 4 & 5 \end{bmatrix} \cdot \begin{bmatrix} 9 & 8 \\ 7 & 6 \end{bmatrix} = \begin{bmatrix} \langle 2, 3 \rangle \cdot \langle 9, 7 \rangle & \langle 2, 3 \rangle \cdot \langle 8, 6 \rangle \\ \langle 4, 5 \rangle \cdot \langle 9, 7 \rangle & \langle 4, 5 \rangle \cdot \langle 8, 6 \rangle \end{bmatrix}$$

$$= \begin{bmatrix} (2 \cdot 9 + 3 \cdot 7) & (2 \cdot 8 + 3 \cdot 6) \\ (4 \cdot 9 + 5 \cdot 7) & (4 \cdot 8 + 5 \cdot 6) \end{bmatrix}$$

$$= \begin{bmatrix} 39 & 34 \\ 71 & 62 \end{bmatrix}$$

In general, matrix multiplication can quickly become tedious, and so a software package is typically used to handle these and other matrix-related calculations.

It is important to note that, in general, matrix multiplication is not a commutative operation. Given matrices $A$ and $B$, the product $A \cdot B$ is usually not equal to the product $B \cdot A$. For example, calculating the product of the matrices from the previous example in the opposite order yields:

$$\begin{bmatrix} 9 & 8 \\ 7 & 6 \end{bmatrix} \cdot \begin{bmatrix} 2 & 3 \\ 4 & 5 \end{bmatrix} = \begin{bmatrix} \langle 9,8 \rangle \cdot \langle 2,4 \rangle & \langle 9,8 \rangle \cdot \langle 2,5 \rangle \\ \langle 7,2 \rangle \cdot \langle 6,4 \rangle & \langle 7,6 \rangle \cdot \langle 3,5 \rangle \end{bmatrix}$$

$$= \begin{bmatrix} (9 \cdot 2 + 8 \cdot 4) & (9 \cdot 3 + 8 \cdot 5) \\ (7 \cdot 2 + 6 \cdot 4) & (7 \cdot 3 + 6 \cdot 5) \end{bmatrix}$$

$$= \begin{bmatrix} 50 & 67 \\ 38 & 51 \end{bmatrix}$$

This fact has a corresponding geometric interpretation as well: the order in which geometric transformations are performed makes a difference. For example, let $T$ represent translation by $\langle 1, 0 \rangle$, and let $R$ represent rotation around the origin by 90°. If $P$ denotes the point $P = (2, 0)$, then $R(T(P)) = R((3, 0)) = (0, 3)$, while $T(R(P)) = T((0, 2)) = (1, 2)$, as illustrated in Figure 3.7. Thus, $R(T(P))$ does not equal $T(R(P))$.

The identity matrix $I$, previously mentioned, is the matrix

$$I = \begin{bmatrix} 1 & 0 \\ 0 & 1 \end{bmatrix}$$

The identity matrix has multiplication properties similar to those of the number 1 in ordinary multiplication. Just as for any number $x$ it is true that $1 \cdot x = x$ and $x \cdot 1 = x$, for any matrix $A$ it can be shown with algebra that $I \cdot A = A$ and $A \cdot I = A$. Because of these properties, both 1 and $I$ are called *identity elements* in their corresponding mathematical contexts. Similarly, the identity function is the identity element in the context of function

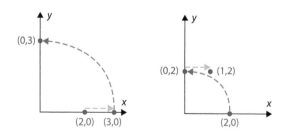

FIGURE 3.7  Geometric transformations (translation and rotation) are not commutative.

composition. Thinking of vector functions as geometric transformations, the identity function does not change the location of any points; the geometric transformations translation by $\langle 0, 0 \rangle$, rotation around the origin by $0°$, and scaling all components by a factor of 1, are all equivalent to the identity function.

The concept of identity elements leads to the concept of *inverse* elements. In a given mathematical context, combining an object with its inverse yields the identity element. For example, a number $x$ multiplied by its inverse equals 1; a function composed with its inverse function yields the identity function. Analogously, a matrix multiplied by its inverse matrix results in the identity matrix. Symbolically, the inverse of a matrix $A$ is a matrix $M$ such that $A \cdot M = I$ and $M \cdot A = I$. The inverse of the matrix $A$ is typically written using the notation $A^{-1}$. Using a fair amount of algebra, one can find a formula for the inverse of the matrix $A$ by solving the equation $A \cdot M = I$ for the entries of $M$:

$$A \cdot M = \begin{bmatrix} a & b \\ c & d \end{bmatrix} \cdot \begin{bmatrix} m & n \\ p & q \end{bmatrix} = \begin{bmatrix} 1 & 0 \\ 0 & 1 \end{bmatrix} = I$$

Solving this equation first involves calculating the product on the left-hand side of the equation and setting each entry of the resulting matrix equal to the corresponding entry in the identity matrix. This yields a system of four equations with four unknowns (the entries of $M$). Solving these four equations yields the following formula for the inverse of a 2-by-2 matrix:

$$M = A^{-1} = \begin{bmatrix} d/(ad-bc) & -b/(ad-bc) \\ -c/(ad-bc) & a/(ad-bc) \end{bmatrix}$$

The value $(a \cdot d - b \cdot c)$ appearing in the denominator of each entry of the inverse matrix is called the *determinant* of the matrix $A$. If this value is equal to 0, then the fractions are all undefined, and the inverse of the matrix $A$ does not exist. Analogous situations, in which certain elements do not have inverse elements, arise in other mathematical contexts. For example, in ordinary arithmetic, the number $x = 0$ does not have a multiplicative inverse, as nothing times 0 equals the identity element 1.

As may be expected, if an invertible vector function $F$ can be represented with matrix multiplication as $F(v) = A \cdot v$, then the inverse function $G$ can be represented with matrix multiplication by the inverse of $A$, as $G(v) = A^{-1} \cdot v$, since

$$F(G(v)) = A \cdot A^{-1} \cdot v = I \cdot v = v$$

$$G(F(v)) = A^{-1} \cdot A \cdot v = I \cdot v = v$$

Once again, thinking of vector functions as geometric transformations, the inverse of a function performs a transformation that is in some sense the "opposite" or "reverse" transformation. As examples: the inverse of translation by $\langle m, n \rangle$ is translation by $\langle -m, -n \rangle$;

the inverse of clockwise rotation by an angle $a$ is counterclockwise rotation by an angle $a$ (which is equivalent to clockwise rotation by an angle $-a$); the inverse of scaling the components of a vector by the values $r$ and $s$ is scaling the components by the values $1/r$ and $1/s$.

### 3.1.3 Vectors and Matrices in Higher Dimensions

All of these vector and matrix concepts can be generalized to three, four, and even higher dimensions. In this section, these concepts will be restated in a 3D context. The generalization to four-dimensional space follows the same algebraic pattern. Four-dimensional vectors and matrices are used quite frequently in computer graphics, for reasons discussed later in this chapter.

Three dimensional coordinate systems are drawn using $xyz$-axes, where each axis is perpendicular to the other two. Assuming that the axes are oriented as in Figure 3.1, so that the plane spanned by the $x$- and $y$-axes are aligned with the window used to display graphics, there are two possible directions for the (positive) $z$-axis: either pointing toward the viewer or away from the viewer. These two systems are called *right-handed* and *left-handed coordinate systems*, respectively, so named due to the hand-based mnemonic rule used to remember the orientation. To visualize the relative orientation of the axes in a right-handed coordinate system, using your right hand, imagine your index finger pointing along the $x$-axis, and your middle finger perpendicular to this (in the direction the palm of your hand is facing), pointing along the $y$-axis. Then your extended thumb will be pointing in the direction of the $z$-axis; this is illustrated in Figure 3.8. If the $z$-axis were pointing in the opposite direction, this would correspond to a left-handed coordinate system, and indeed this would be the orientation indicated by carrying out the steps above with your left hand. Some descriptions of the right-hand rule, instead of indicating the directions of the $x$ and $y$ axes with extended fingers, will suggest curling the fingers of your hand in the direction from the $x$-axis to the $y$-axis; your extended thumb still indicates the direction of the $z$-axis, and the two descriptions have the same result.

In mathematics, physics, and computer graphics, it is standard practice to use a right-handed coordinate system, as shown on the left side of Figure 3.9. In computer graphics, the positive $z$-axis points directly at the viewer. Although the three axes are perpendicular to each other, when illustrated in this way, at first it may be difficult to see that the $z$-axis is perpendicular to the other axes. In this case, it may aid with visualization to imagine the $xyz$-axes as aligned with the edges of a cube hidden from view, illustrated with dashed lines as shown on the right side of Figure 3.9.

FIGURE 3.8   Using a right hand to determine the orientation of $xyz$-axes.

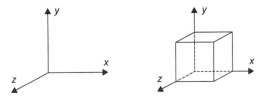

FIGURE 3.9 Coordinate axes in three dimensions.

In 3D space, points are written as $P = (p_x, p_y, p_z)$ or $P = (p_1, p_2, p_3)$, and vectors are written as $v = \langle v_x, v_y, v_z \rangle$ or $v = \langle v_1, v_2, v_3 \rangle$. Sometimes, for clarity, the components may be written as $x$, $y$, and $z$ (and in four-dimensional space, the fourth component may be written as $w$). Vector addition is defined by

$$v + w = \langle v_1, v_2, v_3 \rangle + \langle w_1, w_2, w_3 \rangle = \langle v_1 + w_1, v_2 + w_2, v_3 + w_3 \rangle$$

While scalar multiplication is defined by

$$c \cdot v = c \cdot \langle v_1, v_2, v_3 \rangle = \langle c \cdot v_1, c \cdot v_2, c \cdot v_3 \rangle$$

The standard basis for 3D space consists of the vectors $i = \langle 1, 0, 0 \rangle$, $j = \langle 0, 1, 0 \rangle$, and $k = \langle 0, 0, 1 \rangle$. Every vector $v = \langle x, y, z \rangle$ can be written as a linear combination of these three vectors as follows:

$$v = \langle x, y, z \rangle$$
$$= \langle x, 0, 0 \rangle + \langle 0, y, 0 \rangle + \langle 0, 0, z \rangle$$
$$= x \cdot \langle 1, 0, 0 \rangle + y \cdot \langle 0, 1, 0 \rangle + z \cdot \langle 0, 0, 1 \rangle$$
$$= x \cdot i + y \cdot j + z \cdot k$$

The definition of a linear function is identical for vectors of any dimension, as it only involves the operations of vector addition and scalar multiplication; it does not reference the number of components of a vector at all:

$$F(c \cdot v) = c \cdot F(v)$$
$$F(v + w) = F(v) + F(w)$$

The values of a 3D linear function can be calculated for any vector if the values of $F(i)$, $F(j)$, and $F(k)$ are known, and in general, such a function can be written in the form

$$F\left(\begin{bmatrix} x \\ y \\ z \end{bmatrix}\right) = \begin{bmatrix} a_{11} \cdot x + a_{12} \cdot y + a_{13} \cdot z \\ a_{21} \cdot x + a_{22} \cdot y + a_{23} \cdot z \\ a_{31} \cdot x + a_{32} \cdot y + a_{33} \cdot z \end{bmatrix}$$

As before, the coefficients of $x$, $y$, and $z$ in the formula are typically grouped into a three-by-three matrix:

$$A = \begin{bmatrix} a_{11} & a_{12} & a_{13} \\ a_{21} & a_{22} & a_{23} \\ a_{31} & a_{32} & a_{33} \end{bmatrix}$$

The matrix-vector product $A \cdot v$ is then defined as:

$$A \cdot v = \begin{bmatrix} a_{11} & a_{12} & a_{13} \\ a_{21} & a_{22} & a_{23} \\ a_{31} & a_{32} & a_{33} \end{bmatrix} \begin{bmatrix} x \\ y \\ z \end{bmatrix} = \begin{bmatrix} a_{11} \cdot x + a_{12} \cdot y + a_{13} \cdot z \\ a_{21} \cdot x + a_{22} \cdot y + a_{23} \cdot z \\ a_{31} \cdot x + a_{32} \cdot y + a_{33} \cdot z \end{bmatrix}$$

Matrix multiplication is most clearly described using the dot product, which for 3D vectors is defined as

$$d = v \cdot w = \langle v_1, v_2, v_3 \rangle \cdot \langle w_1, w_2, w_3 \rangle = v_1 \cdot w_1 + v_2 \cdot w_2 + v_3 \cdot w_3$$

Matrix multiplication $A \cdot B$ can be calculated from partitioning the entries of the two matrices into vectors: each row of the first matrix ($A$) is written as a vector, and each column of the second matrix ($B$) is written as a vector. Then, the value in row $m$ and column $n$ of the product is equal to the dot product of row vector $m$ from matrix $A$ (denoted by $a_m$) and column vector $n$ from matrix $B$ (denoted by $b_n$), as illustrated below.

$$A \cdot B = \left[ \begin{array}{ccc} a_{11} & a_{12} & a_{13} \\ \hline a_{21} & a_{22} & a_{23} \\ \hline a_{31} & a_{32} & a_{33} \end{array} \right] \cdot \left[ \begin{array}{c|c|c} b_{11} & b_{12} & b_{13} \\ b_{21} & b_{22} & b_{23} \\ b_{31} & b_{32} & b_{33} \end{array} \right]$$

$$= \left[ \begin{array}{c} a_1 \\ \hline a_2 \\ \hline a_3 \end{array} \right] \cdot \left[ \begin{array}{c|c|c} b_1 & b_2 & b_3 \end{array} \right]$$

$$= \begin{bmatrix} a_1 \cdot b_1 & a_1 \cdot b_2 & a_1 \cdot b_3 \\ a_2 \cdot b_1 & a_2 \cdot b_2 & a_2 \cdot b_3 \\ a_3 \cdot b_1 & a_3 \cdot b_2 & a_3 \cdot b_3 \end{bmatrix}$$

$$= \begin{bmatrix} c_{11} & c_{12} & c_{13} \\ c_{21} & c_{22} & c_{23} \\ c_{31} & c_{32} & c_{33} \end{bmatrix}$$

The three-by-three identity matrix $I$ has the form:

$$I = \begin{bmatrix} 1 & 0 & 0 \\ 0 & 1 & 0 \\ 0 & 0 & 1 \end{bmatrix}$$

As before, this identity matrix is defined by the equations $I \cdot A = A$ and $A \cdot I = A$ for any matrix $A$. Similarly, the inverse of a matrix $A$ (if it exists) is a matrix denoted by $A^{-1}$, defined by the equations $A \cdot A^{-1} = I$ and $A^{-1} \cdot A = I$. The formula for the inverse of a three-by-three matrix in terms of its entries is quite tedious to write down; the code to calculate this will be given in Section 3.3.

## 3.2 GEOMETRIC TRANSFORMATIONS

The previous section introduced linear functions: vector functions that satisfy the linearity equations, functions which can be written with matrix multiplication. It remains to show that the geometric transformations needed in computer graphics (translation, rotation, scaling, and perspective projections) are linear functions, and then formulas must be found for the corresponding matrices. In particular, it must be possible to determine the entries of a matrix corresponding to a description of a transformation, such as "translate along the $x$-direction by 3 units" or "rotate around the $z$-axis by 45°." Formulas for each type of transformation (in both two and three dimensions) will be derived next, in increasing order of difficulty: scaling, rotation, translation, and perspective projection. In the following sections, vectors will be drawn in standard position (the initial point of each vector will be at the origin) and vectors can be identified with their terminal points.

### 3.2.1 Scaling

A scaling transformation multiplies each component of a vector by a constant. For two-dimensional vectors, this has the following form (where $r$ and $s$ are constants):

$$F\left(\begin{bmatrix} x \\ y \end{bmatrix}\right) = \begin{bmatrix} r \cdot x \\ s \cdot y \end{bmatrix}$$

It can quickly be deduced and verified that this transformation can be expressed with matrix multiplication as follows:

$$F\left(\begin{bmatrix} x \\ y \end{bmatrix}\right) = \begin{bmatrix} r \cdot x \\ s \cdot y \end{bmatrix} = \begin{bmatrix} r & 0 \\ 0 & s \end{bmatrix} \cdot \begin{bmatrix} x \\ y \end{bmatrix}$$

Similarly, the 3D version of this transformation, where the $z$-component of a vector is scaled by a constant value $t$, is:

$$F\left(\begin{bmatrix} x \\ y \\ z \end{bmatrix}\right) = \begin{bmatrix} r \cdot x \\ s \cdot y \\ t \cdot z \end{bmatrix} = \begin{bmatrix} r & 0 & 0 \\ 0 & s & 0 \\ 0 & 0 & t \end{bmatrix} \cdot \begin{bmatrix} x \\ y \\ z \end{bmatrix}$$

Observe that if all the scaling constants are equal to one, then the formula for the scaling matrix results in the identity matrix. This corresponds to the following pair of related statements: scaling the components of a vector by one does not change the value of the vector, just as multiplying a vector by the identity matrix does not change the value of the vector.

### 3.2.2 Rotation

In two dimensions, a rotation transformation rotates vectors by a constant amount around the origin point. Unlike the case with the scaling transformation, it is not immediately clear how to write a formula for a rotation function $F(v)$, or whether rotation transformations can even be calculated with matrix multiplication. To establish this fact, it suffices to show that rotation is a linear transformation: that it satisfies the two linearity equations. An informal geometric argument will be presented for each equation.

To see that $F(c \cdot v) = c \cdot F(v)$, begin by considering the endpoint of the vector $v$, and assume that this point is at a distance $d$ from the origin. When multiplying $v$ by $c$, the resulting vector has the same direction, and the endpoint is now at a distance $c \cdot d$ from the origin. Note that rotation transformations fix the origin point and do not change the distance of a point from the origin. Applying the rotation transformation $F$ to the vectors $v$ and $c \cdot v$ yields the vectors $F(v)$ and $F(c \cdot v)$; these vectors have the same direction, and their endpoints have the same distances from the origin: $d$ and $c \cdot d$, respectively. However, the vector $c \cdot F(v)$ is also aligned with $F(v)$ and its endpoint has distance $c \cdot d$ from the origin. Therefore, the endpoints of $F(c \cdot v)$ and $c \cdot F(v)$ must be at the same position, and thus $F(c \cdot v) = c \cdot F(v)$. This is illustrated in Figure 3.10.

To see that $F(v + w) = F(v) + F(w)$, begin by defining $u = v + w$, and let $o$ represent the origin. Due to the nature of vector addition, the endpoints of $u$, $v$, and $w$, together with $o$, form the vertices of a parallelogram. Applying the rotation transformation $F$ to this

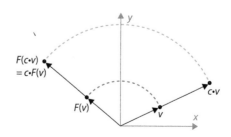

FIGURE 3.10 Illustrating that rotation transformations are linear (scalar multiplication).

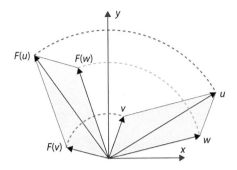

FIGURE 3.11    Illustrating that rotation transformations are linear (vector addition).

parallelogram yields a parallelogram $M$ whose vertices are $o$ and the endpoints of the vectors $F(u)$, $F(v)$, and $F(w)$. Again, due to the nature of vector addition, the endpoints of $F(v)$, $F(w)$, and $F(v)+F(w)$, together with $o$, form the vertices of a parallelogram $N$. Since parallelograms $M$ and $N$ have three vertices in common, their fourth vertex must also coincide, from which it follows that $F(v)+F(w)=F(u)=F(v+w)$. This is illustrated in Figure 3.11.

Given that rotation is a linear transformation, the previous theoretical discussion of linear functions provides a practical method for calculating a formula for the associated matrix. The values of the function at the standard basis vectors – in two dimensions, $F(i)$ and $F(j)$ – are the columns of the associated matrix. Thus, the next step is to calculate the result of rotating the vectors $i=\langle 1, 0\rangle$ and $j=\langle 0, 1\rangle$ around the origin (counterclockwise) by an angle $\theta$.

This calculation requires basic knowledge of trigonometric functions. Given a right triangle with angle $\theta$, adjacent side length $a$, opposite side length $b$, and hypotenuse length $h$, as illustrated in Figure 3.12, then the trigonometric functions are defined as ratios of these lengths: the sine function is defined by $\sin(\theta)=b/h$, the cosine function is defined by $\cos(\theta)=a / h$, and the tangent function is defined by $\tan(\theta)=b/a$.

As illustrated in Figure 3.13, rotating the vector $i$ by an angle $\theta$ yields a new vector $F(i)$, which can be viewed as the hypotenuse of a right triangle. Since rotation does not change lengths of vectors, the hypotenuse has length $h = 1$, which implies $\sin(\theta)=b$ and $\cos(\theta)=a$, from which it follows that $F(i)=\langle \cos(\theta), \sin(\theta)\rangle$. This vector represents the first column of the rotation matrix.

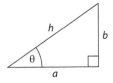

FIGURE 3.12    Right triangle with angle $\theta$, indicating adjacent (a), opposite (b), and hypotenuse (h) side lengths.

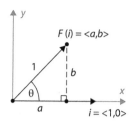

FIGURE 3.13   Rotating the basis vector **i** by an angle θ.

As illustrated in Figure 3.14, rotating the vector **j** by an angle θ yields a new vector $F(j)$, which can once again be viewed as the hypotenuse of a right triangle with $h = 1$, and as before, $\sin(\theta) = b$ and $\cos(\theta) = a$. Note that since the horizontal displacement of the vector $F(j)$ is toward the negative $x$-direction, the value of the first vector component is $-b$, the negative of the length of the side opposite angle θ. From this it follows that $F(j) = \langle -\sin(\theta), \cos(\theta)\rangle$, yielding the second column of the rotation matrix.

Based on these calculations, the matrix corresponding to rotation around the origin by an angle θ in two-dimensional space is given by the matrix:

$$\begin{bmatrix} \cos(\theta) & -\sin(\theta) \\ \sin(\theta) & \cos(\theta) \end{bmatrix}$$

To conclude the discussion of two-dimensional rotations, consider the following computational example. Assume that one wants to rotate the point (7, 5) around the origin by $\theta = 30°$ (or equivalently, $\theta = \pi/6$ radians). The new location of the point can be calculated as follows:

$$\begin{bmatrix} \cos(30°) & -\sin(30°) \\ \sin(30°) & \cos(30°) \end{bmatrix} \begin{bmatrix} 7 \\ 5 \end{bmatrix} = \begin{bmatrix} \sqrt{3}/2 & -1/2 \\ 1/2 & \sqrt{3}/2 \end{bmatrix} \begin{bmatrix} 7 \\ 5 \end{bmatrix} = \begin{bmatrix} (7\sqrt{3}-5)/2 \\ (7+5\sqrt{3})/2 \end{bmatrix} \approx \begin{bmatrix} 3.56 \\ 7.83 \end{bmatrix}$$

In three dimensions, rotations are performed around a line, rather than a point. In theory, it is possible to rotate around any line in a 3D space. For simplicity, only the formulas for

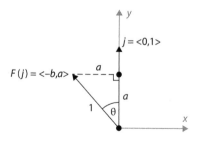

FIGURE 3.14   Rotating the basis vector **j** by an angle θ.

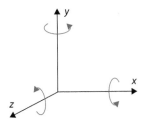

FIGURE 3.15   Rotations around the axes in three-dimensional space.

rotation around each of the three axes, as illustrated in Figure 3.15, will be derived in this section. Note that the rotations appear counterclockwise when looking along each axis from positive values to the origin.

If the $xy$-plane of two-dimensional space is thought of as the set of points in 3D space where $z = 0$, then the two-dimensional rotation previously discussed corresponds to rotation around the $z$-axis. Analogous to the observation that in two dimensions, rotating around a point does not move the point, in three dimensions, rotating around an axis does not move that axis. By the same reasoning as before, rotation (around an axis) is a linear transformation. Therefore, calculating the matrix corresponding to a rotation transformation $F$ can be accomplished by finding the values of $F$ at $i, j$, and $k$ (the standard basis vectors in three dimensions); the vectors $F(i)$, $F(j)$, and $F(k)$ the results will be the columns of the matrix.

To begin, let $F$ denote rotation around the $z$-axis, a transformation which extends the previously discussed two-dimensional rotation around a point in the xy-plane to 3D space. Since this transformation fixes the $z$-axis and therefore all $z$ coordinates, based on previous work calculating $F(i)$ and $F(j)$, it follows that $F(i) = \langle \cos(\theta), \sin(\theta), 0 \rangle$, $F(j) = \langle -\sin(\theta), \cos(\theta), 0 \rangle$, and $F(k) = \langle 0, 0, 1 \rangle$, and therefore the matrix for this transformation is:

$$\begin{bmatrix} \cos(\theta) & -\sin(\theta) & 0 \\ \sin(\theta) & \cos(\theta) & 0 \\ 0 & 0 & 1 \end{bmatrix}$$

Next, let F denote rotation around the x-axis. Evaluating the values of this function requires similar reasoning. This transformation fixes the x-axis, so $F(i) = \langle 1, 0, 0 \rangle$ is the first column of the matrix. Since the transformation fixes all $x$ coordinates, two-dimensional diagrams such as those in Figures 3.13 and 3.14, featuring the $yz$-axes, can be used to analyze $F(j)$ and $F(k)$, this is illustrated in Figure 3.16, where the x-coordinate is excluded for simplicity. One finds that $F(j) = \langle 0, \cos(\theta), \sin(\theta) \rangle$ and $F(k) = \langle 0, -\sin(\theta), \cos(\theta) \rangle$, and thus the corresponding matrix is:

$$\begin{bmatrix} 1 & 0 & 0 \\ 0 & \cos(\theta) & -\sin(\theta) \\ 0 & \sin(\theta) & \cos(\theta) \end{bmatrix}$$

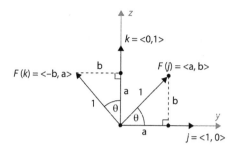

FIGURE 3.16  Calculating rotation around the *x*-axis.

Finally, let $F$ denote the rotation around the *y*-axis. As before, the calculations use the same logic. However, the orientation of the axes illustrated in Figure 3.15 must be kept in mind. Drawing a diagram analogous to Figure 3.16, aligning the *x*-axis horizontally and the *z*-axis vertically (and excluding the *y*-coordinate), a counterclockwise rotation around the *y*-axis in 3D space will appear as a clockwise rotation in the diagram; this is illustrated in Figure 3.17. One may then calculate that $F(i) = \langle \cos(\theta), 0, -\sin(\theta) \rangle$ and $F(k) = \langle \sin(\theta), 0, \cos(\theta) \rangle$, and $F(j) = \langle 0, 1, 0 \rangle$ since the *y*-axis is fixed. Therefore, the matrix for rotation around the *y*-axis is given by:

This completes the analysis of rotations in 3D space; you now have formulas for generating a matrix corresponding to counterclockwise rotation by an angle $\theta$ around each of the axes. As a final note, observe that if the angle of rotation is $\theta = 0$, then since $\cos(0) = 1$ and $\sin(0) = 1$, each of the rotation matrix formulas yields an identity matrix.

### 3.2.3 Translation

A translation transformation adds constant values to each component of a vector. For two-dimensional vectors, this has the following form (where $m$ and $n$ are constants):

$$F\left(\begin{bmatrix} x \\ y \end{bmatrix}\right) = \begin{bmatrix} x+m \\ y+n \end{bmatrix}$$

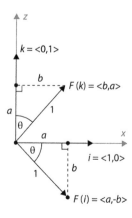

FIGURE 3.17  Calculating rotation around the *y*-axis.

It can quickly be established that this transformation cannot be represented with a two-by-two matrix. For example, consider translation by $\langle 2, 0 \rangle$. If this could be represented as a matrix transformation, then it would be possible to solve the following equation for the constants $a$, $b$, $c$, and $d$:

$$\begin{bmatrix} a & b \\ c & d \end{bmatrix} \begin{bmatrix} x \\ y \end{bmatrix} = \begin{bmatrix} a \cdot x + b \cdot y \\ c \cdot x + d \cdot y \end{bmatrix} = \begin{bmatrix} x + 2 \\ y \end{bmatrix}$$

Matching coefficients of $x$ and $y$ leads to $a = 1$, $c = 0$, $d = 1$, and the unavoidable expression $b = 2/y$, which is not a constant value for $b$. If the value $b = 2$ were chosen, the resulting matrix would not produce a translation – it would correspond to a *shear transformation*.

$$\begin{bmatrix} 1 & 2 \\ 0 & 1 \end{bmatrix} \begin{bmatrix} x \\ y \end{bmatrix} = \begin{bmatrix} x + 2 \cdot y \\ y \end{bmatrix}$$

This particular shear transformation is illustrated in Figure 3.18, where the dot-shaded square on the left side is transformed into the dot-shaded parallelogram on the right side.

Observe that, in Figure 3.18, the points along each horizontal line are being translated by a constant amount that depends on the $y$-coordinate of the points on the line; this is the defining characteristic of any shear transformation. In this particular example, the points along the line $y = 1$ are translated 2 units to the right, the points along $y = 2$ are translated 4 units to the right, and so forth; the points along $y = p$ are translated $2p$ units to the right.

The goal is to find a matrix that performs a constant translation on the *complete* set of points in a space; a shear transformation performs a constant translation on a *subset* of the points in a space. This observation is the key to finding the desired matrix, and requires a new way of thinking about points. Consider a one-dimensional space, which would consist of only an $x$-axis. A translation on this space would consist of adding a constant number $m$ to each $x$ value. To realize this transformation as a matrix, consider a copy of the one-dimensional space embedded in two-dimensional space along the line $y = 1$; symbolically, identifying the one-dimensional point $x$ with the two-dimensional point $(x, 1)$. Then, one-dimensional translation by $m$ corresponds to the matrix calculation:

$$\begin{bmatrix} 1 & m \\ 0 & 1 \end{bmatrix} \begin{bmatrix} x \\ 1 \end{bmatrix} = \begin{bmatrix} x + m \\ 1 \end{bmatrix}$$

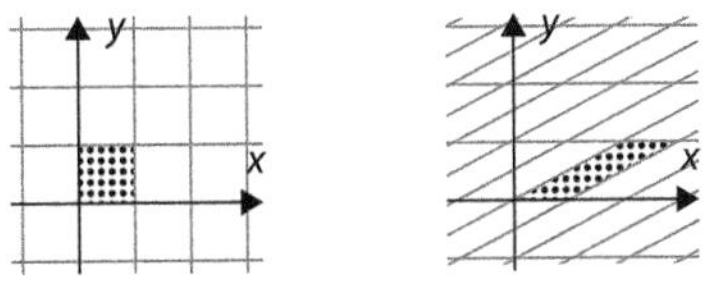

FIGURE 3.18  A shear transformation along the x direction.

Analogously, to perform a two-dimensional translation by $\langle m, n \rangle$, identify each point $(x, y)$ with the point $(x, y, 1)$ and perform the following matrix calculation:

$$\begin{bmatrix} 1 & 0 & m \\ 0 & 1 & n \\ 0 & 0 & 1 \end{bmatrix} \begin{bmatrix} x \\ y \\ 1 \end{bmatrix} = \begin{bmatrix} x+m \\ y+n \\ 1 \end{bmatrix}$$

Finally, to perform a 3D translation by $\langle m, n, p \rangle$, identify each point $(x, y, z)$ with the point $(x, y, z, 1)$ and perform the following matrix calculation:

$$\begin{bmatrix} 1 & 0 & 0 & m \\ 0 & 1 & 0 & n \\ 0 & 0 & 1 & p \\ 0 & 0 & 0 & 1 \end{bmatrix} \begin{bmatrix} x \\ y \\ z \\ 1 \end{bmatrix} = \begin{bmatrix} x+m \\ y+n \\ z+p \\ 1 \end{bmatrix}$$

In other words, to represent translation as a matrix transformation, the space being translated is identified with a subset of a higher dimensional space with the additional coordinate set equal to one. This is the reason that four-dimensional vectors and matrices are used in 3D computer graphics. Even though there is no intuitive way to visualize four spatial dimensions, performing algebraic calculations on four-dimensional vectors is a straightforward process. This system of representing 3D points with four-dimensional points (or representing $n$-dimensional points with $(n + 1)$-dimensional points in general) is called *homogeneous coordinates*. As previously mentioned, each point $(x, y, z)$ is identified with $(x, y, z, 1)$; conversely, each four-dimensional point $(x, y, z, w)$ is associated to the 3D point $(x/w, y/w, z/w)$. This operation is called *perspective division*, and aligns with the previous correspondence when $w = 1$. There are additional uses for perspective division, which will be discussed further in the section on perspective projections.

It is also important to verify that the transformations previously discussed are compatible with the homogeneous coordinate system. In two dimensions, the transformation $F(\langle x, y \rangle) = \langle a \cdot x + b \cdot y, c \cdot x + d \cdot y \rangle$ becomes $F(\langle x, y, 1 \rangle) = \langle a \cdot x + b \cdot y, c \cdot x + d \cdot y, 1 \rangle$, which corresponds to the matrix multiplication:

$$\begin{bmatrix} a & b & 0 \\ c & d & 0 \\ 0 & 0 & 1 \end{bmatrix} \begin{bmatrix} x \\ y \\ 1 \end{bmatrix} = \begin{bmatrix} a \cdot x + b \cdot y \\ c \cdot x + d \cdot y \\ 1 \end{bmatrix}$$

Therefore (when using homogeneous coordinates), all the geometric transformations of interest – translation, rotation, and scaling, collectively referred to as *affine transformations* – can be represented by multiplying by a matrix of the form

$$\begin{bmatrix} a_{11} & a_{12} & m_1 \\ a_{21} & a_{22} & m_2 \\ 0 & 0 & 1 \end{bmatrix}$$

where the two-by-two submatrix in the upper left represents the rotation and/or scaling part of the transformation (or is the identity matrix when there is no rotation or scaling), and the two-component vector $\langle m_1, m_2 \rangle$ within the rightmost column represents the translation part of the transformation (or is the zero vector if there is no translation).

Similarly, in three dimensions (using homogeneous coordinates), affine transformations can be represented by multiplying by a matrix of the form

$$
\begin{bmatrix}
a_{11} & a_{12} & a_{13} & m_1 \\
a_{21} & a_{22} & a_{23} & m_2 \\
a_{31} & a_{32} & a_{33} & m_3 \\
0 & 0 & 0 & 1
\end{bmatrix}
$$

where the three-by-three submatrix in the upper left represents the rotation and/or scaling part of the transformation (or is the identity matrix if there is no rotation or scaling), and the three-component vector $\langle m_1, m_2, m_3 \rangle$ within the rightmost column represents the translation part of the transformation (or is the zero vector if there is no translation).

### 3.2.4 Projections

In this section, the goal is to derive a formula for a perspective projection transformation. In Chapter 1, at the beginning of the chapter and also in the section on geometry processing, some of the core ideas were illustrated and informally introduced. To review: the viewable region in the scene needs to be mapped to the region rendered by OpenGL, a cube where the $x$, $y$, and $z$ coordinates are all between –1 and +1, also referred to as *clip space*. In a perspective projection, the shape of the viewable region is a *frustum*, or truncated pyramid. The pyramid is oriented so that it is "lying on its side": its central axis is aligned with the negative $z$-axis, as illustrated in Figure 3.19, and the viewer or virtual camera is positioned at the origin of the scene, which aligns with the point that was the tip of the original pyramid. The smaller rectangular end of the frustum is nearest to the origin, and the larger rectangular end is farthest from the origin. When the frustum is compressed into a cube, the larger end must be compressed more. This causes objects in the rendered image of the scene to appear smaller the farther they are from the viewer.

The shape of a frustum is defined by four parameters: the *near distance*, the *far distance*, the (vertical) *angle of view*, and the *aspect ratio*. The near and far distances are the most

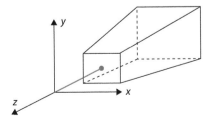

FIGURE 3.19   The frustum for a perspective transformation.

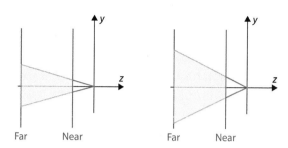

FIGURE 3.20    The effect of the angle of view on the size of a frustum.

straightforward to explain: they refer to distances from the viewer (along the z-axis), and they set absolute bounds on what could potentially be seen by the viewer – any points outside of this range will not be rendered. However, not everything between these bounds will be visible. The *angle of view* is a measure of how much of the scene is visible to the viewer, and is defined as the angle between the top and bottom planes of the frustum (as oriented in Figure 3.19) if those planes were extended to the origin. Figure 3.20 shows two different frustums (shaded regions) as viewed from the side (along the x-axis). The figure also illustrates the fact that for fixed near and far distances, larger angles of view correspond to larger frustums.

In order for the dimensions of the visible part of the near plane to be proportional to the dimensions of the rendered image, the *aspect ratio* (defined as width divided by height) of the rendered image is the final value used to specify the shape of the frustum, illustrated in Figure 3.21, which depicts the frustum as viewed from the front (along the negative z-axis). In theory, a horizontal angle of view could be used to specify the size of the frustum instead of the aspect ratio, but in practice, determining the aspect ratio is simpler.

In a perspective projection, points in space (within the frustum) are mapped to points in the *projection window*: a flat rectangular region in space corresponding to the rendered image that will be displayed on the computer screen. The projection window corresponds to the smaller rectangular side of the frustum, the side nearest to the origin. To visualize how a point P is transformed in a perspective projection, draw a line from P to the origin,

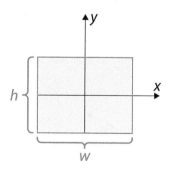

FIGURE 3.21    The aspect ratio r = w/h of the frustum.

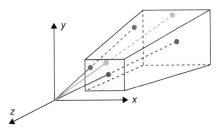

FIGURE 3.22    Projecting points from the frustum to the projection window.

and the intersection of the line with the projection window is the result. Figure 3.22 illustrates the results of projecting three different points within the frustum onto the projection window.

To derive the formula for a perspective projection, the first step is to adjust the position of the projection window so that points in the frustum are projected to $y$-coordinates in the range from $-1$ to $1$. Then the formula for projecting $y$-coordinates will be derived, incorporating both matrix multiplication and the perspective division that occurs with homogeneous coordinates: converting $(x, y, z, w)$ to $(x/w, y/w, z/w)$. Next, the formula for projecting $x$-coordinates will be derived, which is completely analogous to the formula for $y$-coordinates except that the aspect ratio needs to be taken into consideration. Finally, the $z$-coordinates of points in the frustum, which are bounded by the near distance and far distance, will be converted into the range from $-1$ to $1$ and once again will require taking perspective division into account.

To begin, it will help to represent the parameters that define the shape of the frustum – the near distance, far distance, (vertical) angle of view, and aspect ratio – by $n$, $f$, $a$, and $r$, respectively. Consider adjusting the projection window so that the $y$-coordinates range from $-1$ to $1$, while preserving the angle of view $a$, as illustrated on the left side of Figure 3.23 (viewed from the side, along the $x$-axis). This will change the distance $d$ from the origin to the projection window. The value of $d$ can be calculated using trigonometry on the corresponding right triangle, illustrated on the right side of Figure 3.23. By the definition of the tangent function, $\tan(a/2) = 1/d$, from which it follows that $d = 1/\tan(a/2)$. Therefore, all points on the projection window have their $z$ coordinate equal to $-d$.

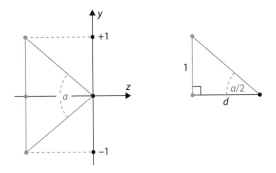

FIGURE 3.23    Adjusting the projection window.

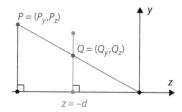

FIGURE 3.24  Calculating y-components of projected points.

Next, ignoring x-coordinates for a moment, consider a point $P=(P_y, P_z)$ in the frustum that will be projected onto this new projection window. Drawing a line from $P$ to the origin, let $Q=(Q_y, Q_z)$ be the intersection of the line with the projection window, as illustrated in Figure 3.24. Adding a perpendicular line from $P$ to the z-axis, it becomes clear that we have two similar right triangles. Note that since the bases of the triangles are located on the negative z-axis, but lengths of sides are positive, the lengths of the sides are the negatives of the z-coordinates. The sides of similar triangles are proportional to each other, so we know that $P_y/(-P_z)=Q_y/(-Q_z)$. Since Q is a point on the adjusted projection window, we also know that $Q_z=-d$. This allows us to write a formula for the y-coordinate of the projection: $Q_y = d \cdot P_y/(-P_z)$.

At first glance, this may appear to be incompatible with our matrix-based approach, as this formula is not a linear transformation, due to the division by the z coordinate. Fortunately, the fact that we are working in homogeneous coordinates (x, y, z, w) will enable us to resolve this problem. Since this point will be converted to (x/w, y/w, z/w) by perspective division (which is automatically performed by the GPU after the vertex shader is complete), the "trick" is to use a matrix to change the value of the w-component (which is typically equal to one) to the value of the z-component (or more precisely, the negative of the z-component). This can be accomplished with the following matrix transformation (where * indicates an as-yet unknown value):

$$
\begin{bmatrix}
* & * & * & * \\
0 & d & 0 & 0 \\
* & * & * & * \\
0 & 0 & -1 & 0
\end{bmatrix}
\begin{bmatrix}
P_x \\
P_y \\
P_z \\
1
\end{bmatrix}
=
\begin{bmatrix}
* \\
d \cdot P_y \\
* \\
-P_z
\end{bmatrix}
$$

Then, after performing the division transformation, the homogeneous point $\left(*, d \cdot P_y, *, -P_z\right)$ is transformed into $\left(*, d \cdot P_y/(-P_z), *\right)$, as desired.

The next step is to derive a formula for the x-component of projected points; the calculations are similar to those for the y-component. The corresponding diagram is illustrated in Figure 3.25, viewed from along the y-axis. Again, there is a pair of similar triangles, and therefore the ratios of corresponding sides are equal, from which we obtain the equation $P_x/(-P_z)=Q_x/(-Q_z)$, and therefore, $Q_x = d \cdot P_x/(-Q_z)$.

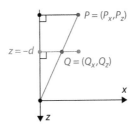

FIGURE 3.25   Calculating x-components of projected points.

However, one additional factor must be taken into account: the aspect ratio $r$. We have previously considered the $y$ values to be in the range from $-1$ to $1$; in accordance with the aspect ratio, the set of points that should be included in the rendered image have $x$ values in the range from $-r$ to $r$. This range needs to be scaled into clip space, from $-1$ to $1$, and therefore the formula for the $x$ coordinate must also be divided by $r$. This leads us to the formula $Q_x = (d/r) \cdot P_x / (-P_z)$, which can be accomplished with the following matrix transformation (again, * indicates undetermined values):

$$\begin{bmatrix} d/r & 0 & 0 & 0 \\ 0 & d & 0 & 0 \\ * & * & * & * \\ 0 & 0 & -1 & 0 \end{bmatrix} \begin{bmatrix} P_x \\ P_y \\ P_z \\ 1 \end{bmatrix} = \begin{bmatrix} (d/r) \cdot P_x \\ d \cdot P_y \\ * \\ -P_z \end{bmatrix}$$

The values in the third row of the matrix remain to be determined and will affect the $z$ component of the point. The $z$ value is used in depth calculations to determine which points will be visible, as specified by the near distance and far distance values. The values of the $x$ and $y$ components of the point are not needed for this calculation, and so the first two values in the row should be 0; refer to the remaining unknown values as $b$ and $c$. Then we have the following matrix transformation:

$$\begin{bmatrix} d/r & 0 & 0 & 0 \\ 0 & d & 0 & 0 \\ 0 & 0 & b & c \\ 0 & 0 & -1 & 0 \end{bmatrix} \begin{bmatrix} P_x \\ P_y \\ P_z \\ 1 \end{bmatrix} = \begin{bmatrix} (d/r) \cdot P_x \\ d \cdot P_y \\ b \cdot P_z + c \\ -P_z \end{bmatrix}$$

After perspective division, the third coordinate $b \cdot P_z + c$ becomes $(b \cdot P_z + c)/(-P_z) = -b - c/P_z$. The values of the constants $b$ and $c$ will be determined soon, after two important points are clarified. First, the near distance $n$ and the far distance $f$ are typically given as positive values, even though the visible region frustum lies along the negative $z$-axis in world space, and thus the nearest visible point $P$ satisfies $P_z = -n$, while the farthest visible point $P$ satisfies $P_z = -f$. Second, we know that we must convert the $z$ coordinates of visible points into clip space coordinates (the range from $-1$ to $1$), and it might seem as though the z coordinates of the nearest points to the viewer should be mapped to the value 1, as the positive z-axis points directly at the viewer in our coordinate system. However, this is not the case! When OpenGL performs depth testing, it determines if one point is closer (to the viewer) than another by comparing their z coordinates. The type of comparison can be specified by the OpenGL function **glDepthFunc**, which has the default value GL_LESS, an OpenGL constant which indicates that a point should be considered closer to the viewer if its z coordinate is *less*. This means that in clip space, the *negative* z-axis points directly at the viewer; this space uses a *left-handed* coordinate system. Combining these two points, we now know that if $P_z = -n$, then $-b - c/P_z$ should equal –1, and if $P_z = -f$, then $-b - c/P_z$ should equal 1. This corresponds to the following system of equations:

$$-b + \frac{c}{n} = -1$$

$$-b + \frac{c}{f} = 1$$

There are a variety of approaches to solve this system; one of the simplest is to multiply the first equation by –1 and then add it to the second equation. This eliminates $b$; solving for $c$ yields $c = 2 \cdot n \cdot f / (n - f)$. Substituting this value for $c$ into the first equation and solving for $b$ yields $b = (n + f)/(n - f)$.

With this calculation finished, the matrix is completely determined. To summarize: the perspective projection transformation for a frustum-shaped region defined by near distance $n$, far distance $f$, (vertical) angle of view $a$, and aspect ratio $r$, when working with homogeneous coordinates, can be achieved with the following matrix:

$$
\begin{bmatrix}
\dfrac{1}{r \cdot \tan(a/2)} & 0 & 0 & 0 \\[3mm]
0 & \dfrac{1}{\tan(a/2)} & 0 & 0 \\[3mm]
0 & 0 & \dfrac{n+f}{n-f} & \dfrac{2 \cdot n \cdot f}{n-f} \\[3mm]
0 & 0 & -1 & 0
\end{bmatrix}
$$

### 3.2.5 Local Transformations

At this point, you are able to produce the matrices corresponding to translation, rotation, and scaling transformations. For example, consider an object in two-dimensional space, such as the turtle on the left side of Figure 3.26, whose shape is defined by some set of points S. Let **T** be the matrix corresponding to translation by $\langle 1, 0 \rangle$ and let **R** be the matrix corresponding to rotation around the origin by 45°. To move the turtle around you could, for example, multiply all the points in the set S by **T**, and then by **R**, and then by **T** again, which would result in the sequence of images illustrated in the remaining parts of Figure 3.26. All these transformations are relative to an external, fixed coordinate system

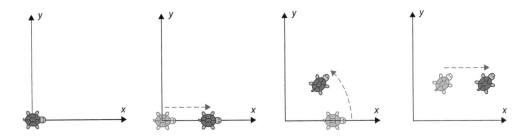

FIGURE 3.26   A sequence of global transformations.

called *world coordinates* or *global coordinates*, and this aspect is emphasized by the more specific term *global transformations*.

The internal or local coordinate system used to define the vertices of a geometric object is somewhat arbitrary – the origin point and the orientation and scale of the local coordinate axes are typically chosen for convenience, without reference to the global coordinate system. For example, the local origin is frequently chosen to correspond to a location on the object that is in some sense the "center" of the object. Locations specified relative to this coordinate system are called *object coordinates* or *local coordinates*. After an object is added to a 3D scene, the object can then be repositioned, oriented, and resized as needed using geometric transformations.

Of particular interest in this section are *local transformations*: transformations relative to the local coordinate system of an object, and how they may be implemented with matrix multiplication. Initially, the local coordinate axes of an object are aligned with the global coordinate axes. As an object is transformed, its local coordinate axes undergo the same transformations. Figure 3.27 illustrates multiple copies of the turtle object together with their local coordinate axes after various transformations have been applied.

Figure 3.28 illustrates several examples of local transformations. Assuming the turtle starts at the state with position and orientation shown in the leftmost image, the remaining images show local translation by $\langle 2, 0 \rangle$, local translation by $\langle 0, 1 \rangle$, and local rotation by 45°, each applied to the starting state. Observe in particular that a local rotation takes place around the center of an object (the origin of its local coordinate system), rather than around the world or global origin.

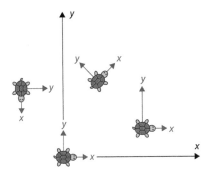

FIGURE 3.27   Transforming local coordinate axes.

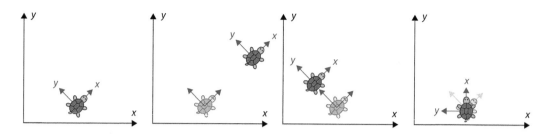

FIGURE 3.28   Various local transformations.

The concepts of local and global transformation are reflected in everyday language. For example, walking forward, backward, left, or right, are examples of local translations that depend on the current orientation of a person's coordinate system: in other words, it matters which way the person is currently facing. If two people are facing in different directions, and they are both asked to step forward, they will move in different directions. If a global translation is specified, which is typically done by referencing the compass directions (North, South, East, and West), then you can be assured that people will walk in the same direction, regardless of which way they may have been facing at first.

The question remains: how can matrix multiplication be used to perform local transformations (assuming that it is possible)? Before addressing this question, it will help to introduce a new concept. When transforming a set of points with a matrix, the points are multiplied by the matrix in the vertex shader and the new coordinates are passed along to the fragment shader, but the new coordinates of the points are not permanently stored. Instead, the accumulated transformations that have been applied to an object are stored as the product of the corresponding matrices, which is a single matrix called the *model matrix* of the object. The model matrix effectively stores the current location, orientation, and scale of an object (although it is slightly complicated to extract some of this information from the entries of the matrix).

Given an object whose shape is defined by a set of points $S$, assume that a sequence of transformations has been applied and let $M$ denote the current model matrix of the object. Thus, the current location of the points of the object can be calculated by $M \cdot P$, where $P$ ranges over the points in the set $S$. Let $T$ be the matrix corresponding to a transformation. If you were to apply this matrix as a global transformation, as described in previous sections, the new model matrix would be $T \cdot M$, since each new matrix that is applied becomes the leftmost element in the product (just as functions are ordered in function composition). In order for the matrix $T$ to have the effect of a local transformation on an object, the local coordinate axes of the object would have to be aligned with the global coordinate axes that suggest the following three-step strategy:

1. Align the two sets of axes by applying $M^{-1}$, the inverse of the model matrix.

2. Apply $T$, since local and global transformations are the same when the axes are aligned.

3. Apply $M$, the original model matrix, which returns the object to its previous state while taking the transformation T into account.

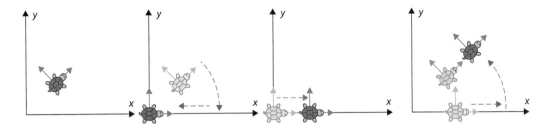

FIGURE 3.29  A sequence of global transformations equivalent to a local translation.

This sequence of transformations is illustrated in Figure 3.29, where the images show an object with model matrix $M$ (in this example, translation and then rotation by 45° was applied), the result of applying $M^{-1}$ (reversing the rotation and then reversing the translation), the result of applying $T$ (in this example, translation), and the result of applying $M$ again (translating and rotating again). The last image also shows the outline of the object in its original placement for comparison.

At the end of this process, combining all these transformations, the model matrix has become $M \cdot T \cdot M^{-1} \cdot M$ (recall that matrices are applied to a point from the right to the left). Since $M^{-1} \cdot M = I$ (the identity matrix), this expression simplifies to $M \cdot T$: the original model matrix $M$ multiplied on the *right* by $T$. This is the answer to the question of interest. To summarize: given an object with model matrix $M$ and a transformation with matrix $T$:

- To apply $T$ as a global transformation, let the new model matrix equal $T \cdot M$.

- To apply $T$ as a local transformation, let the new model matrix equal $M \cdot T$.

As you will see in later sections, being able to use local transformations will be useful when creating interactive 3D scenes. For example, navigating within a scene feels more intuitive and immersive if one is able to move the virtual camera with local transformations. The viewer might not always be aware of the direction of the z-axis, which could lead to unexpected motions when moving in global directions, but the viewer is always able to see what is in front of them, which makes moving forward more natural.

## 3.3  A MATRIX CLASS

Now that you have learned how to derive the various types of matrices that will be needed, the next step will be to create a **Matrix** class. This class will need to store the values contained within a matrix, as well as perform the basic matrix operations previously discussed: multiplying a matrix by a vector, multiply a matrix by another matrix, and calculating the inverse of a matrix. The class will also contain static methods to generate matrices corresponding to each of the previously discussed geometric transformations: identity, translation, rotation (around each axis), scaling, and projection.

Since multiple matrix operations are defined in terms of the dot product of vectors, you will first create a corresponding method to perform this calculation. In the **Vector** class, add the following static method:

```java
public static double dot(Vector v, Vector w)
{
    double c = 0;
    for (int i = 0; i < v.values.length; i++)
        c += v.values[i] * w.values[i];
    return c;
}
```

Next, in the **math** package, create a new Java class named **Matrix** with the following code, which includes the necessary fields, a constructor, a convenience method for setting the values of the matrix, and a method for converting the values from a two-dimensional array (the standard mathematical representation) to a one-dimensional float array (the format used in GLSL).

```java
package math;

public class Matrix
{
    public int rows, cols;

    // standard mathematical representation
    public double[][] values;

    // format required by GLSL
    public float[] flatValues;

    // constructor
    public Matrix(int rows, int cols)
    {
        this.rows = rows;
        this.cols = cols;
        this.values = new double[rows][cols];
        this.flatValues = new float[rows*cols];
    }

    // required format for GLSL;
    //     also helpful for copying data to new matrix
    public float[] flatten()
    {
        for (int rowNum = 0; rowNum < rows; rowNum++)
            for (int colNum = 0; colNum < cols; colNum++)
                flatValues[colNum + rowNum*cols] =
                    (float)values[rowNum][colNum];
```

```
        return flatValues;
    }

    // set matrix values in row order
    public void setValues(double... v)
    {
        for (int i = 0; i < v.length; i++)
        {
            int rowNum = i / cols;
            int colNum = i % cols;
            values[rowNum][colNum] = v[i];
        }
    }
}
```

Next, add the following two methods to the **Matrix** class, which are used to extract the values along a given row or column of the matrix and return the results as a **Vector** object.

```
public Vector getRow(int rowNum)
{
    Vector row = new Vector(this.cols);
    for (int colNum = 0; colNum < cols; colNum++)
        row.values[colNum] = this.values[rowNum][colNum];
    return row;
}

public Vector getCol(int colNum)
{
    Vector col = new Vector(this.rows);
    for (int rowNum = 0; rowNum < rows; rowNum++)
        col.values[rowNum] = this.values[rowNum][colNum];
    return col;
}
```

It will also be convenient to include methods that enable the contents of a vector to be copied into a row or column of a matrix; which can be accomplished with the following methods:

```
public void setRow(int rowNum, Vector row)
{
    int max = Math.min(this.cols, row.values.length);
    for (int colNum = 0; colNum < max; colNum++)
        this.values[rowNum][colNum] = row.values[rowNum];
}
```

```
public void setCol(int colNum, Vector col)
{
    int max = Math.min(this.rows, col.values.length);
    for (int rowNum = 0; rowNum < max; rowNum++)
        this.values[rowNum][colNum] = col.values[rowNum];
}
```

Using these methods, you can now create methods to perform matrix-vector multiplication, as well as matrix-matrix multiplication. For readability, there will be separate methods for matrix multiplication on the left and matrix multiplication on the right, as these correspond to local and global geometric transformations as discussed in Section 3.2. Add the following code to the **Matrix** class:

```
public Vector multiplyVector(Vector vec)
{
    Vector result = new Vector( vec.values.length );
    for (int rowNum = 0; rowNum < rows; rowNum++)
    {
        Vector row = getRow(rowNum);
        result.values[rowNum] = Vector.dot(row, vec);
    }
    return result;
}

public static Matrix multiply(Matrix A, Matrix B)
{
    if (A.cols != B.rows)
        return null;

    Matrix C = new Matrix(A.rows, B.cols);
    for (int rowNum = 0; rowNum < A.rows; rowNum++)
        for (int colNum = 0; colNum < B.cols; colNum++)
            C.values[rowNum][colNum] = Vector.dot(
                A.getRow(rowNum), B.getCol(colNum) );
    return C;
}
// replace this matrix with (M * this)
public void leftMultiply(Matrix M)
{
    this.values = Matrix.multiply(M, this).values;
}

// replace this matrix with (this * M)
public void rightMultiply(Matrix M)
{
    this.values = Matrix.multiply(this, M).values;
}
```

Next, for reversing geometric transformations, as well as calculations involving the virtual camera (briefly mentioned in Section 1.2.2, and which will be discussed in detail in Chapter 4), it is necessary to be able to calculate the inverse of a matrix. The theoretical details would take us too far afield; the interested reader can find the algebraic derivation in any matrix algebra reference text. The related concepts include the *minor* of a matrix (a smaller matrix containing a subset of the values of the original matrix), the *determinant* of a matrix (a value that naturally arises in the calculation of inverse matrices, that can be calculated recursively), and the *transpose* of a matrix (which interchanges the rows and columns of a matrix). To proceed, in the Matrix class, add the following methods:

```
// generate the (rows-1) by (cols-1) submatrix,
//    excluding given row and column.
public Matrix minor(int excludeRowNum, int excludeColNum)
{
    Matrix m = new Matrix(this.rows-1, this.cols-1);

    int minorRowNum = 0, minorColNum = 0;
    for (int rowNum = 0; rowNum < rows; rowNum++)
    {
        if (rowNum == excludeRowNum)
            continue;

        minorColNum = 0;
        for (int colNum = 0; colNum < cols; colNum++)
        {
            if (colNum == excludeColNum)
                continue;

            m.values[minorRowNum][minorColNum] =
                this.values[rowNum][colNum];
            minorColNum++;
        }
        minorRowNum++;
    }

    return m;
}

public double determinant()
{
    if (rows == 1)
        return values[0][0];

    if (rows == 2)
        return values[0][0] * values[1][1]
            - values[0][1] * values[1][0];
```

```java
        // for larger matrices, calculate determinant
        //    using cofactor expansion along first row
        double det = 0;
        for (int colNum = 0; colNum < cols; colNum++)
            det += Math.pow(-1, colNum) * values[0][colNum]
                    * minor(0, colNum).determinant();

        return det;
    }



    // multiply all values in matrix by given number
    public void multiplyScalar(double s)
    {
        for (int rowNum = 0; rowNum < rows; rowNum++)
            for (int colNum = 0; colNum < cols; colNum++)
                values[rowNum][colNum] *= s;
    }

    // interchange rows and columns of matrix
    public Matrix transpose()
    {
        Matrix tr = new Matrix(this.cols, this.rows);
        for (int rowNum = 0; rowNum < rows; rowNum++)
            for (int colNum = 0; colNum < cols; colNum++)
                tr.values[colNum][rowNum] = this.values[rowNum]
[colNum];
        return tr;
    }

    // calculate the inverse of the matrix
    public Matrix inverse()
    {
        Matrix inv = new Matrix(rows, cols);

        for (int rowNum = 0; rowNum < rows; rowNum++)
            for (int colNum = 0; colNum < cols; colNum++)
                inv.values[rowNum][colNum] =
                    Math.pow(-1, rowNum + colNum)
                    * this.minor(rowNum, colNum).determinant();

        double det = determinant();
        inv = inv.transpose();
        inv.multiplyScalar( 1.0f/det );
        return inv;
    }
```

At this point, you may wish to write a test class to test these methods, using some of the numerical examples from Section 3.1.2. To facilitate this, add the following method to the Matrix class to convert a matrix to a more easily readable format:

```java
public String toString()
{
    String s = "";
    for (int rowNum = 0; rowNum < rows; rowNum++)
        s += getRow(rowNum).toString() + "\n";
    return s;
}
```

Before continuing, you will create a test class to verify that the matrix-related functions are working properly. Create a new Java class in the **src** folder named **Test_3_1** and insert the following code:

```java
import static org.lwjgl.glfw.GLFW.*;
import static org.lwjgl.opengl.GL40.*;

import core.*;
import math.*;

// test Matrix class
public class Test_3_1 extends Base
{
    public void initialize()
    {
        System.out.println("Testing matrix class:");

        Matrix m = new Matrix(2,3);
        m.setValues(1,2,3,4,5,6);
        System.out.println(m);

        Matrix n = m.transpose();
        System.out.println(n);

        System.out.println(Matrix.multiply(m, n));
        System.out.println(Matrix.multiply(n, m));

        System.out.println("Testing inverse method:");
        Matrix p = new Matrix(2,2);
        p.setValues(1,2,3,4);
        Matrix pInv = p.inverse();
        System.out.println(p);
        System.out.println(pInv);
        System.out.println("Product should be identity matrix:");
```

```
        System.out.println( Matrix.multiply(p, pInv) );
        System.out.println( Matrix.multiply(pInv, p) );
    }

    public void update()
    {
    }

    // driver method
    public static void main(String[] args)
    {
        new Test_3_1().run();
    }
}
```

If everything is done correctly, then you should see a black window which you can ignore, while displayed in the console terminal will be several matrices and the results of various methods applied to them.

Finally, you will add some static methods to the **Matrix** class that generate matrices corresponding to the geometric transformations that were derived in Section 3.2. Since the transformations will be applied to a 3D space, each method will return a four-by-four matrix. To this end, add the following code, which implements the identity, translation, rotation (around each axis), scale, and perspective projection transformations:

```
public static Matrix makeIdentity()
{
    Matrix m = new Matrix(4,4);
    m.setValues(1,0,0,0,  0,1,0,0,  0,0,1,0,  0,0,0,1);
    return m;
}

public static Matrix makeTranslation(double x, double y, double z)
{
    Matrix m = new Matrix(4,4);
    m.setValues(1,0,0,x,  0,1,0,y,  0,0,1,z,  0,0,0,1);
    return m;
}

public static Matrix makeRotationZ(double angle)
{
    double c = Math.cos(angle);
    double s = Math.sin(angle);
    Matrix m = new Matrix(4,4);
    m.setValues(c,-s,0,0,  s,c,0,0,  0,0,1,0,  0,0,0,1);
    return m;
}
```

```java
public static Matrix makeRotationX(double angle)
{
    double c = Math.cos(angle);
    double s = Math.sin(angle);
    Matrix m = new Matrix(4,4);
    m.setValues(1,0,0,0, 0,c,-s,0, 0,s,c,0, 0,0,0,1);
    return m;
}

public static Matrix makeRotationY(double angle)
{
    double c = Math.cos(angle);
    double s = Math.sin(angle);
    Matrix m = new Matrix(4,4);
    m.setValues(c,0,s,0, 0,1,0,0, -s,0,c,0, 0,0,0,1);
    return m;
}

public static Matrix makeScale(double s)
{
    Matrix m = new Matrix(4,4);
    m.setValues(s,0,0,0, 0,s,0,0, 0,0,s,0, 0,0,0,1);
    return m;
}

public static Matrix makePerspective(double angleOfView,
    double aspectRatio, double near, double far)
{
    double a = Math.toRadians(angleOfView);
    double d = 1.0 / Math.tan(a/2);
    double r = aspectRatio;
    double b = (far + near) / (near - far);
    double c = 2*far*near / (near - far);
    Matrix m = new Matrix(4,4);
    m.setValues(d/r,0,0,0, 0,d,0,0, 0,0,b,c, 0,0,-1,0);
    return m;
}

// default parameters for perspective projection
public static Matrix makePerspective()
{
    return makePerspective(60, 1, 0.1, 1000);
}
```

With this class completed, you are nearly ready to incorporate matrix-based transformations into your scenes.

## 3.4 INCORPORATING WITH GRAPHICS PROGRAMS

Before creating the main application, the **Uniform** class needs to be updated to be able to store the matrices generated by the **Matrix** class. In GLSL, four-by-four matrices correspond to the data type **mat4**, and the corresponding uniform data can be sent to the GPU with the following OpenGL command:

**glUniformMatrix4fv(** *variableRef, matrixCount, transpose, value* **)**

> Specify the value of the uniform variable referenced by the parameter *variableRef* in the currently bound program. The number of matrices is specified by the parameter *matrixCount*. The matrix data is stored as an array of vectors in the parameter *value*. OpenGL expects matrix data to be stored as an array of column vectors; if this is not the case (if data is stored as an array of row vectors), then the Boolean parameter *transpose* should be set to the OpenGL constant GL_TRUE (which causes the data to be re-interpreted as rows), and GL_FALSE otherwise.
>
> In the **Uniform** class located in the **core** package, add the following else-if condition at the end of the block of **else if** statements in the **uploadData** method:

```
else if (dataType.equals("mat4"))
{
    Matrix m = (Matrix)data;
    glUniformMatrix4fv(variableRef, true, m.flatten());
}
```

Since you will now be creating 3D scenes, you will activate a render setting that performs depth testing (in case you later choose to add objects which may obscure other objects). This (and other render settings) can be configured by using the following two OpenGL functions:

**glEnable(** *setting* **)**

> Enables an OpenGL capability specified by an OpenGL constant specified by the parameter *setting*. For example, possible constants include GL_DEPTH_TEST to activate depth testing, GL_POINT_SMOOTH to draw rounded points instead of square points, or GL_BLEND to enable blending colors in the color buffer based on alpha values.

**glDisable(** *setting* **)**

> Disables an OpenGL capability specified by an OpenGL constant specified by the parameter *setting*.

Finally, for completeness, we include the OpenGL function that allows you to configure depth testing, previously mentioned in the section on perspective projection. However, you will not change the function from its default setting, and this function will not be used in what follows.

**glDepthFunc(** *compareFunction* **)**

Specify the function used to compare each pixel depth with the depth value present in the depth buffer. If a pixel passes the comparison test, it is considered to be currently the closest to the viewer, and its values overwrite the current values in the color and depth buffers. The function used is specified by the OpenGL constant *compareFunction*, some of whose possible values include the default setting GL_LESS (indicating that a pixel is closer to the viewer if the depth value is less) and GL_GREATER (indicating that a pixel is closer if the depth value is greater). If depth testing has not been enabled, the depth test always passes, and pixels are rendered on top of each other according to the order in which they are processed.

Now you are ready to create an interactive scene. The first new component will be the vertex shader code: there will be two uniform **mat4** variables. One will store the model transformation matrix, which will be used to translate and rotate a geometric object. The other will store the perspective transformation matrix, which will make objects appear smaller as they move further away. To begin creating this scene, in the **src** directory, create the following files named **Test_3_2, Test_3_2.frag** and **Test_3_2.vert**. First, in the fragment shader file, insert the following code:

```
out vec4 fragColor;
void main()
{
    fragColor = vec4(1.0, 1.0, 0.0, 1.0);
}
```

Inside the vertex shader file, insert the following code:

```
in vec3 position;
uniform mat4 projectionMatrix;
uniform mat4 modelMatrix;
void main()
{
    gl_Position = projectionMatrix * modelMatrix *
        vec4(position, 1.0);
}
```

Finally, inside the main test class, insert the following code:

```
import static org.lwjgl.glfw.GLFW.*;
import static org.lwjgl.opengl.GL40.*;
```

```java
import core.*;
import math.*;

public class Test_3_2 extends Base
{
    public int programRef, vaoRef;
    public Uniform<Matrix> modelMatrix, projectionMatrix;
    public float moveSpeed, turnSpeed;

    public void initialize()
    {
        // load code, send to GPU, and compile;
        //    store program reference
        programRef = OpenGLUtils.initFromFiles(
            "./src/Test_3_2.vert",
            "./src/Test_3_2.frag" );
    }
}
```

Next, you will initialize attribute data for the vertices of an isosceles triangle, uniforms for the model and projection matrices, and variables to store the movement and rotation speed that will be applied to the triangle in the **update** method. To continue, return to the class named **Test_3_2** and add the following code to the **initialize** method:

```java
// specify color used when clearing the screen
glClearColor(0.0f, 0.0f, 0.0f, 1.0f);
glEnable(GL_DEPTH_TEST);

// setup vertex array object
vaoRef = glGenVertexArrays();
glBindVertexArray(vaoRef);

float[] positionData = {
            0.0f,  0.2f, 0.0f,
            0.1f, -0.2f, 0.0f,
           -0.1f, -0.2f, 0.0f  };
Attribute positionAttribute = new Attribute(
    "vec3", positionData );
positionAttribute.associateVariable(
    programRef, "position" );

// set up uniforms
Matrix mMatrix = Matrix.makeTranslation(0, 0, -1);
modelMatrix = new Uniform<Matrix>("mat4", mMatrix);
modelMatrix.locateVariable( programRef, "modelMatrix" );
```

```
Matrix pMatrix = Matrix.makePerspective();
projectionMatrix = new Uniform<Matrix>("mat4", pMatrix);
projectionMatrix.locateVariable( programRef, "projectionMatrix" );

// movement speed, units per second
moveSpeed = 0.5f;
// rotation speed, radians per second
turnSpeed = (float)Math.toRadians(90);
```

Next, you will turn your attention to creating an **update** method. The first step will be to calculate the actual amounts of movement that may be applied, based on the previously set base speed and the time elapsed since the last frame (which is stored in the **Base** class variable **deltaTime**). In the **Test_3_2** class, add the following code:

```
public void update()
{
    // update data
    float moveAmount = moveSpeed * deltaTime;
    float turnAmount = turnSpeed * deltaTime;
}
```

To illustrate the versatility of using matrices to transform objects, both global and local movement will be implemented. Next, there will be many conditional statements, each of which follow the same pattern: check if a particular key is being pressed, and if so, create the corresponding matrix **m** and multiply the model matrix by **m** in the correct order (**m** on the left for global transformations using the method **leftMultiply**, and **m** on the right for local transformations using the method **rightMultiply**). For global translations, you will use the keys W/A/S/D for the up/left/down/right directions, and the keys Z/X for the forward/backward directions. In the **Test_3_2** class, in the **update** method, add the following code:

```
// global translation
if (input.isKeyPressed(GLFW_KEY_W))
    modelMatrix.data.leftMultiply(
        Matrix.makeTranslation(0, moveAmount, 0) );

if (input.isKeyPressed(GLFW_KEY_S))
    modelMatrix.data.leftMultiply(
        Matrix.makeTranslation(0, -moveAmount, 0));

if (input.isKeyPressed(GLFW_KEY_A))
    modelMatrix.data.leftMultiply(
        Matrix.makeTranslation(-moveAmount, 0, 0));

if (input.isKeyPressed(GLFW_KEY_D))
    modelMatrix.data.leftMultiply(
        Matrix.makeTranslation(moveAmount, 0, 0));
```

```
if (input.isKeyPressed(GLFW_KEY_Z))
    modelMatrix.data.leftMultiply(
        Matrix.makeTranslation(0, 0, moveAmount));

if (input.isKeyPressed(GLFW_KEY_X))
    modelMatrix.data.leftMultiply(
        Matrix.makeTranslation(0, 0, -moveAmount));
```

Rotation that makes the object appear to rotate left and right from the viewer's perspective is really a rotation around the z-axis in a 3D space. Since the keys A/D move the object left/right, you will use the keys Q/E to rotate the object left/right, as they lay in the row directly above A/D. Since these keys will be used for a global rotation, they will cause the triangle to rotate around the origin (0,0,0) of the 3D world. Continuing in the **Test_3_2** class, in the **update** method, add the following code:

```
// global rotation
if (input.isKeyPressed(GLFW_KEY_Q))
    modelMatrix.data.leftMultiply(
        Matrix.makeRotationZ(turnAmount));

if (input.isKeyPressed(GLFW_KEY_E))
    modelMatrix.data.leftMultiply(
        Matrix.makeRotationZ(-turnAmount));
```

Next, to incorporate local translation, you will use the keys I/J/K/L for the directions up/left/down/right, as they are arranged in a similar layout to the W/A/S/D keys. Continue by adding the following code to the **update** method:

```
// local translation
if (input.isKeyPressed(GLFW_KEY_I))
    modelMatrix.data.rightMultiply(
        Matrix.makeTranslation(0, moveAmount, 0) );

if (input.isKeyPressed(GLFW_KEY_K))
    modelMatrix.data.rightMultiply(
        Matrix.makeTranslation(0, -moveAmount, 0) );

if (input.isKeyPressed(GLFW_KEY_J))
    modelMatrix.data.rightMultiply(
        Matrix.makeTranslation(-moveAmount, 0, 0) );

if (input.isKeyPressed(GLFW_KEY_L))
    modelMatrix.data.rightMultiply(
        Matrix.makeTranslation(moveAmount, 0, 0) );
```

You will use the keys U/O for local rotation left/right, as they are in the row above the keys used local movement left/right (J/L), analogous to the key layout for global transformations.

Since these keys refer to a local rotation, they will rotate the triangle around its center (where the world origin was located when the triangle was in its original position).

```
// local rotation
if (input.isKeyPressed(GLFW_KEY_U))
    modelMatrix.data.rightMultiply(
        Matrix.makeRotationZ(turnAmount) );

if (input.isKeyPressed(GLFW_KEY_O))
    modelMatrix.data.rightMultiply(
        Matrix.makeRotationZ(-turnAmount) );
```

After processing user input, the buffers need to be cleared before the image is rendered. In addition to clearing the color buffer, since depth testing is now being performed, the depth buffer should also be cleared. Uniform values need to be stored in their corresponding variables, and the **glDrawArrays** function needs to be called to render the triangle. To accomplish these tasks, at the end of the **update** method, add the following code:

```
// render scene

// reset color buffer with specified color
glClear(GL_COLOR_BUFFER_BIT | GL_DEPTH_BUFFER_BIT);

glUseProgram( programRef );
glBindVertexArray( vaoRef );
modelMatrix.uploadData();
projectionMatrix.uploadData();
glDrawArrays( GL_TRIANGLES, 0, 3 );
```

Finally, to run this application, the last lines of code need to instantiate the **Test** class and call the **run** method. At the end of the **Test_3_2** class, add the following code:

```
// driver method
public static void main(String[] args)
{
    new Test_3_2().run();
}
```

At this point, the application class is complete! Run the class and you should see an isosceles triangle in the center of your screen. Press the keyboard keys as described previously to experience the difference between global and local transformations of an object. While the object is located at the origin, local and global rotations will appear identical, but when the object is located far away from the origin, the difference in rotation is more easily seen. Similarly, while the object is in its original orientation (its local right direction aligned with the positive x-axis), local and global translations will appear identical, but after a rotation, the difference in the translations becomes apparent.

## 3.5 SUMMARY AND NEXT STEPS

In this chapter, you learned about the mathematical foundations involved in geometric transformations. You learned about vectors and the operations of vector addition and scalar multiplication, and how any vector can be written as a combination of standard basis vectors using these operations. Then you learned about a particular type of vector function called a linear transformation, which naturally led to the definition of a matrix and matrix multiplication. Then you learned how to create matrices representing the different types of geometric transformations (scaling, rotation, translation, and perspective projection) used in creating animated, interactive 3D graphics applications. You also learned how a model matrix stores the accumulated transformations that have been applied to an object, and how this structure enables you to use matrices for both global and local transformations. Finally, all of this was incorporated into the framework being developed in this book.

In the next chapter, you will turn your attention to automating many of these steps as you begin to create the graphics framework classes in earnest.

# CHAPTER 4

# A Scene Graph Framework

In this chapter, you will begin to create the structure of a three-dimensional (3D) graphics framework in earnest. At the heart of the framework will be a *scene graph*: a data structure that organizes the contents of a 3D scene using a hierarchical or tree-like structure.

In the context of computer science, a *tree* is a collection of *node* objects, each of which stores a value and a list of zero or more nodes called *child* nodes. If a node *A* has a child node *B*, then node *A* is said to be the *parent* node of node *B*. In a tree, each node has exactly one parent, with the exception of a special node called the *root*, from which all other nodes can be reached by a sequence of child nodes. Starting with any node *N*, the set of nodes that can be reached from a sequence of child nodes are called the *descendants* of *N*, while the sequence of parent nodes from N up to and including the root node are called the *ancestors* of *N*. An abstract example of a tree is illustrated in Figure 4.1, where nodes are represented by ovals labeled with the letters from A through G, and arrows point from a node to its children. In the diagram, node A is the root and has child nodes B, C, and D; node B has child nodes E and F; node D has child node G. Nodes E, F, and G do not have any child nodes.

In a scene graph, each node represents a 3D object in the scene. As described previously, the current position, orientation, and scale of an object is stored in a matrix called the model matrix, which is calculated from the accumulated transformations that have been applied to the object. For convenience, the position, orientation, and scale of an object will be collectively referred to as the *transform* of the object. The model matrix stores the transform of an object relative to its parent object in the scene graph. The transform of an object relative to the root of the scene graph, which is often called a *world transformation*, can be calculated from the product of the model matrix of the object and those of each of its ancestors. This structure enables complicated transformations to be expressed in terms of simpler ones. For example, the motion of the moon relative to the sun, illustrated in Figure 4.2 (gray dashed line), can be more simply expressed in terms of the combination of two circular motions: the moon relative to the Earth and the Earth relative to the sun (blue dotted line).

DOI: 10.1201/9781003153375-4

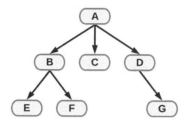

FIGURE 4.1   A tree with seven nodes.

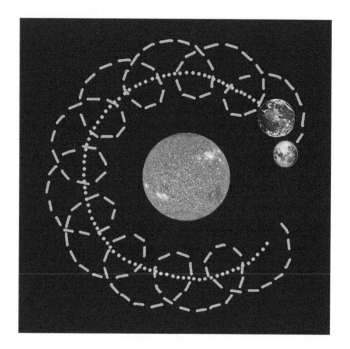

FIGURE 4.2   Motion of moon and earth relative to sun.

A scene graph structure also allows for simple geometric shapes to be grouped together into a compound object that can then be easily transformed as a single unit. For example, a simple model of a table may be created using a large, flat box shape for the top surface and four narrow, tall box shapes positioned underneath near the corners for the table legs, as illustrated by Figure 4.3. Let each of these objects be stored in

FIGURE 4.3   A table composed of five boxes.

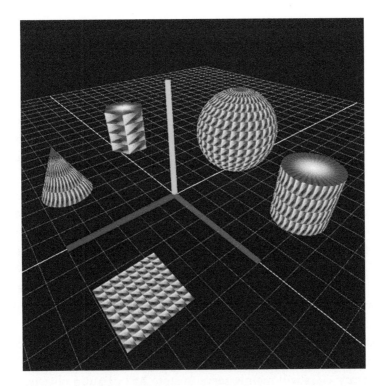

FIGURE 4.4    A scene containing multiple geometric shapes.

a node, and all five nodes share the same parent node. Then, transforming the parent node affects the entire table object. (It is also worth noting that each of these boxes may reference the same vertex data; the different sizes and positions of each may be set with a model matrix.)

In the next section, you will learn about the overall structure of a scene graph based framework, what the main classes will be, and how they encapsulate the necessary data and perform the required tasks to render a 3D scene. Then, in the following sections, you will implement the classes for the framework, building on the knowledge and code from earlier chapters. The framework will enable you to rapidly create interactive scenes containing complex objects, such as the one illustrated in Figure 4.4.

## 4.1  OVERVIEW OF CLASS STRUCTURE

In a scene graph framework, the nodes represent objects located in a 3D space. The corresponding class will be named **Object3D**, and will contain three items:

- a matrix to store its transform data
- a list of references to child objects
- a reference to a parent object

Many classes will extend the **Object3D** class, each with a different role in the framework. The root node will be represented by the **Scene** class. Interior nodes that are only used for grouping purposes will be represented by the **Group** class. Nodes corresponding to objects that can be rendered will be represented by the **Mesh** class. There are other objects with 3D characteristics that affect the appearance of the scene but are not themselves rendered. One such object is a virtual camera from whose point of view the scene will be rendered; this will be represented by the **Camera** class. Another such object is a virtual light source that affects shading and shadows; this will be represented by the **Light** class (but will not be created until a future chapter).

To keep the framework code modular, each mesh will consist of a **Geometry** class object and a **Material** class object. The **Geometry** class will specify the general shape and other vertex-related properties, while the **Material** class will specify the general appearance of an object. Since each instance of a mesh stores a transformation matrix, multiple versions of a mesh (based on the same geometry and material data) can be rendered with different positions and orientations. Each mesh will also store a reference to a vertex array object, which associates vertex buffers (whose references will be stored by attribute objects stored in the geometry) to attribute variables (specified by shaders stored in the material). This will allow geometric objects to be reused and rendered with different materials in different meshes.

The **Geometry** class will mainly serve to store **Attribute** objects, which describe vertex properties, such as position and color, as seen in examples in prior chapters. In later chapters, geometric objects will also store texture coordinates, for applying images to shapes, and normal vectors, for use in lighting calculations. This class will calculate the total number of vertices, which is equal to the length of the data array stored in any attribute. Extensions of the **Geometry** class will be created to realize each particular shape. In some cases, such as rectangles and boxes, the data for each attribute will be listed directly. For other shapes, such as polygons, cylinders, and spheres, the attribute data will be calculated from mathematical formulas.

The **Material** class will serve as a repository for three types of information related to the rendering process and the appearance of an object: shader code (and the associated program reference), **Uniform** objects, and render settings: the properties which are set by calling OpenGL functions, such as the type of geometric primitive (points, lines, or triangles), point size, line width, and so forth. The base **Material** class will initialize collections to store uniform objects and render setting data, and will define functions to perform tasks such as compiling the shader program code and locating uniform variable references. Extensions of this class will supply the actual shader code, a collection of uniform objects corresponding to uniform variables defined in the shaders, and a collection of render setting variables applicable to the type of geometric primitive being rendered.

A **Renderer** class will handle the general OpenGL initialization tasks as well as rendering the image. The rendering function will require a scene object and a camera object as parameters. For each mesh in the scene graph, the renderer will perform the tasks necessary before the **glDrawArrays** function is called, including activating the correct shader program, binding a vertex array object, configuring OpenGL render settings, and sending values to be used in uniform variables. Regarding uniform variables, there are three required by most shaders whose values are naturally stored outside the material: the transformation of a mesh, the transformation of the virtual camera used to view the scene, and the perspective transformation applied to all objects in the scene. While the uniform objects will be stored in the material for consistency, this matrix data will be copied into the corresponding uniform objects by the renderer before they send their values to the graphics processing unit (GPU).

Now that you have an idea of the initial classes that will be used by the framework, it is time to begin writing the code for each class.

## 4.2 3D OBJECTS

The **Object3D** class represents a node in the scene graph tree structure, and as such, it will store a list of references to child objects and a parent object, as well as **add** and **remove** methods to update parent and child references when needed. In addition, each object stores transform data and will have a method called **getWorldMatrix** to calculate the world transformation. When rendering the scene, the nodes in the tree will be collected into a list to simplify iterating over the set of nodes; this will be accomplished with a method called **getDescendantList**. To implement this, in the **core** package, create a new Java class named **Object3D** containing the following code:

```java
package core;

import java.util.ArrayList;
import math.*;

public class Object3D
{
    public Matrix transform;
    public Object3D parent;
    public ArrayList<Object3D> children;

    public Object3D()
    {
        transform = Matrix.makeIdentity();
        parent = null;
        children = new ArrayList<Object3D>();
    }

    public void add(Object3D child)
    {
        children.add(child);
        child.parent = this;
    }
```

```java
public void remove(Object3D child)
{
    children.remove(child);
    child.parent = null;
}

// calculate transformation of this Object3D relative
//    to the root Object3D of the scene graph
public Matrix getWorldMatrix()
{
    if (parent == null)
        return transform;
    else
        return Matrix.multiply( parent.getWorldMatrix(),
            transform );
}

// return a single list containing all descendants
public ArrayList<Object3D> getDescendentList()
{
    ArrayList<Object3D> descendents =
        new ArrayList<Object3D>();

    // nodes to be added to descendant list,
    //    and whose children will be added to this list
    ArrayList<Object3D> nodesToProcess =
        new ArrayList<Object3D>();
    nodesToProcess.add(this);

    // continue processing nodes while any are left
    while ( nodesToProcess.size() > 0 )
    {
        // remove first node from list
        Object3D node = nodesToProcess.remove(0);
        // add this node to descendant list
        descendents.add(node);
        // children of this node must also be processed
        for (Object3D child : node.children)
            nodesToProcess.add(0, child);
    }
    return descendents;
}
}
```

It will also be convenient for this class to contain a set of functions that translate, rotate, and scale the object by creating and applying the corresponding matrices from the **Matrix** class to the model matrix. Recall that each of these transformations can be applied as either a local transformation or a global transformation, depending on the order in which the model matrix and the new transformation matrix are multiplied. (In this context, a global transformation means a transformation performed with respect to the coordinate axes of the parent object in the scene graph.) This distinction – whether a matrix should be applied as a local transformation – will be specified with an additional parameter. To incorporate this functionality, add the following code to the **Object3D** class:

```
// apply geometric transformations
public void applyMatrix(Matrix m, boolean local)
{
    if (local)
        transform.rightMultiply(m);
    else
        transform.leftMultiply(m);
}

public void translate(double x, double y, double z,
    boolean local)
{
    applyMatrix(Matrix.makeTranslation(x,y,z), local);
}

public void rotateX(double angle, boolean local)
{
    applyMatrix(Matrix.makeRotationX(angle), local);
}

public void rotateY(double angle, boolean local)
{
    applyMatrix(Matrix.makeRotationY(angle), local);
}

public void rotateZ(double angle, boolean local)
{
    applyMatrix(Matrix.makeRotationZ(angle), local);
}

public void scale(double s, boolean local)
{
    applyMatrix(Matrix.makeScale(s), local);
}
```

Finally, the position of an object can be determined from entries in the last column of the transform matrix, as discussed in the previous chapter. Making use of this fact, functions to get and set the position of an object are implemented with the following code, which you should add to the **Object3D** class. Two functions are included to get the position of an object: one which returns its local position (with respect to its parent), and one which returns its global or world position, extracted from the world transform matrix previously discussed.

```java
// get/set position components of transform
public Vector getPosition()
{
    return new Vector(
        transform.values[0][3],
        transform.values[1][3],
        transform.values[2][3] );
}

public Vector getWorldPosition()
{
    Matrix worldTransform = getWorldMatrix();
    return new Vector(
        worldTransform.values[0][3],
        worldTransform.values[1][3],
        worldTransform.values[2][3] );
}

public void setPosition(Vector position)
{
    transform.values[0][3] = position.values[0];
    transform.values[1][3] = position.values[1];
    transform.values[2][3] = position.values[2];
}
```

The next few classes correspond to particular types of elements in the scene graph, and therefore each will extend the **Object3D** class.

## 4.2.1 Scene and Group

The **Scene** and **Group** classes will both be used to represent nodes in the scene graph that do not correspond to visible objects in the scene. The **Scene** class represents the root node of the tree, while the **Group** class represents an interior node to which other nodes are attached to more easily transform them as a single unit. These classes do not add any functionality to the **Object3D** class; their primary purpose is to make the application code easier to understand.

In the **core** package, create a new Java class named **Scene** with the following code:

```java
package core;

public class Scene extends Object3D
{
}
```

Then create a new Java class named **Group** with the following code.

```
package core;

public class Group extends Object3D
{
}
```

## 4.2.2 Camera

The **Camera** class represents the virtual camera used to view the scene. As with any 3D object, it has a position and orientation, and this information is stored in its transform matrix. The camera itself is not rendered, but its transform affects the apparent placement of the objects in the rendered image of the scene. Understanding this relationship is necessary to creating and using a **Camera** object. Fortunately, the key concept can be illustrated by a couple of examples.

Consider a scene containing multiple objects in front of the camera, and imagine that the camera shifts two units to the left. From the perspective of the viewer, all the objects in the scene would appear to have shifted two units to the right. In fact, these two transformations (shifting the camera left versus shifting all world objects right) are *equivalent*, in the sense that there is no way for the viewer to distinguish between them in the rendered image. As another example, imagine that the camera rotates 45° clockwise about its vertical axis. To the viewer, this appears equivalent to all objects in the world having rotated 45° counterclockwise around the camera. These examples illustrate the general notion that each transformation of the camera affects the scene objects in the opposite way. Mathematically, this relationship is captured by defining the *view matrix*, which describes the placement of objects in the scene with respect to the camera, as the inverse of the camera's transform matrix.

As cameras are used to define the position and orientation of the viewer, this class is also a natural place to store data describing the visible region of the scene, which is encapsulated by the projection matrix. Therefore, the Camera class will store both a view matrix and a projection matrix. The view matrix will be updated as needed, typically once during each iteration of the application main loop, before the meshes are drawn. To implement this class, in your **core** package, create a new Java class named **Camera** with the following code:

```
package core;
import math.Matrix;

public class Camera extends Object3D
{
    public Matrix viewMatrix;
    public Matrix projectionMatrix;
```

```java
    public Camera()
    {
        viewMatrix = Matrix.makeIdentity();
        projectionMatrix = Matrix.makePerspective();
    }

    public Camera(double angleOfView, double aspectRatio,
double near, double far)
    {
        viewMatrix = Matrix.makeIdentity();
        projectionMatrix = Matrix.makePerspective(angleOfView,
    aspectRatio, near, far);
    }

    public void updateViewMatrix()
    {
        viewMatrix = getWorldMatrix().inverse();
    }
}
```

## 4.2.3 Mesh

The **Mesh** class will represent the visible objects in the scene. It will contain geometric data that specifies vertex-related properties and material data that specifies the general appearance of the object. Since a vertex array object links data between these two components, the **Mesh** class is also a natural place to create and store this reference and set up the associations between vertex buffers and shader variables. For convenience, this class will also store a boolean variable used to indicate whether or not the mesh should appear in the scene. To proceed, in the **core** package, create a new Java class named **Mesh** with the following code:

```java
package core;
import static org.lwjgl.opengl.GL40.*;
import geometry.*;
import material.*;

public class Mesh extends Object3D
{
    public Geometry geometry;
    public Material material;

    // should this object be rendered?
    public boolean visible;

    // vertex array object reference
    public int vaoRef;
```

```
    public Mesh(Geometry geometry, Material material)
    {
        this.geometry = geometry;
        this.material = material;
        this.visible = true;

        // set up associations between
        // attributes stored in geometry
    // and shader program stored in material
        vaoRef = glGenVertexArrays();
        glBindVertexArray(vaoRef);

        for (String variableName : geometry.attributes.keySet())
        {
            Attribute attribute =
                geometry.attributes.get(variableName);
            attribute.associateVariable(
                material.programRef, variableName);
        }

        // unbind this vertex array object
        glBindVertexArray(0);
    }
}
```

Now that the **Object3D** and the associated **Mesh** class have been created, the next step is to focus on the two main components of a mesh: the **Geometry** class and the **Material** class, and their various extensions. Before moving forward, there are a few important static methods to add to the **Vector** class. The method **flattenList** is used to convert a list of vectors to an array of floats (a process sometimes called "flattening"), as required by vertex buffers in the GPU. The method **unflattenList** reverses this process. To proceed, in the **Vector** class, insert the following methods:

```
// used by geometry/attribute classes
public static float[] flattenList(List<Vector> vecList)
{
    int listSize = vecList.size();
    int vecSize  = vecList.get(0).values.length;
    float[] flattened = new float[listSize * vecSize];
    for (int vecNumber = 0; vecNumber < listSize; vecNumber++)
    {
        Vector v = vecList.get(vecNumber);
        for (int i = 0; i < vecSize; i++)
            flattened[vecNumber * vecSize + i] =
                (float)v.values[i];
    }
    return flattened;
}
```

```java
public static List<Vector> unflattenList(float[] flatArray,
    int vecSize)
{
    List<Vector> vecList = new ArrayList<Vector>();
    double[] tempData = new double[vecSize];
    for (int i = 0; i < flatArray.length; i += vecSize)
    {
        for (int j = 0; j < vecSize; j++)
            tempData[j] = flatArray[i + j];

        vecList.add( new Vector(tempData) );
    }
    return vecList;
}
```

## 4.3 GEOMETRY OBJECTS

Geometry objects will store attribute data and the total number of vertices. The base **Geometry** class will define a HashMap to store attributes, a function named **addAttribute** to simplify adding attributes, and a variable **vertexCount** to store the number of vertices. Classes that extend the base class will add attribute data and set the actual number of vertices for that particular object.

Since there will be many geometry-related classes, they will be organized into a separate package. In your **src** folder, create a new package called **geometry**. Then, in the **geometry** package, create a new Java class called **Geometry** with the following code:

```java
package geometry;

import java.util.HashMap;
import core.Attribute;
import java.util.List;
import java.util.ArrayList;

public class Geometry
{
    // Store Attribute objects,
    //    indexed by name of associated variable in shader.
    // Shader variable associations set up later
    //    and stored in vertex array object in Mesh.
    public HashMap<String, Attribute> attributes;

    public int vertexCount;

    public Geometry()
    {
        attributes = new HashMap<String, Attribute>();
        vertexCount = -1;
    }
```

```
public void addAttribute(String dataType,
        String variableName, float[] dataArray)
{
    attributes.put(variableName,
        new Attribute(dataType, dataArray));
}
}
```

The next step is to create a selection of classes that extend the **Geometry** class that contain the data for commonly used shapes. Many applications can make use of these basic shapes or combine basic shapes into compound shapes by virtue of the underlying structure of the scene graph.

In this chapter, these geometric objects will contain two attributes: vertex positions (which are needed for every vertex shader) and a default set of vertex colors. Until intermediate topics such as applying images to surfaces or lighting and shading are introduced in later chapters (along with their corresponding vertex attributes, texture coordinates and normal vectors), vertex colors will be necessary to distinguish the faces of a 3D object. For example, Figure 4.5 illustrates a cube with and without vertex colors applied; without these distinguishing features, a cube is indistinguishable from a hexagon. If desired, a developer can always change the default set of vertex colors in a geometric object by overwriting the array data in the corresponding attribute and calling its **uploadData** function to resend the data to its buffer.

### 4.3.1 Rectangles

After a triangle, a rectangle is the simplest shape to render, as it is composed of four vertices grouped into two triangles. To provide flexibility when using this class, the constructor will take two parameters, the width and height of the rectangle, each with a default value of one. Assuming that the rectangle is centered at the origin, this means that the vertex $x$ and $y$ coordinates will be $\pm width / 2$ and $\pm height / 2$, as illustrated in Figure 4.6. (The $z$ coordinates will be set to zero.) Also, with the points denoted by **P0**, **P1**, **P2**, **P3** as shown in the diagram, they will be grouped into the triangles (*P0*, *P1*, *P3*) and (*P0*, *P3*, *P2*). Note that the vertices in each

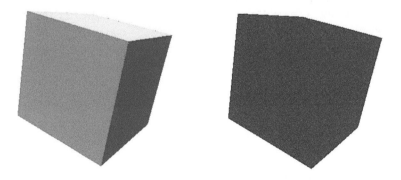

FIGURE 4.5    A cube rendered with (left) and without (right) vertex colors.

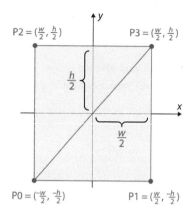

FIGURE 4.6    Vertex coordinates for a rectangle with width w and height h.

triangle are consistently listed in counterclockwise order, as OpenGL uses counterclockwise ordering by default to distinguish between the front side and back side of a triangle; back sides of shapes are frequently not rendered in order to improve rendering speed.

To implement this geometric shape, in the **geometry** package, create a new Java class called **RectangleGeometry** containing the following code:

```java
package geometry;

import java.util.Arrays;
import java.util.List;
import math.Vector;

public class RectangleGeometry extends Geometry
{
    public RectangleGeometry()
    {
        this(1,1);
    }

    public RectangleGeometry(double width, double height)
    {
        Vector P0 = new Vector(-width/2, -height/2, 0);
        Vector P1 = new Vector( width/2, -height/2, 0);
        Vector P2 = new Vector(-width/2,  height/2, 0);
        Vector P3 = new Vector( width/2,  height/2, 0);

        Vector C0 = new Vector(1f,1f,1f);
        Vector C1 = new Vector(1f,0f,0f);
        Vector C2 = new Vector(0f,1f,0f);
        Vector C3 = new Vector(0f,0f,1f);

        List positionList = Arrays.asList(P0,P1,P3, P0,P3,P2);
        float[] positionData = Vector.flattenList(positionList);
```

```
        List colorList = Arrays.asList(C0,C1,C3, C0,C3,C2);
        float[] colorData = Vector.flattenList(colorList);

        addAttribute("vec3", "vertexPosition", positionData);
        addAttribute("vec3", "vertexColor", colorData);
        vertexCount = 6;
    }
}
```

Note that the colors corresponding to the vertices, denoted by **C0**, **C1**, **C2**, **C3**, are listed in precisely the same order as the positions; this will create a consistent gradient effect across the rectangle. Alternatively, to render each triangle with a single solid color, the color data array could have been entered as the array {**C0, C0, C0, C1, C1, C1**}, for example. Although you are not able to create an application to render this data yet, when it can be rendered, it will appear as shown on the left side of Figure 4.7; the right side illustrates the alternative color data arrangement described in this paragraph.

In the next few subsections, classes for geometric shapes of increasing complexity will be developed. At this point, you may choose to skip ahead to the section titled "Material Objects," or you may continue creating as many of the geometric classes below as you wish before proceeding.

### 4.3.2 Boxes

A box is a particularly simple 3D shape to render. Although some other 3D shapes (such as some pyramids) may have fewer vertices, the familiarity of the shape and the symmetries in the positions of its vertices make it a natural choice for a first 3D shape to implement. A box has eight vertices and six sides composed of two triangles each, for a total of 12 triangles. Since each triangle is specified with three vertices, the data arrays for each attribute will contain 36 elements. Similar to the **Rectangle** class just created, the constructor of the **Box** class will take three parameters: the width, height, and depth of the box, referring to lengths of the box edges parallel to the $x$-, $y$-, and $z$-axis, respectively. As before, the parameters will each have a default value of one, and the box will be centered at the origin.

FIGURE 4.7    Rendering RectangleGeometry with gradient coloring (left) and solid coloring (right).

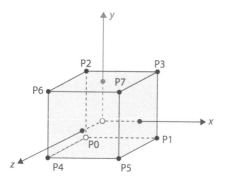

FIGURE 4.8   Vertices of a cube.

The points will be denoted P0 through P7, as illustrated in Figure 4.8, where the dashed lines indicate parts of the lines which are obscured from view by the box. To more easily visualize the arrangement of the triangles in this shape, Figure 4.9 depicts an "unfolded" box lying in a flat plane, sometimes called a *net diagram*. For each face of the box, the vertices of the corresponding triangles will be ordered in the same sequence as they were in the **Rectangle** class.

To aid with visualization, the vertices will be assigned colors (denoted C1 through C6) depending on the corresponding face. The faces perpendicular to the *x*-axis, *y*-axis, and *z*-axis will be tinted shades of red, green, and blue, respectively. Note that each of the vertices is present on three different faces: for instance, the vertex with position P7 is part of the right (x+) face, the top (y+) face, and the front (z+) face, and thus each point will be associated with multiple colors, in contrast to the **Rectangle** class. To create this class, in the **geometry** package, create a new Java class called **BoxGeometry** containing the following code:

```
package geometry;

import java.util.Arrays;
import java.util.List;
import math.Vector;
```

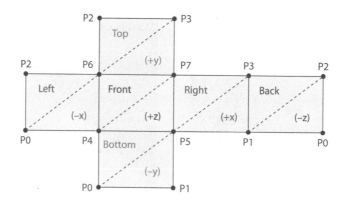

FIGURE 4.9   Vertex arrangement of an unfolded cube.

```java
public class BoxGeometry extends Geometry
{
    public BoxGeometry()
    {
        this(1,1,1);
    }

    public BoxGeometry(double width, double height, double depth)
    {
        // corners of a cube
        Vector P0 = new Vector(-width/2, -height/2, -depth/2);
        Vector P1 = new Vector( width/2, -height/2, -depth/2);
        Vector P2 = new Vector(-width/2,  height/2, -depth/2);
        Vector P3 = new Vector( width/2,  height/2, -depth/2);
        Vector P4 = new Vector(-width/2, -height/2,  depth/2);
        Vector P5 = new Vector( width/2, -height/2,  depth/2);
        Vector P6 = new Vector(-width/2,  height/2,  depth/2);
        Vector P7 = new Vector( width/2,  height/2,  depth/2);

        // colors for faces in order: x+, x-, y+, y-, z+, z-
        Vector C1 = new Vector(1.0f, 0.5f, 0.5f);
        Vector C2 = new Vector(0.5f, 0.0f, 0.0f);
        Vector C3 = new Vector(0.5f, 1.0f, 0.5f);
        Vector C4 = new Vector(0.0f, 0.5f, 0.0f);
        Vector C5 = new Vector(0.5f, 0.5f, 1.0f);
        Vector C6 = new Vector(0.0f, 0.0f, 0.5f);

        List positionList = Arrays.asList(
                P5,P1,P3,P5,P3,P7, P0,P4,P6,P0,P6,P2,
                P6,P7,P3,P6,P3,P2, P0,P1,P5,P0,P5,P4,
                P4,P5,P7,P4,P7,P6, P1,P0,P2,P1,P2,P3  );
        float[] positionData = Vector.flattenList(positionList);

        List colorList = Arrays.asList(
                C1,C1,C1,C1,C1,C1, C2,C2,C2,C2,C2,C2,
                C3,C3,C3,C3,C3,C3, C4,C4,C4,C4,C4,C4,
                C5,C5,C5,C5,C5,C5, C6,C6,C6,C6,C6,C6  );
        float[] colorData = Vector.flattenList(colorList);

        addAttribute("vec3", "vertexPosition", positionData);
        addAttribute("vec3", "vertexColor", colorData);
        vertexCount = 36;
    }
}
```

Figure 4.10 illustrates how this box will appear from multiple perspectives once you are able to render it later in this chapter.

FIGURE 4.10   Rendering BoxGeometry from multiple perspectives.

### 4.3.3 Polygons

*Polygons* (technically, *regular polygons*) are two-dimensional shapes such that all sides have the same length and all angles have equal measure, such as equilateral triangles, squares, pentagons, hexagons, and so forth. The corresponding class will be designed so that it may produce a polygon with any number of sides (three or greater). The coordinates of the vertices can be calculated by using equally spaced points on the circumference of a circle. A circle with radius $R$ can be expressed with the parametric equations $x = R \cdot \cos(t)$ and $y = R \cdot \sin(t)$. Note that these parametric equations also satisfy the implicit equation of a circle of radius $R$, $x^2 + y^2 = R^2$, which can be verified with the use of the trigonometric identity $\sin^2(t) + \cos^2(t) = 1$. The key is to find the required values of the angle $t$ that correspond to these equally spaced points. This in turn is calculated using multiples of a base angle $A$, equal to $2\pi$ divided by the number of sides of the polygon being generated, as illustrated with a nonagon in Figure 4.11.

Once it is understood how the vertices of a polygon can be calculated, one must also consider how the vertices will be grouped into triangles. In this case, each triangle will have one vertex at the origin (the center of the polygon) and two adjacent vertices on the circumference of the polygon, ordered counterclockwise, as usual. In addition, the same three vertex colors will be repeated in each triangle for simplicity. To proceed, in the **geometry** package, create a new Java class called **PolygonGeometry** with the following code:

```
package geometry;

import java.util.Arrays;
import java.util.ArrayList;
import math.Vector;
```

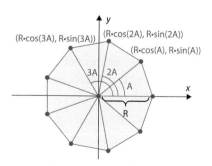

FIGURE 4.11   Calculating the vertices of a regular polygon.

```java
public class PolygonGeometry extends Geometry
{
    // default constructor creates a triangle
    public PolygonGeometry()
    {
        this(3, 1);
    }

    public PolygonGeometry(int sides, double radius)
    {
        float A = (float)(2 * Math.PI / sides);
        ArrayList<Vector> positionList =
            new ArrayList<Vector>();
        ArrayList<Vector> colorList    =
            new ArrayList<Vector>();
        Vector Z  = new Vector(0,0,0);
        Vector C1 = new Vector(1,1,1);
        Vector C2 = new Vector(1,0,0);
        Vector C3 = new Vector(0,0,1);

        for (int n = 0; n < sides; n++)
        {
            positionList.add( Z );
            positionList.add( new Vector(
              radius * Math.cos(n*A),
              radius * Math.sin(n*A), 0) );
            positionList.add( new Vector(
              radius * Math.cos((n+1)*A),
              radius * Math.sin((n+1)*A), 0) );
            colorList.add( C1 );
            colorList.add( C2 );
            colorList.add( C3 );
        }

        float[] positionData = Vector.flattenList(positionList);
        float[] colorData = Vector.flattenList(colorList);

        addAttribute("vec3", "vertexPosition", positionData);
        addAttribute("vec3", "vertexColor", colorData);
        vertexCount = sides * 3;
    }
}
```

Figure 4.12 illustrates a few different polygons that you will eventually be able to render with this class, with 3, 8, and 32 sides, respectively. Note that with sufficiently many sides, the polygon closely approximates a circle. In fact, due to the discrete nature of computer graphics, it is not possible to render a perfect circle, and so this is how circular shapes are implemented in practice.

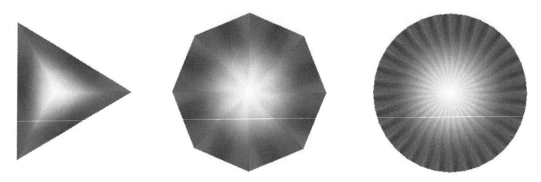

FIGURE 4.12  Polygons with 3 sides, 8 sides, and 32 sides.

For convenience, you may decide to extend the **Polygon** class to generate particular polygons with preset numbers of sides (or even a circle, as previously discussed), while still allowing the developer to specify a value for the radius, which will be passed along to the base class. For example, you could optionally create a **Hexagon** class with a file in the **geometry** package named **HexagonGeometry** containing the following code:

```
package geometry;

public class HexagonGeometry extends PolygonGeometry
{
    // default radius is 1
    public HexagonGeometry()
    {
        super(6, 1);
    }

    public HexagonGeometry(float radius)
    {
        super(6, radius);
    }
}
```

### 4.3.4 Parametric Surfaces and Planes

Similar to the two-dimensional polygons just presented, there are a variety of surfaces in three dimensions that can be expressed with mathematical functions. The simplest type of surface arises from a function of the form $z = f(x, y)$, but this is too restrictive to express many common surfaces, such as cylinders and spheres. Instead, each of the coordinates $x$, $y$, and $z$ will be expressed by a function of two independent variables $u$ and $v$. Symbolically,

$$x = f(u,v), \quad y = g(u,v), \quad z = h(u,v)$$

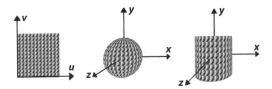

FIGURE 4.13   A rectangular region (left), transformed into a sphere (center) and a cylinder (right).

or, written in a different format,

$$(x, y, z) = \left( f(u,v), \ g(u,v), \ h(u,v) \right) = S(u,v)$$

Generally, the variables $u$ and $v$ are limited to a rectangular domain such as $0 \le u \le 1$ and $0 \le v \le 1$, and thus the function $S$ can be thought of as transforming a two-dimensional square or rectangular region, embedding it in 3D space. The function $S$ is called a *parametric function*. Graphing the set of output values $(x, y, z)$ yields a surface that is said to be *parameterized* by the function $S$. Figure 4.13 depicts a rectangular region (subdivided into triangles) and the result of transforming it into the surface of a sphere or a cylinder.

To incorporate this into the graphics framework you are creating, the first step is to create a class that takes as inputs a parametric function $S(u, v)$ that defines a surface, whose format is defined by an interface, and in practice will be specified by a lambda expression. Additional parameters will include bounds for $u$ and $v$, and the resolution – in this context, the number of sample values to be used between the $u$ and $v$ bounds. With this data, the space between $u$ and $v$ coordinates (traditionally called **deltaU** and **deltaV**) can be calculated, and a set of points on the surface can be calculated and stored in a two-dimensional array (called **positions**) for convenience. Finally, the vertex positions (and related vertex data, such as colors) must be grouped into triangles and stored in a dictionary of **Attribute** objects for use in the **Geometry** class. To accomplish this task, in your **math** package, create a new Java class named **Surface** containing the following code:

```java
package math;

public class Surface
{
    public interface Function
    {
        Vector apply(double u, double v);
    }

    public Function function;

    public Surface(Function function)
    {
        this.function = function;
    }
```

```java
    // get a 2D array of points on the surface
    //    represented by this function
    public Vector[][] getPoints(
        double uStart, double uEnd, int uResolution,
        double vStart, double vEnd, int vResolution)
    {

        Vector[][] points =
            newVector[uResolution+1][vResolution+1];
        double deltaU = (uEnd - uStart) / uResolution;
        double deltaV = (vEnd - vStart) / vResolution;

        for (int uIndex=0; uIndex < uResolution+1; uIndex++)
        {
            for (int vIndex=0; vIndex < vResolution+1; vIndex++)
            {
                double u = uStart + uIndex * deltaU;
                double v = vStart + vIndex * deltaV;
                points[uIndex][vIndex] =
                    this.function.apply(u,v);
            }
        }
        return points;
    }
}
```

Immediately afterwards, in your **geometry** package, create a new Java class named
**SurfaceGeometry** containing the following code:

```java
package geometry;

import java.util.Arrays;
import java.util.List;
import java.util.ArrayList;
import math.*;

public class SurfaceGeometry extends Geometry
{
    public SurfaceGeometry( Surface.Function function,
        double uStart, double uEnd, int uResolution,
        double vStart, double vEnd, int vResolution  )
    {
        Surface surface = new Surface(function);

        Vector[][] positions = surface.getPoints(
            uStart, uEnd, uResolution,
            vStart, vEnd, vResolution);
```

```
List<Vector> quadColors = Arrays.asList(
        new Vector(1,0,0), new Vector(0,1,0),
        new Vector(0,0,1), new Vector(0,1,1),
        new Vector(1,0,1), new Vector(1,1,0) );

ArrayList<Vector> positionList =
    new ArrayList<Vector>();
ArrayList<Vector> colorList    =
    new ArrayList<Vector>();

for (int uIndex=0; uIndex<uResolution; uIndex++)
{
    for (int vIndex=0; vIndex<vResolution; vIndex++)
    {
        // position coordinates
        Vector pA = positions[uIndex+0][vIndex+0];
        Vector pB = positions[uIndex+1][vIndex+0];
        Vector pD = positions[uIndex+0][vIndex+1];
        Vector pC = positions[uIndex+1][vIndex+1];
        positionList.addAll(
            Arrays.asList(pA,pB,pC, pA,pC,pD) );
        colorList.addAll(quadColors);
    }
}

float[] positionData = Vector.flattenList(positionList);
float[] colorData = Vector.flattenList(colorList);

addAttribute("vec3", "vertexPosition", positionData);
addAttribute("vec3", "vertexColor", colorData);
vertexCount = uResolution * vResolution * 6;
}
}
```

The **SurfaceGeometry** class should be thought of as an abstract class: it will not be instantiated directly; instead, it will be extended by other classes that supply specific functions and variable bounds that yield different surfaces. The simplest case is a *plane*, a flat surface that can be thought of as a subdivided rectangle, similar to the **Rectangle** class previously developed. The equation for a plane (extending along the *x* and *y* directions, and where *z* is always 0) is:

$$S(u,v) = (u,v,0)$$

As was the case with the **Rectangle** class, the plane will be centered at the origin, and parameters will be included in the constructor to specify the width and height of the plane. Additional parameters will be included to allow the user to specify the resolution for the u and v variables, but given the more relevant variable names **widthSegments** and

**heightSegments**. To create this class, create a new Java class named **PlaneGeometry** in the **geometry** package, containing the following code:

```
package geometry;

import math.Vector;

public class PlaneGeometry extends SurfaceGeometry
{
    public PlaneGeometry( double width, double height,
                      int widthSegments, int heightSegments )
    {
        super( (u,v) -> { return new Vector(u,v,0); },
               -width/2,   width/2, widthSegments,
               -height/2, height/2, heightSegments  );
    }

    public PlaneGeometry()
    {
        this(1,1, 8,8);
    }
}
```

A plane geometry with the default parameter values above will appear as shown in Figure 4.14.

## 4.3.5 Spheres and Related Surfaces

Along with boxes, spheres are one of the most familiar 3D shapes, illustrated on the left side of Figure 4.15. In order to render a sphere in this framework, you will need to know the parametric equations of a sphere. For simplicity, assume that the sphere is centered at the origin and has radius one. The starting point for deriving this formula is the parametric equation of a circle of radius $R$, since the cross-sections of a sphere are circles. Assuming that cross-sections will be analyzed along the $y$-axis, let $z = R \cdot \cos(u)$ and $x = R \cdot \sin(u)$, where $0 \leq u \leq 2\pi$. The radius $R$ of the cross-section will depend on the value of $y$. For example, in the central cross section, when $y = 0$, the radius is $R = 1$. At the top and bottom of the sphere (where $y = 1$ and $y = -1$), the cross-sections are single points, which can be considered as

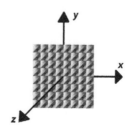

FIGURE 4.14   Plane geometry.

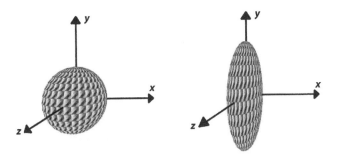

FIGURE 4.15   Sphere and ellipsoid.

$R = 0$. Since the equations for $x$, $y$, and $z$ must also satisfy the implicit equation of a unit sphere, $x^2 + y^2 + z^2 = 1$, you can substitute the formulas for $x$ and $z$ into this equation and simplify to get the equation $R^2 + y^2 = 1$. Rather than solve for $R$ as a function of $y$, it is more productive to once again use the parametric equations for a circle, letting $R = \cos(v)$ and $y = \sin(v)$. For $R$ and $y$ to have the values previously described, the values of $v$ must range from $-\pi/2$ to $\pi/2$. This yields the full parameterization of the unit sphere:

$$(x, y, z) = \left( \sin(u) \cdot \cos(v), \sin(v), \cos(u) \cdot \cos(v) \right)$$

For additional flexibility, you may scale the parametric equations for $x$, $y$, and $z$ by different amounts, resulting in a shape called an *ellipsoid*, illustrated on the right side of Figure 4.15. Then a sphere can be considered as a special case of an ellipsoid, where the scaling amounts are equal along each direction.

To implement these shapes, you will start with an ellipsoid. The size parameters will be called *width*, *height*, and *depth*, and used in the same way as the corresponding parameters that define the size of a box. In the **geometry** package, create a new Java class named **EllipsoidGeometry**, containing the following code:

```java
package geometry;
import math.Vector;

public class EllipsoidGeometry extends SurfaceGeometry
{
    public EllipsoidGeometry(
            double width, double height, double depth,
            int radiusSegments, int heightSegments )
    {
        super( (u,v) -> { return new Vector(
                    width/2 * Math.sin(u)  * Math.cos(v),
                    height/2 * Math.sin(v),
                    depth/2 * Math.cos(u)  * Math.cos(v)); },
                0, 2*Math.PI, radiusSegments,
                -Math.PI/2, Math.PI/2, heightSegments  );
    }
```

```java
    public EllipsoidGeometry()
    {
        this(1,1,1, 32,16);
    }
}
```

Next, you will extend this class to create a sphere. In the **geometry** package, create a new Java class named **SphereGeometry**, containing the following code:

```java
package geometry;

public class SphereGeometry extends EllipsoidGeometry
{
    public SphereGeometry( double radius,
                    int radiusSegments, int heightSegments )
    {
        super( 2*radius, 2*radius, 2*radius,
                radiusSegments, heightSegments );
    }

    public SphereGeometry( double radius )
    {
        this(radius, 32,16);
    }

    public SphereGeometry()
    {
        this(1, 32,16);
    }
}
```

## 4.3.6 Cylinders and Related Surfaces

As was the case for spheres, the starting point for deriving the equation of a cylinder (illustrated in Figure 4.16) is the parametric equation of a circle, since the cross-sections of a cylinder are also circles. For the central axis of the cylinder to be aligned with the $y$-axis, as

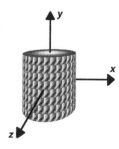

FIGURE 4.16   Cylinder.

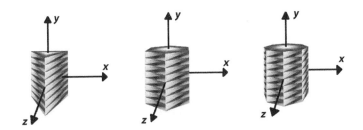

FIGURE 4.17    Triangular, hexagonal, and octagonal prism.

illustrated in Figure 4.16, let $z = R \cdot \cos(u)$ and $x = R \cdot \sin(u)$, where $0 \leq u \leq 2\pi$. Furthermore, for the cylinder to have height $h$ and be centered at the origin, you will use the parameterization $y = h \cdot (v - 1/2)$, where $0 \leq v \leq 1$.

This parameterization yields an "open-ended" cylinder or tube; the parameterization does not include top or bottom sides. The data for these sides can be added from polygon geometries, modified so that the circles are perpendicular to the $y$-axis and centered at the top and bottom of the cylinder. This requires additional code that will be described later.

To approximate a circular cross-section, a large number of radial segments will typically be used. Choosing a significantly smaller number of radial segments will result in a solid whose cross-sections are clearly polygons: these 3D shapes are called *prisms*, three of which are illustrated in Figure 4.17. Note that a square prism has the shape of a box, although due to the way the class is structured, it will contain more triangles and is aligned differently: in the **BoxGeometry** class, the coordinates were chosen so that the sides were perpendicular to the coordinate axes; a square prism will appear to have been rotated by 45° (around the $y$-axis) from this orientation.

By generalizing the cylinder equations a bit more, you gain the ability to produce more 3D shapes, as illustrated in Figure 4.18. For example, cones are similar to cylinders in that their cross-sections are circles, with the difference that the radius of each circle becomes smaller the closer the cross-section is to the top of the cylinder; the top is a single point, a circle with radius zero. Furthermore, by replacing the circular cross-sections of a cone with polygon cross-sections, the result is a pyramid. Square pyramids may come to mind most readily, but one may consider triangular pyramids, pentagonal pyramids, hexagonal

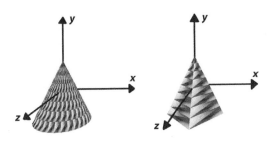

FIGURE 4.18    Cone and pyramid.

pyramids, and so on. To provide maximum generality, the base class for all of these shapes will include parameters where the radius at the top and the radius at the bottom can be specified, and the radius of each cross-section will be linearly interpolated from these two values. In theory, this would even enable frustum (truncated pyramid) shapes to be created.

To efficiently code this set of shapes, the most general class will be named **CylindricalGeometry**, and the classes that extend it will be named **CylinderGeometry**, **PrismGeometry**, **ConeGeometry**, and **PyramidGeometry**. (To create a less common shape such as a frustum, you can use the **CylindricalGeometry** class directly.) To begin, in the **geometry** package, create a new Java class named **CylindricalGeometry**, containing the following code:

```java
package geometry;
import math.Vector;
import math.Matrix;

public class CylindricalGeometry extends SurfaceGeometry
{
    public CylindricalGeometry(
        double radiusTop, double radiusBottom, double height,
        int radialSegments, int heightSegments,
        boolean closedTop, boolean closedBottom )
    {
        super( (u,v) -> { return new Vector(
            (v*radiusTop + (1-v)*radiusBottom) * Math.sin(u),
            height * (v - 0.5),
            (v*radiusTop + (1-v)*radiusBottom) * Math.cos(u)); },
                0, 2*Math.PI, radialSegments,
                0, 1, heightSegments  );
    }

    public CylindricalGeometry()
    {
        this(1,1,1, 32, 4, true,true);
    }
}
```

The most natural way to create a top and bottom for the cylinder is to use the data generated by the **PolygonGeometry** class. For the polygons to be correctly aligned with the top and bottom of the cylinder, there needs to be a way to transform the vertex position data of a polygon. Furthermore, once the data has been transformed, all the attribute data from the polygon objects will need to be merged into the attribute data for the cylindrical object. Since these operations may be useful in multiple situations, methods to perform these tasks will be implemented in the **Geometry** class. In order to complete these methods though, an additional method must be added to the **Vector** class for ease of use in the coming changes. Inside the **math** package, in the **Vector** class, insert the following method:

```
// resize values array (can be larger or smaller)
public void resize(int newSize)
{
    double[] newValues = new double[newSize];
    int smaller = Math.min(values.length, newValues.length);
    for (int i = 0; i < smaller; i++)
        newValues[i] = values[i];
    values = newValues;
}
```

Afterwards, in the **Geometry** class in the **geometry** package, add the following two methods:

```
// transform vertex position data using a matrix
public void applyMatrix(Matrix matrix)
{
    float[] oldPositionData =
        attributes.get("vertexPosition").dataArray;
    // convert flattened array back into list of vectors
    List<Vector> oldPositionList
        = Vector.unflattenList(oldPositionData, 3);
    List<Vector> newPositionList = new ArrayList<Vector>();
    for (Vector oldPos : oldPositionList)
    {
        // add homogeneous fourth coordinate
        oldPos.resize(4);
        oldPos.values[3] = 1;
        // multiply by matrix
        Vector newPos = matrix.multiplyVector(oldPos);
        // remove homogeneous coordinate
        newPos.resize(3);
        // add to new data list
        newPositionList.add( newPos );
    }
    float[] newPositionData =
        Vector.flattenList(newPositionList);
    attributes.get("vertexPosition").dataArray =
        newPositionData;
    // new data must be uploaded
    attributes.get("vertexPosition").uploadData();
}
```

```java
// merge data from attributes of other geometry
//    requires both geometries to have attributes with same names
public void merge(Geometry other)
{
    for ( String variableName : attributes.keySet() )
    {
        // merge two arrays
        float[] data1 =
            this.attributes.get(variableName).dataArray;
        float[] data2 =
            other.attributes.get(variableName).dataArray;
        float[] data3 = new float[data1.length + data2.length];
        for (int i = 0; i < data3.length; i++)
            if (i < data1.length)
                data3[i] = data1[i];
            else
                data3[i] = data2[i - data1.length];

        // new data must be set and uploaded
        this.attributes.get(variableName).dataArray = data3;
        this.attributes.get(variableName).uploadData();
    }
    // update the number of vertices
    this.vertexCount = this.vertexCount + other.vertexCount;
}
```

With these additions to the **Geometry** class, you can now use these functions as described above. In the class **CylindricalGeometry**, add the following code to the initialization method, after which the **CylindricalGeometry** class will be complete.

```java
if (closedTop)
{
    Geometry topGeometry =
        new PolygonGeometry(radialSegments, radiusTop);
    Matrix transform = Matrix.makeTranslation(0, height/2, 0);
    transform.rightMultiply( Matrix.makeRotationY(-Math.PI/2) );
    transform.rightMultiply( Matrix.makeRotationX(-Math.PI/2) );
    topGeometry.applyMatrix( transform );
    this.merge( topGeometry );
}
if (closedBottom)
{
    Geometry bottomGeometry =
        new PolygonGeometry(radialSegments, radiusBottom);
    Matrix transform = Matrix.makeTranslation(0, -height/2, 0);
    transform.rightMultiply( Matrix.makeRotationY(-Math.PI/2) );
```

```
    transform.rightMultiply( Matrix.makeRotationX( Math.PI/2) );
    bottomGeometry.applyMatrix( transform );
    this.merge( bottomGeometry );
}
```

To create cylinders, the same radius is used for the top and bottom, and the top and bottom sides will both be closed (present) or not. In the **geometry** package, create a new Java class named **CylinderGeometry**, containing the following code:

```
package geometry;

public class CylinderGeometry extends CylindricalGeometry
{
    public CylinderGeometry( double radius, double height,
        int radialSegments, int heightSegments, boolean closed )
    {
        super( radius, radius, height,
            radialSegments, heightSegments, closed, closed );
    }

    public CylinderGeometry()
    {
        this(1,1, 32,4, true);
    }
}
```

To create prisms, the parameter **radialSegments** is replaced by **sides** for clarity in this context. In the **geometry** package, create a new Java class named **PrismGeometry**, containing the following code:

```
package geometry;

public class PrismGeometry extends CylindricalGeometry
{
    public PrismGeometry( double radius, double height,
            int sides, int heightSegments, boolean closed )
    {
        super( radius, radius, height,
                sides, heightSegments, closed, closed );
    }

    public PrismGeometry()
    {
        this(1,1, 6,4, true);
    }
}
```

To create cones, the top radius will always be zero, and the top polygon side never needs to be rendered. In the **geometry** package, create a new Java class named **ConeGeometry**, containing the following code:

```java
package geometry;

public class ConeGeometry extends CylindricalGeometry
{
    public ConeGeometry( double radius, double height,
        int radialSegments, int heightSegments, boolean closed )
    {
        super( 0, radius, height,
            radialSegments, heightSegments, false, closed  );
    }

    public ConeGeometry()
    {
        this(1,1, 32,4, true);
    }
}
```

Finally, creating pyramids is similar to creating cones, and as was the case for prisms, the parameter **radialSegments** is replaced by **sides** for clarity in this context. In the **geometry** package, create a new Java class named **PyramidGeometry** containing the following code:

```java
package geometry;

public class PyramidGeometry extends CylindricalGeometry
{
    public PyramidGeometry( double radius, double height,
            int sides, int heightSegments, boolean closed )
    {
        super( 0, radius, height,
                sides, heightSegments, false, closed  );
    }

    public PyramidGeometry()
    {
        this(1,1, 4,4, true);
    }
}
```

## 4.4 MATERIAL OBJECTS

Material objects will store three types of data related to rendering: shader program references, **Uniform** objects, and OpenGL render settings. As was the case with the base **Geometry** class, there will be many extensions of the base **Material** class.

For example, different materials will exist for rendering geometric data as a collection of points, as a set of lines, or as a surface. Some basic materials will implement vertex colors or uniform base colors, while advanced materials (developed in later chapters) will implement texture mapping, lighting, and other effects. The framework will also enable developers to easily write customized shaders in applications.

The tasks handled by the base **Material** class will include:

- compiling the shader code and initializing the program

- initializing collections to store uniforms

- defining uniforms corresponding to the model, view, and projection matrices, whose values are stored outside the material (in mesh and camera objects)

- define a method named **addUniform** to simplify creating and adding **Uniform** objects

- defining a method named **locateUniforms** that determines and stores all the uniform variable references in the shaders

Classes that extend this class will:

- contain the actual shader code

- add any extra uniform objects required by the shaders

- call the **locateUniforms** method once all uniform objects have been added

- add OpenGL render settings (as Java variables) to the settings dictionary

- implement a method named **addRenderSettings**, which will call the OpenGL functions needed to configure the render settings

## 4.4.1 Material Class

Since there will be many extensions of this class, all the material-related classes will be organized into a separate folder. To this end, in your main folder, create a new package called **material**. To create the base class, in the **material** package, create a new Java class called **Material** with the following code. (The **RenderSetting** class referenced here will be introduced immediately after this code listing.)

```
package material;
import static org.lwjgl.opengl.GL40.*;
import java.util.HashMap;
import core.OpenGLUtils;
import core.Uniform;
import core.RenderSetting;
```

```java
public class Material
{
    public int programRef;

    public int drawStyle;

    // Store Uniform objects,
    //    indexed by name of associated variable in shader.
    public HashMap<String, Uniform> uniforms;

    // Store OpenGL render settings,
    //    indexed by variable name.
    // Additional settings added by extending classes.
    public HashMap<String, RenderSetting> renderSettings;

    public Material(String vertexShaderFileName,
                    String fragmentShaderFileName)
    {
        programRef = OpenGLUtils.initFromFiles(
            vertexShaderFileName, fragmentShaderFileName );

        drawStyle = GL_TRIANGLES;

        uniforms = new HashMap<String, Uniform>();

        // Each shader typically contains these uniforms;
        //    values set during render process from Mesh/Camera.
        // Additional uniforms added by extending classes.
        addUniform("mat4", "modelMatrix", null);
        addUniform("mat4", "viewMatrix", null);
        addUniform("mat4", "projectionMatrix", null);

        renderSettings = new HashMap<String, RenderSetting>();
    }

    public void addUniform(String dataType,
          String variableName, Object data)
    {
        uniforms.put(variableName, new Uniform(dataType, data));
    }

    // initialize all uniform variable references
    public void locateUniforms()
    {
        for (String variableName : uniforms.keySet())
        {
            Uniform uniform = uniforms.get(variableName);
```

```
                uniform.locateVariable(programRef, variableName);
        }
    }

    public void addRenderSetting(String settingName,
        Object data)
    {
        renderSettings.put(settingName,
            new RenderSetting(settingName, data));
    }
}
```

The **RenderSetting** class referred to in the **Material** class is used to configure OpenGL settings efficiently. Based on the setting name associated with this object, an OpenGL function will be called using the associated data. To proceed, in the **core** directory, create a new Java class named **RenderSetting**, with the following code:

```java
package core;
import static org.lwjgl.opengl.GL40.*;

public class RenderSetting
{
    // setting name
    public String settingName;

    // default data value
    public Object data;

    public RenderSetting(String settingName, Object data)
    {
        this.settingName = settingName;
        this.data = data;
    }

    public void apply()
    {
        if (settingName.equals("pointSize"))
        {
            glPointSize( (int)data );
        }
        else if (settingName.equals("roundedPoints"))
        {
            if ( (boolean)data )
                glEnable(GL_POINT_SMOOTH);
            else
                glDisable(GL_POINT_SMOOTH);
        }
```

```
        else if (settingName.equals("lineWidth"))
        {
            glLineWidth( (int)data );
        }
        else if (settingName.equals("doubleSide"))
        {
            if ( (boolean)data )
                glDisable(GL_CULL_FACE);
            else
                glEnable(GL_CULL_FACE);
        }
        else if (settingName.equals("wireframe"))
        {
            if ( (boolean)data )
                glPolygonMode(GL_FRONT_AND_BACK, GL_LINE);
            else
                glPolygonMode(GL_FRONT_AND_BACK, GL_FILL);
        }
        else
        {
            System.out.println("Unknown render setting: "
                + settingName);
        }
    }
}
```

With this class completed, you will next turn your attention to creating extensions of the **Material** class.

## 4.4.2 Basic Materials

In this section you will create an extension of the **Material** class, called **BasicMaterial**, which contains shader code and a set of corresponding uniforms. The shaders can be used to render points, lines, or surfaces. Keeping modular design principles in mind, this class will in turn be extended into classes called **PointMaterial**, **LineMaterial**, and **SurfaceMaterial**, each of which will contain the relevant OpenGL parameters and render settings for the corresponding type of geometric primitive. Figure 4.19 illustrates

FIGURE 4.19 Rendering the six vertices of a Rectangle geometry with a point material (left), line material (center), and surface material (right).

the results of rendering the six vertices of a **Rectangle** object with each of these types of materials using vertex colors. Note that since the bottom-left vertex color has been changed to gray so that it is visible against a white background, and that the line material groups points into pairs and thus does not produce a full wireframe (although this will be possible with the surface material settings).

The shaders for the basic material will use two attributes: vertex positions and vertex colors. As before, attribute variables are designated with the type qualifier **in**. The vertex color data will be sent from the vertex shader to the fragment shader using the variable **color**. The uniform variables used by the vertex shader will include the model, view, and projection matrices, as usual, which are used to calculate the final position of each vertex. The two main options for coloring fragments are either to use interpolated vertex colors, or to apply a single color to all vertices. To this end, there will be two additional uniform variables used by this shader. The first variable, **baseColor**, will be a **vec3** containing a color applied to all vertices, with the default value (1,1,1), corresponding to white. The second variable, **useVertexColors**, will be a boolean value that determines whether the data stored in the vertex color attribute will be applied to the base color. You do not need to include a boolean variable specifying whether base color should be used (in other words, there is no **useBaseColor** variable), because if the base color is left at its default value of (1,1,1), then combining this with other colors (by multiplication) will have no effect.

To begin, in the **material** package create two additional files named **BasicMaterial. frag** and **BasicMaterial.vert**. In the fragment shader file, insert the following code:

```
uniform vec3 baseColor;
uniform bool useVertexColors;

in vec3 color;
out vec4 fragColor;

void main()
{
    vec4 tempColor = vec4(baseColor, 1.0);
    if ( useVertexColors )
        tempColor *= vec4(color, 1.0);
    fragColor = tempColor;
}
```

And inside the vertex shader file, insert the following code:

```
uniform mat4 projectionMatrix;
uniform mat4 viewMatrix;
uniform mat4 modelMatrix;

in vec3 vertexPosition;
in vec3 vertexColor;
out vec3 color;
```

```
void main()
{
    gl_Position = projectionMatrix * viewMatrix * modelMatrix
        * vec4(vertexPosition, 1.0);
    color = vertexColor;
}
```

To fully implement the basic material class, in the **material** package, create a new Java class called **BasicMaterial** with the following code:

```
package material;
import math.Vector;

public class BasicMaterial extends Material
{
    public BasicMaterial()
    {
        super(
                "./src/material/BasicMaterial.vert",
                "./src/material/BasicMaterial.frag"  );

        addUniform("vec3", "baseColor", new Vector(1,1,1) );
        addUniform("bool", "useVertexColors", 0);
        locateUniforms();
    }
}
```

Next, the render settings and **drawStyle** need to be specified. As previously mentioned, this will be accomplished with three classes that extend the **BasicMaterial** class.

The first extension will be the **PointMaterial** class, which renders vertices as points. The draw style is the OpenGL constant GL_POINTS. The applicable render settings are "**pointSize**" and "**roundedPoints**." To implement this class, in the **material** package, create a new Java class called **PointMaterial** with the following code:

```
package material;
import static org.lwjgl.opengl.GL40.*;

public class PointMaterial extends BasicMaterial
{
    public PointMaterial()
    {
        drawStyle = GL_POINTS;
        addRenderSetting( "pointSize", 16 );
        addRenderSetting( "roundedPoints", true );
    }
}
```

The second extension will be the **LineMaterial** class, which renders vertices as lines. In this case, there are three different ways to group vertices: as a connected set of points, a loop (additionally connecting the last point to the first), and as a disjoint set of line segments. These are specified by the OpenGL constants GL_LINE_STRIP, GL_LINE_LOOP, and GL_LINES, respectively, but for readability will be specified by the constructor parameter "**lineStyle**" with the values "**connected**," "**loop**," or "**segments**." The only render setting is the thickness or width of the lines, specified by "**lineWidth**." To implement this class, in the **material** package, create a new Java class called **LineMaterial** with the following code:

```
package material;
import static org.lwjgl.opengl.GL40.*;

public class LineMaterial extends BasicMaterial
{
    public LineMaterial()
    {
        drawStyle = GL_LINES;
        addRenderSetting( "lineWidth", 1 );
    }

    public LineMaterial(String lineStyle)
    {
        if (lineStyle.equals("segments"))
            drawStyle = GL_LINES;
        else if (lineStyle.equals("connected"))
            drawStyle = GL_LINE_STRIP;
        else if (lineStyle.equals("loop"))
            drawStyle = GL_LINE_LOOP;
        else
        {
            System.out.println("Unknown line style: "
                + lineStyle);
            drawStyle = GL_LINES;
        }
        addRenderSetting( "lineWidth", 1 );

    }
}
```

The third extension will be the **SurfaceMaterial** class, which renders vertices as a surface. In this case, the draw style is specified by the OpenGL constant GL_TRIANGLES. For rendering efficiency, OpenGL only renders the front side of triangles by default; the front side is defined to be the side from which the vertices appear to be listed in counterclockwise order. Both sides of each triangle can be rendered by changing the render setting "**doubleSide**" to **true**. A surface can be rendered in wireframe style by changing the

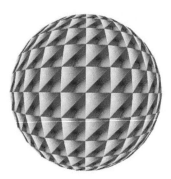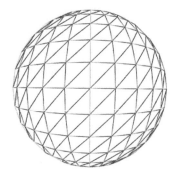

FIGURE 4.20   Rendering a sphere with triangles and as a wireframe.

render setting "**wireframe**" to **true**, in which case the thickness of the lines may also be set as with line-based materials with the render setting "**lineWidth**." The results of rendering a shape in wireframe style (with double sided rendering set to False) are illustrated in Figure 4.20. To implement this class, in the **material** package, create a new Java class called **SurfaceMaterial** with the following code:

```
package material;
import static org.lwjgl.opengl.GL40.*;

public class SurfaceMaterial extends BasicMaterial
{
    public SurfaceMaterial()
    {
        drawStyle = GL_TRIANGLES;
        addRenderSetting( "doubleSide", true );
        addRenderSetting( "wireframe", false );
        addRenderSetting( "lineWidth", 1 );
    }
}
```

At this point, you have completed many geometry and material classes, which store all the information required to render an object. In the next section, you will create a class that uses this information in the process of rendering mesh objects.

## 4.5 RENDERING SCENES WITH THE FRAMEWORK

The final class required in the framework at this stage is the **Renderer** class. When initialized, this class will perform general rendering tasks, including enabling depth testing, antialiasing, and setting the color used when clearing the color buffer (the default background color). A method named **render** will take a **Scene** and a **Camera** object as input, and perform all of the rendering related tasks that you have seen in earlier examples. The color and depth buffers are cleared, and the camera's view matrix is updated. Next, a list of all the **Mesh** objects in the scene is created by first extracting all elements in the scene using the **getDescendentList** method, and then filtering this list using a for loop. Then, for each mesh that is visible, the following tasks need to be performed:

- the shader program being used must be specified
- the vertex array object that specifies the associations between vertex buffers and shader variables must be bound
- the values corresponding to the model, view, and projection matrices (stored in the mesh and camera) must be stored in the corresponding uniform objects
- the values in all uniform objects must be uploaded to the GPU
- render settings are applied via OpenGL functions
- the **glDrawArrays** function is called, specifying the correct draw mode and the number of vertices to be rendered

To continue, in the **core** package, create a new Java class called **Renderer** with the following code:

```java
package core;
import static org.lwjgl.opengl.GL40.*;
import java.util.List;
import java.util.ArrayList;
import math.Vector;

public class Renderer
{
    public Renderer()
    {
        glClearColor(0, 0, 0, 1);
        glEnable( GL_DEPTH_TEST );

        // required for antialiasing
        glEnable( GL_MULTISAMPLE );
    }

    public void setClearColor( Vector color )
    {
        glClearColor( (float)color.values[0],
            (float)color.values[1], (float)color.values[2], 1);
    }

    public void render(Scene scene, Camera camera)
    {
        // clear color and depth buffers
        glClear(GL_COLOR_BUFFER_BIT | GL_DEPTH_BUFFER_BIT);

        // update camera view (calculate inverse)
        camera.updateViewMatrix();
```

```java
        // extract list of all Mesh objects in scene
        List<Object3D> descendentList =
            scene.getDescendentList();
        ArrayList<Mesh> meshList = new ArrayList<Mesh>();

        for (Object3D obj : descendentList)
            if (obj instanceof Mesh)
                meshList.add( (Mesh)obj );

        for (Mesh mesh : meshList)
        {
            // if this object is not visible,
            // continue to next object in list
            if (!mesh.visible)
                continue;

            glUseProgram( mesh.material.programRef );

            // bind VAO
            glBindVertexArray( mesh.vaoRef );
            // update uniform values stored outside of material
            mesh.material.uniforms.get("modelMatrix").data =
                mesh.getWorldMatrix();
            mesh.material.uniforms.get("viewMatrix").data =
                camera.viewMatrix;
            mesh.material.uniforms.get("projectionMatrix").data
                = camera.projectionMatrix;

            // update uniforms stored in material
    for ( Uniform uniform :
            mesh.material.uniforms.values() )
                uniform.uploadData();

            // update render settings
            for ( RenderSetting setting :
                    mesh.material.renderSettings.values() )
                setting.apply();

            glDrawArrays( mesh.material.drawStyle,
              0, mesh.geometry.vertexCount );
        }
    }
}
```

At this point, you are now ready to create an application using the graphics framework! Most applications will require at least seven classes to be imported: **Base**, **Renderer**, **Scene**, **Camera**, **Mesh**, and at least one geometry and one material class to be used in the mesh. To create the application that consists of a spinning cube, in your main project folder, create a new Java class named **Test_4_1**, containing the following code:

```java
import static org.lwjgl.glfw.GLFW.*;
import static org.lwjgl.opengl.GL40.*;
import core.*;
import math.*;
import geometry.*;
import material.*;

public class Test_4_1 extends Base
{
    public Renderer renderer;
    public Scene scene;
    public Camera camera;
    public Mesh mesh;

    public void initialize()
    {
        renderer = new Renderer();
        scene    = new Scene();
        camera   = new Camera();
        camera.setPosition( new Vector(0,0,3) );
        Geometry geometry = new BoxGeometry();
        Material material = new SurfaceMaterial();
        // to change value from default, for example:
        // material.renderSettings.get("pointSize").data = 32;
        material.uniforms.get("useVertexColors").data = 1;

        mesh = new Mesh( geometry, material );
        scene.add( mesh );
    }

    public void update()
    {
        mesh.rotateY( 0.0123f, true );
        mesh.rotateX( 0.0237f, true );
        renderer.render(scene, camera);
    }

    // driver method
    public static void main(String[] args)
    {
        new Test_4_1().run();
    }
}
```

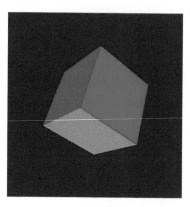

FIGURE 4.21    Rendering a spinning cube with the graphics framework classes.

Running this code should produce a result similar to that illustrated in Figure 4.21, where the dark background is due to the default clear color in the renderer being used.

Hopefully, the first thing you noticed about the application code was that it is quite short, and focuses on high-level concepts. This is thanks to all the work that went into writing the framework classes in this chapter. At this point you should try displaying the other geometric shapes that you have implemented to confirm that they appear as expected. In addition, you should also try out the other materials and experiment with changing the default uniform values and render settings. For example, you could configure the material in the previous example by adding this line of code:

```
material.renderSettings.get("wireframe").data = true;
```

This would produce a result similar to that shown in Figure 4.22.

Before proceeding, it will be very helpful to create a template file containing most of this code. In your main src folder, copy the code in the file named **Test_4_1**, save it as a new Java class named **Test_Template** and comment out the two lines of code in the **update** method that rotate the mesh.

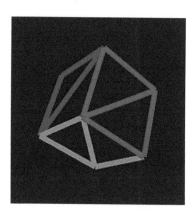

FIGURE 4.22    Rendering a cube with alternate material properties.

The following examples will illustrate how to create custom geometry and custom material objects in an application.

## 4.6 CUSTOM GEOMETRY AND MATERIAL OBJECTS

The first example will demonstrate how to create a custom geometry object by explicitly listing the vertex data, similar to the geometry classes representing rectangles and boxes; the result will be as shown in Figure 4.23.

To begin, create a copy of the file **Test_Template**, save it as **Test_4_2**. Whenever you want to create your own customized geometry, you will need to import the **Geometry** class. However, the template class you just created already has it imported. Next, add the following import statements to your code:

```
import java.util.Arrays;
import java.util.List;
```

To continue, replace the line of code where the geometry object is initialized with the following block of code:

```
Geometry geometry = new Geometry();
Vector P0 = new Vector(-0.1, 0.1, 0.0);
Vector P1 = new Vector( 0.0, 0.0, 0.0);
Vector P2 = new Vector( 0.1, 0.1, 0.0);
Vector P3 = new Vector(-0.2, -0.2, 0.0);
Vector P4 = new Vector( 0.2, -0.2, 0.0);
List positionList =
    Arrays.asList(P0,P3,P1, P1,P3,P4, P1,P4,P2);
float[] positionData = Vector.flattenList(positionList);

Vector R = new Vector(1, 0, 0);
Vector Y = new Vector(1, 1, 0);
Vector G = new Vector(0, 0.25, 0);
List colorList = Arrays.asList(R,G,Y, Y,G,G, Y,G,R);
float[] colorData = Vector.flattenList(colorList);
```

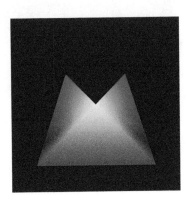

FIGURE 4.23   A custom geometry.

```
geometry.addAttribute("vec3", "vertexPosition", positionData);
geometry.addAttribute("vec3", "vertexColor", colorData);
geometry.vertexCount = 9;
Material material = new SurfaceMaterial();
material.uniforms.get("useVertexColors").data = 1;
```

With these changes, save and run your file, and you should see a result similar to that in Figure 4.23.

For all but the simplest models, listing the vertices by hand can be a tedious process, and so you may wish to generate vertex data using functions. The next example generates the image from Figure 4.24 from vertices generated along the graph of a sine function. This particular appearance is generated by drawing the same geometric data twice: once using a point-based material, and once using a line-based material.

To begin, create a copy of the file **Test_Template**, save it as **Test_4_3**. As before, you will need to import the Geometry and Attribute classes. Add the following import statement to your code:

```
import java.util.ArrayList;
```

Next, in the **initialize** method, delete the code in that function that occurs after the camera position is set, replacing it with the following:

```
Geometry geometry = new Geometry();
ArrayList<Vector> positionList = new ArrayList<Vector>();
for (double x=-3.2; x <= 3.2; x += 0.3)
    positionList.add( new Vector(x, Math.sin(x), 0) );

float[] positionData = Vector.flattenList(positionList);
geometry.addAttribute("vec3", "vertexPosition", positionData);

geometry.vertexCount = positionList.size();
```

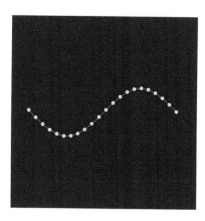

FIGURE 4.24   A custom geometry with data generated from a function.

```
Material lineMaterial = new LineMaterial("connected");
lineMaterial.uniforms.get("baseColor").data = new Vector(1,0,1);
lineMaterial.renderSettings.get("lineWidth").data = 4;
Mesh lineMesh = new Mesh( geometry, lineMaterial );
scene.add( lineMesh );


Material pointMaterial = new PointMaterial();
pointMaterial.uniforms.get("baseColor").data =
    new Vector(1,1,0);
pointMaterial.renderSettings.get("pointSize").data = 8;
Mesh pointMesh = new Mesh( geometry, pointMaterial );
scene.add(pointMesh);
```

Note that vertex color data does not need to be generated, since the material's base color is used when rendering. Save and run this file, and the result will be similar to Figure 4.24.

Next, you will turn your attention to customized materials, where the shader code, uniforms, and render settings are part of the application code. In the next example, you will color the surface of an object based on the coordinates of each point on the surface. In particular, you will take the fractional part of the x, y, and z coordinates of each point and use these for the red, green, and blue components of the color. The fractional part is used because this is a value between zero and one, which is the range of color components. Figure 4.25 shows the effect of applying this shader to a sphere of radius three.

As before, create a copy of the file **Test_Template**, this time saving it with the file name **Test_4_4**. Whenever you want to create your own customized material, you will need to import the **Material** class, however as before, it is already imported in our template class.

FIGURE 4.25    Coloring the surface of a sphere based on point coordinates.

Before continuing with this test class, create two new shader files named **Test_4_4. frag** and **Test_4_4.vert**. Inside the fragment shader file, insert the following code:

```
in vec3 position;
out vec4 fragColor;
void main()
{
    vec3 color = mod(position, 1.0);
    fragColor = vec4(color, 1.0);
}
```

And inside the vertex shader file, insert the following code:

```
in vec3 vertexPosition;
out vec3 position;
uniform mat4 modelMatrix;
uniform mat4 viewMatrix;
uniform mat4 projectionMatrix;
void main()
{
vec4 pos = vec4(vertexPosition, 1.0);
gl_Position = projectionMatrix * viewMatrix * modelMatrix
        * pos;
position = vertexPosition;
}
```

Note that there are **out** and **in** variables named **position**, which are used to transmit position data from the vertex shader to the fragment shader (which, as usual, is interpolated for each fragment). Additionally, to obtain the fractional part of each coordinate, the values are reduced modulo one using the GLSL function **mod**. In this example, uniform objects do not need to be created for the matrices, as this is handled by the **Mesh** class.

Next, in the initialize method in the file **Test_4_4**, delete the code that is present after the camera object is initialized, and replace it with the following code.

```
Geometry geometry = new SphereGeometry(3);

Material material = new Material(
    "./src/Test_4_4.vert", "./src/Test_4_4.frag");
material.locateUniforms();

mesh = new Mesh( geometry, material );
scene.add( mesh );
```

It is easy to see the red and green color gradients on the rendered sphere, but not the blue gradient, due to the orientation of the sphere and the position of the camera (looking along

FIGURE 4.26 A sphere with periodic displacement and color shifting.

the z-axis). If desired, you may add code to the **update** method that will rotate this mesh around the y-axis, to get a fuller understanding of how the colors are applied across the surface.

The final example in this section will illustrate how to create animated effects in both the vertex shader and the fragment shader, using a custom material. Once again, you will use a spherical shape for the geometry. In the material's vertex shader, you will add an offset to the y-coordinate, based on the sine of the x-coordinate, and shift the displacement over time. In the material's fragment shader, you will shift between the geometry's vertex colors and a shade of red in a periodic manner. A still image from this animation is shown in Figure 4.26.

First create three new files, one copy of the **Test_Template** named **Test_4_5** and two files named **Test_4_5.frag** and **Test_4_5.vert**. Inside the fragment shader file, insert the following code:

```
in vec3 color;
uniform float time;
out vec4 fragColor;

void main()
{
    float r = abs(sin(time));
    vec4 c = vec4(r, -0.5*r, -0.5*r, 0.0);
    fragColor = vec4(color, 1.0) + c;
}
```

Second, insert the following code into the vertex shader file:

```
uniform mat4 modelMatrix;
uniform mat4 viewMatrix;
uniform mat4 projectionMatrix;

in vec3 vertexPosition;
in vec3 vertexColor;
```

```
out vec3 color;
uniform float time;

void main()
{
    float offset = 0.2 * sin(8.0 * vertexPosition.x + time);
    vec3 pos = vertexPosition + vec3(0.0, offset, 0.0);
    gl_Position = projectionMatrix * viewMatrix * modelMatrix
        * vec4(pos, 1);
    color = vertexColor;
}
```

Next, in the **initialize** method of the main **Test_4_5** file, delete the code that occurs after the camera position is set and replace it with the following code:

```
Geometry geometry = new SphereGeometry(3, 128, 64);

Material material = new Material(
    "./src/Test_4_5.vert", "./src/Test_4_5.frag");
material.addUniform("float", "time", 0);
material.locateUniforms();

mesh = new Mesh( geometry, material );
scene.add( mesh );

time = 0;
```

Note that in this example, there is a uniform variable called **time** present in both the vertex shader and the fragment shader, for which a Uniform object will need to be created. Also note the Java variable **time**, which will be used to supply the value to the uniform later.

Finally, to produce the animated effect, you must increment and update the value of the **time** variable. In the **update** method, add the following code before the **render** method is called:

```
time += 1/60f;
mesh.material.uniforms.get("time").data = time;
```

With these additions, this example is complete. Run the code and you should see an animated rippling effect on the sphere, as the color shifts back and forth from the red end of the spectrum.

## 4.7 EXTRA COMPONENTS

Now that you are familiar with writing customized geometric objects, there are several useful, reusable classes you will add to the framework: axes and grids, to more easily orient the viewer. Following this, you will create a movement rig, enabling you to more easily create interactive scenes by moving the camera or objects in the scene in an intuitive way.

### 4.7.1 Axes and Grids

At present, there is no easy way to determine one's orientation relative to the scene, or a sense of scale, within a 3D scene built in this framework. One approach that can partially alleviate these issues is to create 3D axis and grid objects, illustrated separately and together in Figure 4.27.

For convenience, each of these objects will extend the Mesh class, and set up their own Geometry and Material within the class. Since they are not really of core importance to the framework, in order to keep the file system organized, in your main **src** folder, create a new package called **extras**.

First you will implement the object representing the (positive) coordinate axes. By default, the x, y, and z axes will have length one and be rendered with red, green, and blue lines, using a basic line material, although these parameters will be able to be adjusted in the constructor. In the **extras** package, create a new Java class named **AxesGeometry** with the following code:

```
package extras;
import geometry.Geometry;
import math.Vector;
import java.util.Arrays;
import java.util.List;

public class AxesGeometry extends Geometry
{
    public AxesGeometry(double axisLength)
    {
        List positionList = Arrays.asList(
                new Vector(0,0,0), new Vector(axisLength,0,0),
                new Vector(0,0,0), new Vector(0,axisLength,0),
                new Vector(0,0,0), new Vector(0,0,axisLength)   );
        float[] positionData = Vector.flattenList(positionList);

        List colorList = Arrays.asList(
                new Vector(0.5, 0, 0), new Vector(1, 0.5, 0.5),
```

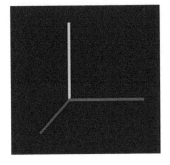 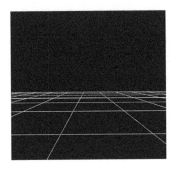 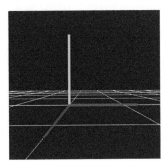

FIGURE 4.27   Coordinate axes (left), a grid (center), and in combination (right).

```
                    new Vector(0, 0.5, 0), new Vector(0.5, 1, 0.5),
                    new Vector(0, 0, 0.5), new Vector(0.5, 0.5, 1)  );
            float[] colorData = Vector.flattenList(colorList);

            addAttribute("vec3", "vertexPosition", positionData);
            addAttribute("vec3", "vertexColor", colorData);
            vertexCount = 6;
        }

        public AxesGeometry()
        {
            this(1);
        }
    }
```

You can now proceed to create the **AxesHelper** Java class in the same package. This is the file that will be called utilizing the class you just created. Inside this file, insert the following code:

```
package extras;
import core.Mesh;
import material.LineMaterial;

public class AxesHelper extends Mesh
{
    public AxesHelper(float axisLength, int lineWidth)
    {
        super( new AxesGeometry(axisLength),
                new LineMaterial() );
        this.material.uniforms.get("useVertexColors").data = 1;
        this.material.renderSettings.get("lineWidth").data =
            lineWidth;
    }
}
```

Next, you will create a (square) grid object. Settings that you will be able to customize will include the dimensions of the grid, the number of divisions on each side, the color of the grid lines, and a separate color for the central grid line. In the **extras** package, create a new Java class named **GridGeometry** containing the following code:

```
package extras;
import geometry.Geometry;
import math.Vector;
import java.util.List;
import java.util.ArrayList;
```

```java
public class GridGeometry extends Geometry
{
    public GridGeometry(double size, int divisions,
                        Vector gridColor, Vector centerColor )
    {
        double deltaSize = size / divisions;

        List<Double> values = new ArrayList<Double>();
        for (int n = 0; n < divisions + 1; n++)
            values.add( -size/2 + n * deltaSize );

        List<Vector> positionList = new ArrayList<Vector>();
        List<Vector> colorList    = new ArrayList<Vector>();

        // add vertical lines
        for (Double x : values)
        {
            positionList.add( new Vector(x, -size/2, 0) );
            positionList.add( new Vector(x,  size/2, 0) );
            if (x == 0)
            {
                colorList.add(centerColor);
                colorList.add(centerColor);
            }
            else
            {
                colorList.add(gridColor);
                colorList.add(gridColor);
            }
        }

        // add horizontal lines
        for (Double y : values)
        {
            positionList.add( new Vector(-size/2, y, 0) );
            positionList.add( new Vector( size/2, y, 0) );
            if (y == 0)
            {
                colorList.add(centerColor);
                colorList.add(centerColor);
            }
            else
            {
                colorList.add(gridColor);
                colorList.add(gridColor);
            }
        }
```

```
        float[] positionData = Vector.flattenList(positionList);
        float[] colorData = Vector.flattenList(colorList);

        addAttribute("vec3", "vertexPosition", positionData);
        addAttribute("vec3", "vertexColor", colorData);
        vertexCount = positionList.size();
    }

    public GridGeometry()
    {
        this(10,10, new Vector(0.5,0.5,0.5),
                    new Vector(0.8,0.8,0.8));
    }
}
```

Next, create a new Java class in the same package named **GridHelper**. This will be the class called in the main application to generate the grid structure. Inside this file, insert the following code:

```
package extras;
import core.Mesh;
import math.Vector;
import material.LineMaterial;

public class GridHelper extends Mesh
{
    public GridHelper(double size, int divisions,
                      Vector gridColor, Vector centerColor, int
lineWidth )
    {
        super( new GridGeometry(size, divisions,
                                gridColor, centerColor),
               new LineMaterial() );
        this.material.uniforms.get("useVertexColors").data = 1;
        this.material.renderSettings.get("lineWidth").data =
            lineWidth;
    }

    public GridHelper()
    {
        this(10, 10,
             new Vector(0.5,0.5,0.5),
             new Vector(0.8,0.8,0.8), 1);
    }
}
```

Note that the grid will by default be parallel to the xy-plane. For it to appear horizontal, as in Figure 4.27, you could rotate it by 90° around the x-axis. In order to see how these classes are used in code, to produce an image like the right side of Figure 4.27, make a copy of the file **Test_Template**, and save it as **Test_4_6**. First, in the beginning of this new class, add the following import statement:

```
import extras.*;
```

Then, in the **initialize** method, delete the code that occurs after the camera object is initialized, and replace it with the following code, which adds coordinate axes and a grid to the scene, and demonstrates use of some of the available customization parameters.

```
camera.setPosition( new Vector(0.5, 1, 4) );

Mesh grid = new GridHelper(10,10,
    new Vector(1,1,0), new Vector(1,1,1), 2);
grid.rotateX(-Math.PI/2, true);
scene.add( grid );

Mesh axes = new AxesHelper(2, 8);
axes.translate(0, 0.01, 0, true);
scene.add( axes );
```

When running this test application, you should see axes and a grid as previously described.

## 4.7.2 Movement Rig

As the final topic in this chapter, you will learn how to create a movement rig: an object with a built-in control system that can be used to move the camera or other attached objects within a scene in a natural way, similar to the way person might move around a field: moving forwards and backwards, left and right (all local translations), as well as turning left and right, and looking up and down. Here, the use of the verb "look" indicates that even if a person's point of view tilts up or down, their movement is still aligned with the horizontal plane. The only unrealistic movement feature that will be incorporated will be that the attached object will also be able to move up and down along the direction of the y-axis (perpendicular to the horizontal plane).

To begin, this class, which will be called **MovementRig**, naturally extends the **Object3D** class. In addition, to support the "look" feature, it will take advantage of the scene graph structure, by way of including a child Object3D; the move and turn motions will be applied to the base Object3D, while the look motions will be applied to the child Object3D (and thus the orientation resulting from the current look angle will have no effect on the move and turn motions). However, in order to properly attach objects to the movement rig (to the child object within the rig) will require the Object3D functions **add** and **remove** to be overridden. For convenience, the rate of each motion will be able to be specified. To begin, in the **extras** package, create a new Java class named **MovementRig** with the following code:

```java
package extras;
import core.Object3D;
import java.util.HashMap;
import static org.lwjgl.glfw.GLFW.*;
import core.Input;

public class MovementRig extends Object3D
{
    public Object3D lookAttachment;
    public double unitsPerSecond;
    public double degreesPerSecond;
    public HashMap<String, Integer> keyMap;

    public MovementRig(double unitsPerSecond,
                        double degreesPerSecond)
    {
        this.lookAttachment = new Object3D();
        this.add(lookAttachment);
        this.unitsPerSecond = unitsPerSecond;
        this.degreesPerSecond = degreesPerSecond;
        this.keyMap = new HashMap<String, Integer>();
    }

    public MovementRig()
    {
        this(1, 60);
    }

    public void attach(Object3D obj)
    {
        lookAttachment.add(obj);
    }
}
```

Next, in order to conveniently handle movement controls, this class will have an **update** method that takes an **Input** object as a parameter, and if certain keys are pressed, transforms the movement rig correspondingly. In order to provide the developer the ability to easily configure the keys being used, they will be assigned to variables in the class, and in theory, one could even disable certain types of motion by assigning the value None to any of these motions. The default controls will follow the standard practice of using the "w" / "a" / "s" / "d" keys for movement forwards / left / backwards / right. The letters "q" and "e" will be used for turning left and right, as they are positioned above the keys for moving left and right. Movement up and down will be assigned to the keys "r" and "f," which can be remembered with the mnemonic words "rise" and "fall," and "r" is positioned in the row above "f." Finally, looking up and down will be assigned to the keys "t" and "g," as they are positioned adjacent to the keys for moving up and down. To implement this, in the main **constructor**, add the following code:

```
// customizable key mappings
// defaults: WASDRF (move), QE (turn), TG (look)
this.keyMap.put("move_forwards",  GLFW_KEY_W);
this.keyMap.put("move_backwards", GLFW_KEY_S);
this.keyMap.put("move_left",      GLFW_KEY_A);
this.keyMap.put("move_right",     GLFW_KEY_D);
this.keyMap.put("move_up",        GLFW_KEY_R);
this.keyMap.put("move_down",      GLFW_KEY_F);
this.keyMap.put("turn_left",      GLFW_KEY_Q);
this.keyMap.put("turn_right",     GLFW_KEY_E);
this.keyMap.put("look_up",        GLFW_KEY_T);
this.keyMap.put("look_down",      GLFW_KEY_G);
```

Finally, in the **MovementRig** class, add the following method which also calculates the amount of motion that should occur based on **deltaTime**: the amount of time that has elapsed since the previous update.

```
public void update(Input input, double deltaTime)
{
    double moveAmount = unitsPerSecond * deltaTime;
    double rotateAmount = Math.toRadians(degreesPerSecond) *
        deltaTime;
    if (input.isKeyPressed(keyMap.get("move_forwards")))
        translate( 0, 0, -moveAmount, true );
    if (input.isKeyPressed(keyMap.get("move_backwards")))
        translate( 0, 0, moveAmount, true );
    if (input.isKeyPressed(keyMap.get("move_right")))
        translate( moveAmount, 0, 0, true );
    if (input.isKeyPressed(keyMap.get("move_left")))
        translate( -moveAmount, 0, 0, true );
    if (input.isKeyPressed(keyMap.get("move_up")))
        translate( 0, moveAmount, 0, true );
    if (input.isKeyPressed(keyMap.get("move_down")))
        translate( 0, -moveAmount, 0, true );
    if (input.isKeyPressed(keyMap.get("turn_right")))
        rotateY( -rotateAmount, true );
    if (input.isKeyPressed(keyMap.get("turn_left")))
        rotateY( rotateAmount, true );
    if (input.isKeyPressed(keyMap.get("look_up")))
        lookAttachment.rotateX( rotateAmount, true );
    if (input.isKeyPressed(keyMap.get("look_down")))
        lookAttachment.rotateX( -rotateAmount, true );
}
```

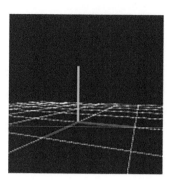 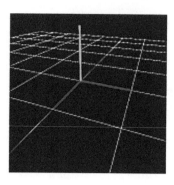 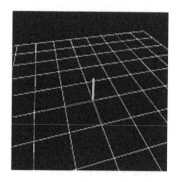

FIGURE 4.28    Multiple views of the coordinate axes and grid.

To see one way to use this class, in the previous application file (**Test_4_6**), add the line of code to the class level definition (right under the mesh):

```
public MovementRig rig;
```

Next, in the **initialize** method, delete the line of code that sets the position of the camera, and add the following code instead:

```
rig = new MovementRig();
rig.attach( camera );
rig.setPosition( new Vector(0.5, 1, 4) );
scene.add( rig );
```

Finally, in the **update** method, add the following line of code:

```
rig.update(input, deltaTime);
```

When you run this application, it will initially appear similar to the right side of Figure 4.27. However, by pressing the motion keys as previously indicated, you should easily be able to view the scene from many different perspectives, some of which are illustrated in Figure 4.28.

Another way the **MovementRig** class may be used is by adding a cube or other geometric object to the rig, instead of a camera. While the view from the camera will remain fixed, this approach will enable you to move an object around the scene in a natural way. You may now add a MovementRig definition to your template class because it will be used in the rest of the book.

## 4.8 SUMMARY AND NEXT STEPS

Building on your knowledge and work from previous chapters, in this chapter, you have seen the graphics framework truly start to take shape. You learned about the advantages of a scene graph framework, and began by developing classes corresponding to the nodes: Scene, Group, Camera, and Mesh. Then you created many classes that generate geometric data corresponding to many different shapes you may want to render: rectangles, boxes, polygons, spheres, cylinders, and more. You also created classes that enabled these objects to be rendered as collections of points, lines, or triangulated surfaces. After learning how to render objects in this new framework, you also learned how customized geometry or material objects can be created. Finally, you created some extra classes representing coordinate axes and grids, to help the viewer to have a sense of orientation and scale within the scene, and a movement rig class, to help the viewer interact with the scene, by moving the camera or other objects with a natural control scheme.

In the next chapter, you will move beyond vertex colors, and learn about textures: images applied to surfaces of objects, which can add realism and sophistication to your 3D scenes.

# CHAPTER 5

# Textures

In many computer graphics applications, you will want to use *textures*: images applied to surfaces of geometric shapes in three-dimensional scenes, such as Figure 5.1, which shows an image applied to a box to create the appearance of a wooden crate. Textures and some related concepts (such as UV coordinates) were briefly mentioned in Chapter 1. In this chapter, you will learn all the details necessary to use textures in your scenes, including creating a **Texture** class that handles uploading pixel data to the graphics processing unit (GPU), assigning UV coordinates to geometric objects, associating textures to uniform variables, and sampling pixel data from a texture in a shader. Once you have learned the basics, you will learn how to create animated effects such as blending and distortion. In the last part of the chapter, there are some optional sections that introduce advanced techniques, such as procedurally generating textures, displaying sprite sheet animations, rendering the scene to a texture, and applying postprocessing effects such as pixelation and vignette shading. In theory, textures may also be one-dimensional and three-dimensional, but the discussion in this chapter will be limited to two-dimensional textures.

## 5.1 A TEXTURE CLASS

In OpenGL, a *texture object* is a data structure that stores pixel data from an image. In addition, a texture object stores information about which algorithms to use to determine the colors of the surface the texture is being applied to; this requires some type of computation whenever the texture and the surface are different sizes. In this section, you will create a **Texture** class to more easily manage this information and perform related tasks, similar to the motivation for creating an **Attribute** class in Chapter 2. Working with textures involves some additional OpenGL functions, introduced and discussed in this section.

Similar to the process for working with vertex buffers, you must first identify an available texture name or reference, and bind it to a particular type of target. OpenGL functions that affect a texture in some way do not directly reference a particular texture object; they also contain a target parameter and affect the texture object currently bound

DOI: 10.1201/9781003153375-5

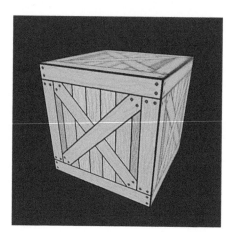

FIGURE 5.1   A wooden crate.

to that target, similar to the use of **glBindBuffer** and GL_ARRAY_BUFFER when working with attributes.

**glGenTextures(** *textureCount* **)**
> Returns a set of nonzero integers representing available texture references. The number of references returned is specified by the integer parameter *textureCount*.

**glBindTexture(** *bindTarget, textureRef* **)**
> The texture referenced by the parameter *textureRef* is bound to the target specified by the parameter *bindTarget*, whose value is an OpenGL constant such as GL_TEXTURE_1D or GL_TEXTURE_2D (for one-dimensional and two-dimensional textures, respectively). Future OpenGL operations affecting the same *bindTarget* will be applied to the referenced texture.

Another necessary task is to upload the corresponding pixel data to the GPU. In addition to the raw pixel data itself, there is additional information required to parse this data, including the resolution (width and height) and precision (number of bits used in the components of each color) of the image. Some image formats (such as JPEG, the Joint Photographics Expert Group image format) do not support transparency, and thus each pixel only stores three-component red, green, and blue (RGB) values. Image formats that do support transparency (such as PNG, the Portable Network Graphics image format) also store alpha (A) values, and thus each pixel stores four-component RGBA values. All of this information (and more) must be transmitted to the GPU along with the pixel data in order for it to be parsed properly; this is handled by the following OpenGL function:

**glTexImage2D(** *bindTarget, level, internalFormat, width, height, border, format, type, pixelData* **)**
> Create storage and upload *pixelData* for the texture currently bound to *bindTarget*. The dimensions of the image are given by the integers *width* and *height*. The parameter *border* is usually zero, indicating that the texture has no border. The parameter

*level* is usually zero, indicating this is the base image level in the associated mipmap image. The other parameters describe how the image data is stored in memory. The format of the data stored in *pixelData* and the desired format that should be used by the GPU are defined by the parameters *format* and *internalFormat*, respectively, and are specified using OpenGL constants such as GL_RGB or GL_RGBA. The parameter *type* indicates the precision used for the color data, and is often GL_UNSIGNED_BYTE, indicating that 8 bits are used for each component.

When applying a texture to a surface, the pixels of the texture (referred to as *texels*) are usually not precisely the same size as the pixels in the rendered image of the scene. If the texture is smaller than the area of the surface it is being applied to, then the texture needs to be scaled up, a process called *magnification*. This requires an algorithm to determine a color for each pixel on the surface based on the colors of the texels. The simplest algorithm is *nearest neighbor filtering*, which assigns the pixel the color of the closest texel; this will result in a blocky or pixelated appearance, as illustrated in Figure 5.2. Another algorithm is *bilinear filtering*, which interpolates the colors of the four closest texels (calculating a weighted average, similar to the rasterization process described in Chapters 1 and 2); the result is a smoother appearance, also illustrated in Figure 5.2.

If the texture is larger than the area of the surface it is being applied to, then the texture needs to be scaled down, a process called *minification*. After minification, the texels will be smaller than the pixels; multiple texels will overlap each pixel. As before, an algorithm is required to determine the color of each pixel from the texture data. A nearest neighbor filter can be used, where the pixel color is set to the color of the texel whose center is closest to the center of the pixel, but this may cause unwanted visual artifacts. A linear filter can be used, where the pixel color is calculated from a weighted average of the colors of the texels overlapping the pixel, but if a very large number of texels correspond to each pixel, calculating this average can take a relatively large amount of time. A computer graphics technique called *mipmapping* provides a more efficient approach to this calculation.

A *mipmap* is a sequence of images, each of which is half the width and height of the previous image; the final image in the sequence consists of a single pixel. A sample mipmap is illustrated in Figure 5.3. The images in the sequence only need to be calculated once, when the original image is uploaded to the GPU. Then, when a texture needs to be minified, the GPU can select the image from the corresponding mipmap that is closest to the desired size, and perform linear filtering on that image, a much more efficient calculation as it will involve only four texels.

FIGURE 5.2 Original image (left), magnified using nearest neighbor (center) and bilinear (right) filters.

FIGURE 5.3   Example of a mipmap.

Mipmap images are generated using the following OpenGL function:

**glGenerateMipmap(** *bindTarget* **)**
> This generates a sequence of mipmap images for the texture currently bound to *bindTarget*.

The next function enables you to select the filters used for magnification and minification, as well as configure other texture-related settings.

**glTexParameteri(** *bindTarget, parameterName, parameterValue* **)**
> This is a general-purpose function used to set parameter values for the texture currently bound to *bindTarget*. In particular, the parameter with the symbolic name specified by the OpenGL constant *parameterName* is assigned the value specified by the OpenGL constant *parameterValue*.

For example, the magnification and minification filters are specified by the OpenGL constants GL_TEXTURE_MAG_FILTER and GL_TEXTURE_MIN_FILTER, respectively. Possible values for either include:

- GL_NEAREST, for nearest-neighbor filtering
- GL_LINEAR, for linear filtering

When performing minification, mipmap-based filter options are also available, such as:

- GL_NEAREST_MIPMAP_NEAREST, to select the closest mipmap and use nearest-neighbor filtering on it

- GL_NEAREST_MIPMAP_LINEAR, to select the closest mipmap and use linear filtering on it

- GL_LINEAR_MIPMAP_LINEAR, to select the two closest mipmaps, use linear filtering on each, and then linearly interpolate between the two results

Another use of the OpenGL function **glTexParameteri** relates to texture coordinates. Similar to the red, green, blue, and alpha components of a color, the components in texture coordinates range from zero to one. You can specify how to handle values outside this range by setting the parameters referenced by the OpenGL constants GL_TEXTURE_WRAP_S and GL_TEXTURE_WRAP_T. (You can think of $(s, t)$ as an alternative notation for texture coordinates, which are typically written using the variables $(u, v)$, although some distinguish $(s, t)$ as *surface coordinates* that may extend beyond the range of texture coordinate values and must be projected into this range.) Some of the possible values for the wrap parameters are:

- GL_REPEAT: only the fractional part of the values are used (the integer parts are ignored), equivalent to reducing the values modulo one, creating a periodic, repeating pattern; this is the default setting

- GL_CLAMP_TO_EDGE: clamps values to the range from zero to one while avoiding sampling from the border color set for the texture

- GL_CLAMP_TO_BORDER: when values are outside the range from zero to one, the value returned by sampling from a texture will be the border color set for the texture

The effects of these wrap settings are illustrated by Figure 5.4.

Finally, before creating the **Texture** class, it is important to understand how Java handles image data. Image data can be created by loading an image from a file or by manipulating pixel data directly. In this framework, you will always convert image data to a string buffer containing RGBA data (red, green, blue, alpha values for each pixel), and therefore

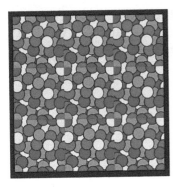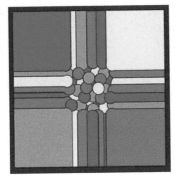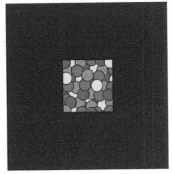

FIGURE 5.4   Texture wrap settings: repeat, clamp to edge, clamp to border.

the *format* and *internalFormat* parameters of the **glTexImage2D** function can always be set to GL_RGBA.

With this knowledge, you are ready to implement the **Texture** class. In the **core** package, create a new Java class called **Texture** with the following code:

```java
package core;

import static org.lwjgl.glfw.GLFW.*;
import static org.lwjgl.opengl.GL40.*;

import java.nio.ByteBuffer;
import java.nio.IntBuffer;
import org.lwjgl.BufferUtils;
import static org.lwjgl.stb.STBImage.*;


public class Texture
{
    // reference of available texture from GPU
    public int textureRef;

    public int magFilter;
    public int minFilter;
    public int wrap;

    public int width, height;
    public ByteBuffer pixelData;

    // load texture from file
    public Texture(String fileName)
    {
        magFilter = GL_LINEAR;
        minFilter = GL_LINEAR_MIPMAP_LINEAR;
        wrap = GL_REPEAT;

        IntBuffer widthBuf  = BufferUtils.createIntBuffer(1);
        IntBuffer heightBuf = BufferUtils.createIntBuffer(1);
        IntBuffer compBuf   = BufferUtils.createIntBuffer(1);

        // prevents inverted images
        stbi_set_flip_vertically_on_load(true);
        // last argument as 4: generates RGBA formatted buffer
        pixelData = stbi_load(fileName,
            widthBuf, heightBuf, compBuf, 4);

        width = widthBuf.get();
        height = heightBuf.get();
```

```java
        uploadData();
    }

    // generate an empty texture - used by RenderTarget class
// RenderTarget will be implemented later
    public Texture(int width, int height)
    {
        this.width = width;
        this.height = height;

        magFilter = GL_LINEAR;
        minFilter = GL_LINEAR;
        wrap = GL_CLAMP_TO_EDGE;

        uploadData();
    }

    // upload pixel data to GPU
    public void uploadData()
    {
        textureRef = glGenTextures();

        // specify texture used by the following functions
        glBindTexture(GL_TEXTURE_2D, textureRef);

        // send pixel data (ByteBuffer) to texture buffer
        if (pixelData != null)
            glTexImage2D(GL_TEXTURE_2D, 0, GL_RGBA, width,
                height, 0, GL_RGBA, GL_UNSIGNED_BYTE, pixelData);
        else
            glTexImage2D(GL_TEXTURE_2D, 0, GL_RGBA, width,
                height, 0, GL_RGBA, GL_UNSIGNED_BYTE, 0);

        // generate mipmap image from uploaded pixel data
        glGenerateMipmap(GL_TEXTURE_2D);
        // specify technique for magnifying/minifying textures
        glTexParameteri(GL_TEXTURE_2D,
            GL_TEXTURE_MAG_FILTER, magFilter );
        glTexParameteri(GL_TEXTURE_2D,
            GL_TEXTURE_MIN_FILTER, minFilter );
        // specify what happens to texture coordinates
        //     outside range [0, 1]
        glTexParameteri(GL_TEXTURE_2D, GL_TEXTURE_WRAP_S,
            wrap );
        glTexParameteri(GL_TEXTURE_2D, GL_TEXTURE_WRAP_T,
            wrap );
        // set default border color to white;
```

```
//    important for rendering shadows
float[] borderColor = new float[] {1,1,1,1};
glTexParameterfv(GL_TEXTURE_2D,
    GL_TEXTURE_BORDER_COLOR, borderColor);
    }
}
```

Note that the constructor for the class is designed so that creating a texture object from an image file is optional; this allows for the possibility of creating an empty image by other means and assigning it to a Texture object directly, which will be explored later in this chapter.

## 5.2 TEXTURE COORDINATES

*Texture coordinates* (also known as *UV coordinates*) are used to specify which points of an image correspond to which vertices of a geometric object. Each coordinate ranges from zero to one, with the point (0,0) corresponding to the lower-left corner of the image, and the point (1,1) corresponding to the upper-right corner of the image. Typically, these values are passed from the vertex shader to the fragment shader (automatically interpolated for each fragment), and then the UV coordinates are used to select a point on the texture from which the color of the fragment will be generated. Figure 5.5 shows a sample image, and two of the many different ways that UV coordinates can be applied to the vertices of a triangle, in order to map different parts of the image to the triangle.

The next step will be to add a new attribute containing UV coordinates to the previously created geometry classes: rectangles, boxes, polygons, and parametric surfaces. The shader code that will be created later in this chapter will access this data through a shader variable named **vertexUV**.

### 5.2.1 Rectangles

The simplest class to add UV coordinates is the **Rectangle** class. The four vertices of the rectangle correspond to the four corners of a texture; coordinates will be assigned as shown in Figure 5.6.

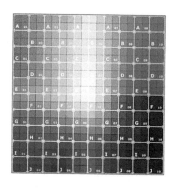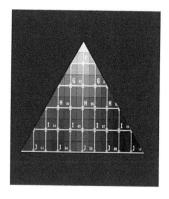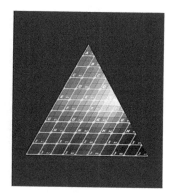

FIGURE 5.5   Texture coordinates used to apply an image (left) to a triangle (center, right).

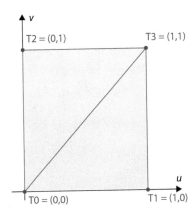

FIGURE 5.6   Texture coordinates for a rectangle shape.

It will be important to keep in mind that UV coordinates for each vertex need to be stored in a list in the same order as the vertex positions. In the **RectangleGeometry** class in the **geometry** package, add the following code to the constructor:

```
// texture coordinates
Vector T0 = new Vector(0,0);
Vector T1 = new Vector(1,0);
Vector T2 = new Vector(0,1);
Vector T3 = new Vector(1,1);

List uvList = Arrays.asList(T0,T1,T3, T0,T3,T2);
float[] uvData = Vector.flattenList(uvList);

addAttribute("vec2", "vertexUV", uvData);
```

At this point, this code cannot yet be tested. If you wish to test this code as soon as possible, you may skip ahead to Section 5.3 and learn how to use textures in shaders, or you may continue implementing UV coordinates for other geometric shapes as described in what follows.

### 5.2.2  Boxes

Since each of the six sides of a box is a rectangle, and the vertices were ordered in the same way, the code for adding UV coordinates to the **BoxGeometry** class is straightforward. In the **BoxGeometry** class in the **geometry** package, add the following code to the constructor:

```
// texture coordinates
Vector T0 = new Vector(0,0);
Vector T1 = new Vector(1,0);
Vector T2 = new Vector(0,1);
Vector T3 = new Vector(1,1);
```

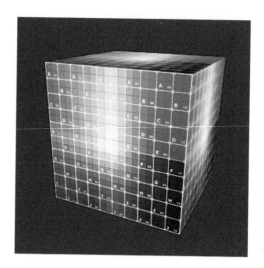

FIGURE 5.7    Box geometry with grid texture applied.

```
List uvList = Arrays.asList(
    T0,T1,T3,T0,T3,T2,  T0,T1,T3,T0,T3,T2,
    T0,T1,T3,T0,T3,T2,  T0,T1,T3,T0,T3,T2,
    T0,T1,T3,T0,T3,T2,  T0,T1,T3,T0,T3,T2  );
float[] uvData = Vector.flattenList(uvList);

addAttribute("vec2", "vertexUV", uvData);
```

When you are able to render this shape with a grid texture later on in this chapter, it will appear similar to Figure 5.7.

### 5.2.3 Polygons

To apply a texture to a polygon without distorting the texture, you will use UV coordinates corresponding to the arrangement of the vertices of the polygon, effectively appearing to "cut out" a portion of the texture, as illustrated for various polygons in Figure 5.8.

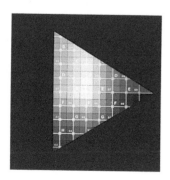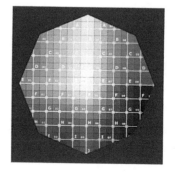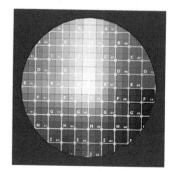

FIGURE 5.8    Textured polygons with 3 sides, 8 sides, and 32 sides.

Recall that the vertices of the polygon are arranged around the circumference of a circle centered at the origin with a user-specified radius, and that a circle is parameterized by the sine and cosine functions. To stay within the range of UV coordinates (from zero to one), you will use a circle of radius 0.5, centered at the point (0.5, 0.5). To implement this, in the **PolygonGeometry** class in the **geometry** package, add the following code immediately before the **for** loop:

```
ArrayList<Vector> uvList  = new ArrayList<Vector>();
Vector uvCenter = new Vector(0.5, 0.5);
```

Within the **for** loop, add the following code:

```
uvList.add( uvCenter );
uvList.add( new Vector( Math.cos(n*A) * 0.5 + 0.5,
                        Math.sin(n*A) * 0.5 + 0.5 ) );
uvList.add( new Vector( Math.cos((n+1)*A) * 0.5 + 0.5,
                        Math.sin((n+1)*A) * 0.5 + 0.5 ) );
```

Finally, following the **for** loop, add the following lines:

```
float[] uvData = Vector.flattenList(uvList);
addAttribute("vec2", "vertexUV", uvData);
```

### 5.2.4 Parametric Surfaces

The positions of vertices on a parametric surface are calculated using a parametric function, which maps a two-dimensional rectangular region onto a surface in three-dimensional space. Therefore, UV coordinates can be generated by rescaling points in the domain of the parametric function to values in the domain of texture coordinates: from zero to one. This will be accomplished in a sequence of steps, similar to the process by which vertex positions were generated. The first step will be to generate UV coordinates for each point in the domain; these will be stored in a two-dimensional list called **uvs**. Then, this data will be grouped into triangles and stored in a two-dimensional list called **uvData**, which will be used for the corresponding attribute.

To begin, in the **Surface** class in the **math** package, add the following method:

```
public Vector[][] getUVs(
      double uStart, double uEnd, int uResolution,
      double vStart, double vEnd, int vResolution)
{
    Vector[][] uvs = new Vector[uResolution+1][vResolution+1];
    for (int uIndex = 0; uIndex < uResolution+1; uIndex++)
    {
        for (int vIndex = 0; vIndex < vResolution+1; vIndex++)
        {
            double u = (double)uIndex/uResolution;
```

```
        double v = (double)vIndex/vResolution;
        uvs[uIndex][vIndex] = new Vector(u,v);
    }
}
    return uvs;
}
```

Note that dividing each of the u and v index values by the corresponding resolution values produces a sequence of evenly-spaced values between zero and one. Next, in the **SurfaceGeometry** class, add the following lines of code in the constructor before the **for** loop:

```
Vector[][] uvs = surface.getUVs(
        uStart, uEnd, uResolution, vStart, vEnd, vResolution);
ArrayList<Vector> uvList = new ArrayList<Vector>();
```

Next, to group this data into triangles, add the following code in the nested **for** loop that follows, after the line of code where data is added to the **colorList**:

```
// uv coordinates
Vector uvA = uvs[uIndex + 0][vIndex + 0];
Vector uvB = uvs[uIndex + 1][vIndex + 0];
Vector uvD = uvs[uIndex + 0][vIndex + 1];
Vector uvC = uvs[uIndex + 1][vIndex + 1];
uvList.addAll( Arrays.asList(uvA,uvB,uvC, uvA,uvC,uvD) );
```

Finally, after the code where the other Attribute objects are created, add the following line of code:

```
addAttribute("vec2", "vertexUV", uvData);
```

After you are able to test this code, you will be able to create textured parametric surfaces, like those shown in Figure 5.9. No special modifications need to be made to the

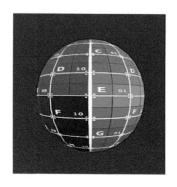
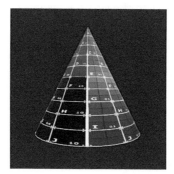
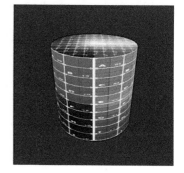

FIGURE 5.9   A sphere, cone, and cylinder with grid image textures applied.

**CylindricalGeometry** class, since the **merge** method used by that class copies all attributes from the **PolygonGeometry** objects used for the top and bottom sides, including the recently added UV coordinates.

## 5.3 USING TEXTURES IN SHADERS

Once you have implemented UV coordinates for at least one geometric shape, the next step is to focus on adding shader code that supports this new functionality. *Sampling* refers to the process of calculating a color based on the information stored in a texture object; this calculation is performed by a *texture unit*, to which a texture object is assigned. To perform sampling in a shader program, you will use a uniform variable of type **sampler2D**, which stores a reference to a texture unit. You will also use the function **texture**, which takes a sampler2D and a vector (containing UV coordinates) as inputs, then performs the sampling calculation.

There are a limited number of texture units available for use by a shader at any given time. In OpenGL 3.0 and above, there are a minimum of 16 texture units available. This number may be greater for some systems depending on the implementation of OpenGL, but only 16 texture units are guaranteed to exist. It may be possible to create many more texture objects than this, depending on the size of the image data in each texture object and the storage capacity of the GPU. However, when rendering any particular geometric primitive, you may be limited to using the data from at most 16 of these texture objects, as they are accessed through the texture units.

In order to work with multiple texture units (as you will later on in this chapter), you will need to use the following OpenGL function:

**glActiveTexture(** *textureUnitRef* **)**
> Activates a texture unit specified by the parameter *textureUnitRef*; any texture objects that are bound using the function glBindTexture are assigned to the active texture unit. The value of *textureUnitRef* is an OpenGL constant GL_TEXTURE0, GL_TEXTURE1, GL_TEXTURE2, etc., with maximum value depending on the number of texture units supported by the particular OpenGL implementation. These constants form a consecutive set of integers, so that for any positive integer $n$, GL_TEXTURE$n$ is equal to GL_TEXTURE0 + $n$.

Due to the intermediate step of assigning the texture object to a texture unit that whose reference is stored in a shader variable, each **Uniform** object that represents a sampler2D will store a list in its **data** field containing the reference for the texture object, followed by the number of the texture unit to be used. Unlike texture object references, which must be generated by the OpenGL function **glGenTextures**, texture units may be chosen by the developer. In addition, you will need to use the previously discussed OpenGL function **glUniform1i** to upload the number of the texture unit (not the OpenGL constant) to the sampler2D variable. In other words, using the previously established notation, if the active texture unit is GL_TEXTURE$n$, then the integer $n$ should be uploaded to the sampler2D variable.

With this knowledge, you are ready to modify the **Uniform** class. In the **Uniform** class in the **core** package, add the following code to the **if** statement block in the **uploadData** method:

```
else if (dataType.equals("sampler2D"))
{
    Vector v = (Vector)data;
    int textureObjectRef = (int)v.values[0];
    int textureUnitRef   = (int)v.values[1];
    // activate texture unit
    glActiveTexture( GL_TEXTURE0 + textureUnitRef );
    // associate texture object reference
    //   to currently active texture unit
    glBindTexture( GL_TEXTURE_2D, textureObjectRef );
    // upload texture unit number (0...15)
    //   to uniform variable in shader
    glUniform1i( variableRef, textureUnitRef );
}
```

Since certain image formats (such as PNG images) use transparency, you will next make a few additions to the **Renderer** class to support this feature. Blending colors in the color buffer based on alpha values is enabled with the OpenGL function **glEnable**. The formula used when blending colors needs to be specified as well, with the use of the following OpenGL function:

> **glBlendFunc(** *sourceFactor, destinationFactor* **)**
>
> Specifies values to be used in the formula applied when blending an incoming "source" color with a "destination" color already present in the color buffer. The components of the source and destination colors are multiplied by values specified by the corresponding parameters, *sourceFactor* and *destinationFactor*. The values of these parameters are calculated based on the specified OpenGL constant, some possible values including: GL_SRC_ALPHA, GL_ONE_MINUS_SRC_ALPHA, GL_DST_ALPHA, GL_ONE_MINUS_DST_ALPHA, GL_ZERO, and GL_ONE.

The formula that will be used for blending will be a weighted average based on the alpha value of the source color. To implement this, in the **Renderer** class in the **core** package, add the following code to the initialization method:

```
glEnable(GL_BLEND)
glBlendFunc(GL_SRC_ALPHA, GL_ONE_MINUS_SRC_ALPHA)
```

When using alpha blending, careful attention must be paid to the render order, as described in Chapter 1, in the section on pixel processing. Figure 5.10 illustrates an image of a circle applied to two rectangle geometries; the pixels of the image outside the circle are completely transparent. The top-left circle is nearer to the camera than the bottom-right circle. The left side of the figure shows the circles rendered correctly. The right side of the figure

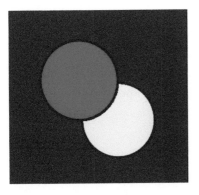 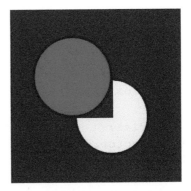

FIGURE 5.10    Transparency rendering issues caused by render order.

shows the result of rendering the front circle before the back circle: the transparent pixels of the front image are blended with the background color and stored in the color buffer, and then when the back image is processed later, the fragments that appear behind the front circle – including those behind transparent pixels – are automatically discarded, as they are a greater distance away from the camera. This causes part of the back circle to be incorrectly removed from the final rendered image.

The next step is to create an extension of the **Material** class with a corresponding shader that incorporates UV coordinates, a uniform sampler2D variable, and the GLSL function **texture**. Unlike the basic materials created in the previous chapter, which included point-based and line-based versions, the only material developed here will be a surface-based version. Therefore, there only needs to be a single class that will contain the shader code, add the **Uniform** objects, and initialize the render settings. In addition, this material will not make use of the vertex color attribute, but will keep the base color uniform, which can be used to tint textures by a particular color. This shader will also include uniform variables **repeatUV** and **offsetUV**, which can be used to scale and translate UV coordinates, allowing textures to appear multiple times on a surface as illustrated by Figure 5.11. Finally, the fragment shader will make use of the GLSL command **discard**,

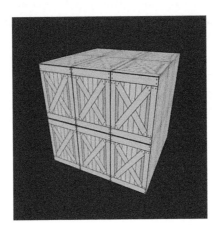

FIGURE 5.11    Applying a repeated crate texture to a box geometry.

which will be used to stop processing fragments with small alpha values. This will automatically resolve some of the rendering issues previously described when the pixels are transparent, but not when the pixels are translucent (partially transparent).

To implement this texture-supporting material, in the **material** package, create a new Java class named **TextureMaterial** and add the following code:

```java
package material;
import math.Vector;
import core.Texture;

public class TextureMaterial extends Material
{
    public TextureMaterial(Texture texture)
    {
        super(
            "./src/material/TextureMaterial.vert",
            "./src/material/TextureMaterial.frag"   );

        addUniform("vec3", "baseColor", new Vector(1,1,1) );
        addUniform("sampler2D", "tex",
            new Vector(texture.textureRef, 1));
        addUniform("vec2", "repeatUV", new Vector(1,1) );
        addUniform("vec2", "offsetUV", new Vector(0,0) );
        locateUniforms();

        addRenderSetting( "doubleSide", true );
        addRenderSetting( "wireframe", false );
        addRenderSetting( "lineWidth", 1 );
    }
}
```

Next, you will have to create the vertex and fragment shader files. Create two new files named **TextureMaterial.vert** and **TextureMaterial.frag**. In the vertex shader file, insert the following code:

```glsl
uniform mat4 projectionMatrix;
uniform mat4 viewMatrix;
uniform mat4 modelMatrix;

in vec3 vertexPosition;
in vec2 vertexUV;

uniform vec2 repeatUV;
uniform vec2 offsetUV;

out vec2 UV;
```

```
void main()
{
    gl_Position = projectionMatrix * viewMatrix * modelMatrix *
        vec4(vertexPosition, 1.0);
    UV = vertexUV * repeatUV + offsetUV;
}
```

In the fragment shader file, insert the following code:

```
uniform vec3 baseColor;
uniform sampler2D tex;

in vec2 UV;
out vec4 fragColor;

void main()
{
    vec4 color = vec4(baseColor, 1.0) * texture(tex, UV);

    if (color.a < 0.10)
        discard;

    fragColor = color;
}
```

With these classes finished, the graphics framework now supports texture rendering.

## 5.4 RENDERING SCENES WITH TEXTURES

At this point, you can now create applications where textures are applied to surfaces. Your first texture-based application will be a simple example – applying a grid image to a rectangle shape – to verify that the code entered up to this point works correctly. To continue to keep your codebase organized, in your main project folder, add a new folder named **images**; this is where all image files will be stored. The image files used in this book will be available to download from an online project repository. Alternatively, you may replace the provided images with image files of your own choosing.

As previously mentioned when you first added shader files to this framework, it is important to understand how your Java development environment interprets file name references. In particular, what directory is considered the root directory, in the case of relative file path references? If not configured properly, the image files will not be accessible, which may cause your program to crash, or may cause textured surfaces to appear solid black. If you are using the IntelliJ development environment, you will need to right-click on the **images** directory in your project hierarchy and select **mark directory as > resources folder**.

In your main project folder, make a copy of the class **Test_Template** and name it **Test_5_1**. In this new file, change the position of the camera to (0, 0, 2) and replace

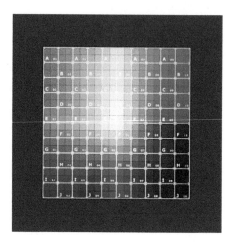

FIGURE 5.12    Texture applied to a rectangle.

the lines of code where the geometry and material variables are defined with the following code:

```
Geometry geometry = new RectangleGeometry();
Material material = new TextureMaterial(
    new Texture("images/grid.png") );
mesh = new Mesh(geometry, material);
scene.add(mesh);
```

When you run this application, you should see a result similar to that of Figure 5.12.

As you have seen earlier in this chapter, the same image used in Figure 5.12 can be applied to other surfaces, such as Spheres, Cones, and Cylinders, as seen in Figure 5.9; the result is that the image will appear stretched in some locations, and compressed in other locations. A *spherical texture* is an image that appears correctly proportioned when applied to a sphere; such an image will appear distorted in some areas (such as being stretched out near the top and bottom) when viewed as a rectangular image. One well-known example is a map of the Earth, illustrated on the left side of Figure 5.13 and applied to a sphere on the right side of the figure.

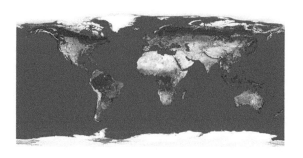

FIGURE 5.13    A spherical texture of the Earth's surface (left), applied to a sphere (right).

FIGURE 5.14   Multiple views of a scene featuring a skysphere texture.

Spherical textures can be particularly useful in generating virtual environments. A *skysphere* is a spherical texture used to create a background in a three-dimensional scene. As the name suggests, the texture is applied to a large sphere that surrounds the virtual camera; the back sides of the triangles must be set to render. The same concept can be used to create backgrounds from textures based on other shapes; *skybox* and *skydome* textures are also frequently used in practice together with the corresponding shape. The next application illustrates how to use a skysphere texture, combined with a large plane containing a repeating grass texture, and adds a **MovementRig** object to enable the viewer to look around the scene. Figure 5.14 shows the resulting scene, viewed from multiple angles: from left to right, the camera rotates right and tilts upward.

To implement this scene, make a copy of the file **Test_Template** and name it **Test_5_2**. In the **initialize** method, replace the code in that function starting from the line where the camera position is set, with the following code:

```
rig = new MovementRig();
rig.attach( camera );
rig.setPosition( new Vector(0, 1, 4) );
scene.add( rig );

Geometry skyGeometry = new SphereGeometry(50);
Material skyMaterial = new TextureMaterial(
    new Texture("images/sky-earth.jpg") );
Mesh sky = new Mesh( skyGeometry, skyMaterial );
scene.add( sky );

Geometry grassGeometry = new RectangleGeometry(100, 100);
Material grassMaterial = new TextureMaterial(
    new Texture("images/grass.jpg") );
grassMaterial.uniforms.get("repeatUV").data = new Vector(50,50);
Mesh grass = new Mesh( grassGeometry, grassMaterial );
grass.rotateX(-3.14/2, true);
scene.add( grass );
```

Finally, in the **update** method, add the following line of code:

```
rig.update(input, deltaTime);
```

When you run this application, you can use the keyboard to navigate around the scene and see results similar to those in Figure 5.14.

## 5.5 ANIMATED EFFECTS WITH CUSTOM SHADERS

In this section, you will write some custom shaders and materials to create animated effects involving textures. In the first example, you will create a rippling effect in a texture, by adding a sine-based displacement to the V component of the UV coordinates in the fragment shader. The overall structure of the application will be similar to the applications involving custom materials from the previous chapter. Besides the use of the **sin** function, the other significant addition to the code is the inclusion of a uniform float variable that stores the time that has elapsed since the application began; this value will be incremented in the **update** method.

To create this effect, make a copy of the file **Test_Template** and name it **Test_5_3** as well as two additional files named **Test_5_3.vert** and **Test_5_3.frag**. To start, insert the following code into the vertex shader file:

```
uniform mat4 projectionMatrix;
uniform mat4 viewMatrix;
uniform mat4 modelMatrix;

in vec3 vertexPosition;
in vec2 vertexUV;
out vec2 UV;

void main()
{
    gl_Position = projectionMatrix * viewMatrix * modelMatrix *
        vec4(vertexPosition, 1.0);
    UV = vertexUV;
}
```

Next, add the following code to the fragment shader file:

```
uniform sampler2D tex;
in vec2 UV;
uniform float time;
out vec4 fragColor;

void main()
{
    vec2 shiftUV = UV + vec2(0, 0.2 * sin(6.0*UV.x + time));
    fragColor = texture(tex, shiftUV);
}
```

Then, in **Test_5_3** inside the **initialize** method, replace the code in that function, starting from the line where the camera position is set, with the following code:

```
camera.setPosition( new Vector(0,0,1.5) );
Geometry geometry = new RectangleGeometry();
Texture gridTex = new Texture("images/grid.png");
Material waveMaterial = new Material(
    "./src/Test_5_3.vert", "./src/Test_5_3.frag");
waveMaterial.addUniform("sampler2D", "texture",
    new Vector(gridTex.textureRef, 1));
waveMaterial.addUniform("float", "time", 0.0);
waveMaterial.locateUniforms();
mesh = new Mesh( geometry, waveMaterial );
scene.add(mesh);
```

Finally, in the **update** method, add the following line of code:

```
mesh.material.uniforms.get("time").data = time;
```

When you run this application, you should see an animated effect as illustrated in Figure 5.15. Note that in this and the following examples, the customized material is applied to a rectangle, but can just as easily be applied to other geometric shapes, with visually interesting results.

In the next example, you will cyclically blend between two different textures. This example also illustrates the importance of assigning texture objects to different texture units. The main idea of this shader is to sample colors from both textures at each fragment, and then linearly interpolate between these colors to determine the fragment color. The amount of interpolation varies periodically between zero and one, calculated using the absolute value of the sine of the time that has elapsed since the application was started.

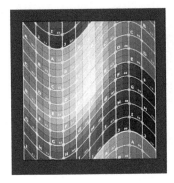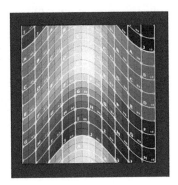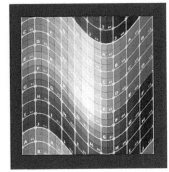

FIGURE 5.15   Images from an animated ripple effect on a grid texture.

Since this example is similar in structure to the previous example, make a copy of the file **Test_5_3** and name it **Test_5_4**. In the initialize method, replace the code there, starting after the line where the grid texture is created, with the following code:

```
Texture crateTex = new Texture("images/crate.png");
Material blendMaterial = new Material(
    "./src/Test_5_3.vert", "./src/Test_5_4.frag");
blendMaterial.addUniform("sampler2D", "texture1",
    new Vector(gridTex.textureRef, 1));
blendMaterial.addUniform("sampler2D", "texture2",
    new Vector(crateTex.textureRef, 2));
blendMaterial.addUniform("float", "time", 0.0);
blendMaterial.locateUniforms();

mesh = new Mesh( geometry, blendMaterial );
```

Next you will create a new fragment shader for this example, create a new file named **Test_5_4.frag** and insert the following code:

```
uniform sampler2D texture1;
uniform sampler2D texture2;
in vec2 UV;
uniform float time;
out vec4 fragColor;

void main()
{
    vec4 color1 = texture(texture1, UV);
    vec4 color2 = texture(texture2, UV);
    float s = abs(sin(time));
    fragColor = s * color1 + (1.0 - s) * color2;
}
```

When copying classes, make sure to change the class name and the driver method to run the proper file. This test class will utilize the vertex shader from the previous example. When you run this application, you should see an animated effect as illustrated in Figure 5.16.

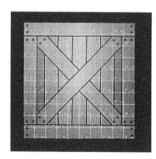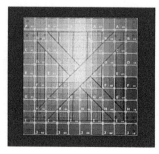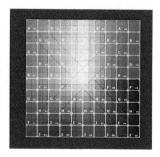

FIGURE 5.16   Images from an animated blend effect between a crate texture and a grid texture.

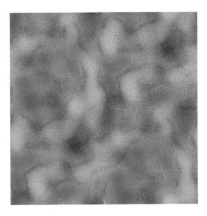

FIGURE 5.17    A "noise" texture used to generate pseudo-random values.

In the final example in this section, you will again use two textures. One of these textures, shown in Figure 5.17, will be used to produce pseudo-random values (also called *noise*) to distort a texture over time, as shown in Figure 5.18. These values are generated by sampling red, green, or blue values from the noise texture, whose colors appear to be a random pattern, but whose components change continuously throughout the image. In this shader, the distortion effect is created by continuously shifting the UV coordinates, using them to obtain values from the noise texture, and then the final fragment color is sampled from the image texture at the original UV coordinates offset by the noise value.

Once again, this example is similar in structure to the previous examples. To begin, make a copy of the file **Test_5_3** and name it **Test_5_5**. In the **initialize** method, replace the code in that function, starting from the line after the grid texture is created, with the following code:

```
Texture noiseTex = new Texture("images/noise.png");
Material distortMaterial = new Material(
    "./src/Test_5_3.vert", "./src/Test_5_5.frag");
distortMaterial.addUniform("sampler2D", "image",
```

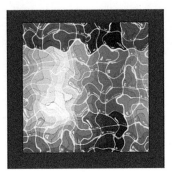

FIGURE 5.18    Images from an animated distortion effect applied to a grid texture.

```
    new Vector(gridTex.textureRef, 1));
distortMaterial.addUniform("sampler2D", "noise",
    new Vector(noiseTex.textureRef, 2));
distortMaterial.addUniform("float", "time", 0.0);
distortMaterial.locateUniforms();
mesh = new Mesh( geometry, distortMaterial );
```

Next create a new fragment shader file named **Test_5_5.frag** and insert the following code:

```
uniform sampler2D image;
uniform sampler2D noise;
in vec2 UV;
uniform float time;
out vec4 fragColor;

void main()
{
    vec2 uvShift = UV + vec2( -0.033, 0.07 ) * time;
    vec4 noiseValues = texture( noise, uvShift );
    vec2 uvNoise = UV + 0.4 * noiseValues.rg;
    fragColor = texture( image, uvNoise );
}
```

When you run this application, you should see an animated effect as illustrated in Figure 5.17. A shader such as this can be used to add realistic dynamic elements to an interactive three-dimensional scene. For example, by applying this shader to a texture such as the water or lava textures shown in Figure 5.19, one can create a fluid-like appearance.

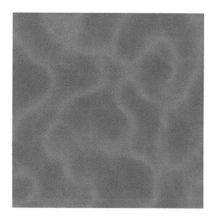 

FIGURE 5.19  Water and lava textures.

## 5.6 PROCEDURALLY GENERATED TEXTURES

A *procedurally generated texture* is a texture that is created using a mathematical algo-rithm, rather than using an array of pixels stored in an image file. Procedural textures can yield noise textures (similar to Figure 5.17) and simulations of naturally occurring patterns such as clouds, water, wood, marble, and other patterns (similar to those in Figure 5.19).

The first step in generating a noise texture is to create a function that can produce pseudo-random values in a shader. This can be accomplished by taking advantage of the limited precision of the fractional part of floating-point numbers, which can be obtained using the GLSL function **fract**. While a function such as $sin(x)$ is perfectly predictable, the output of the function $fract(235711 \cdot sin(x))$ is effectively random for generating images. With regards to the number that sin(x) is being multiplied by, only the magnitude (and not the particular digits) is important. To produce random values across a two-dimensional region, one could define a similar function, such as $fract(235711 \cdot sin(14.337 \cdot x + 42.418 \cdot y))$.

Next, you will create a sample application with a custom material that illustrates how this function can be used in a shader. To begin, make two new files named **Test_5_6.vert** and **Test_5_6.frag**. Additionally, you can make a copy of the file **Test_Template** and name it **Test_5_6**. Inside the vertex shader file, insert the following code:

```
uniform mat4 projectionMatrix;
uniform mat4 viewMatrix;
uniform mat4 modelMatrix;
in vec3 vertexPosition;
in vec2 vertexUV;
out vec2 UV;
void main()
{
    vec4 pos = vec4(vertexPosition, 1.0);
    gl_Position = projectionMatrix * viewMatrix * modelMatrix
        * pos;
    UV = vertexUV;
}
```

Inside the fragment shader file, insert the following code:

```
// return a random value in [0, 1]
float random(vec2 UV)
{
    return fract(235711.0 * sin(14.337*UV.x + 42.418*UV.y));
}

in vec2 UV;
out vec4 fragColor;
```

```
void main()
{
    float r = random(UV);
    fragColor = vec4(r, r, r, 1);
}
```

Note that this code contains the first example of a function defined in GLSL, in this case the random function defined in the fragment shader.

In the main **Test_5_6** class, inside the **initialize** method, replace the code there, starting from the line where the camera position is set, with the following code.

```
camera.setPosition( new Vector(0,0,1.5) );
Geometry geometry = new RectangleGeometry();

Material material = new Material(
    "./src/Test_5_6.vert", "./src/Test_5_6.frag");
material.locateUniforms();

mesh = new Mesh( geometry, material );
```

Don't forget to remove everything in the **update** method before proceeding. When you run this example, it will produce an image similar to the one illustrated in Figure 5.20, where the random value generated from the UV coordinates at each fragment are used for the red, green, and blue components of the fragment color, yielding a shade of gray. The overall image resembles the static pattern seen on older analog televisions resulting from weak broadcasting signals.

For the applications that follow, this texture is actually *too* random. The next step will be to scale up and round the UV coordinates used as inputs for the random function, which will produce a result similar to the left side of Figure 5.21, in which the corners of each square correspond to points whose scaled UV coordinates are integers, and the color of each square corresponds the the random value at the lower-left corner. Next, the random

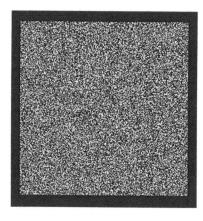

FIGURE 5.20   A randomly generated texture.

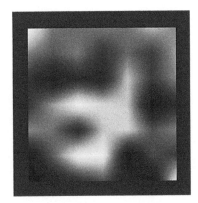

FIGURE 5.21    Scaled and smoothed random textures.

value (and thus the color) at each point will be replaced with a weighted average of the random values at the vertices of the square in which the point is contained, thus producing a smoothed version of the left side of Figure 5.21, illustrated on the right side of Figure 5.21. The GLSL function **mix** will be used to linearly interpolate the two values at the bottom corners of each square, followed by interpolating the values at the top corners of each square, and then interpolating these results.

To produce these images, first add the following functions to the code in the fragment shader:

```
float boxRandom(vec2 UV, float scale)
{
    vec2 iScaleUV = floor(scale * UV);
    return random(iScaleUV);
}

float smoothRandom(vec2 UV, float scale)
{
    vec2 iScaleUV = floor(scale * UV);
    vec2 fScaleUV = fract(scale * UV);
    float a = random(iScaleUV);
    float b = random(round(iScaleUV + vec2(1, 0)));
    float c = random(round(iScaleUV + vec2(0, 1)));
    float d = random(round(iScaleUV + vec2(1, 1)));
    return mix( mix(a, b, fScaleUV.x),
                mix(c, d, fScaleUV.x),
                fScaleUV.y );
}
```

Then, to produce the image on the left of Figure 5.21, in the **main** function in the fragment shader, replace the line of code where the variable **r** is declared with the following.

```
float r = boxRandom(UV, 6);
```

FIGURE 5.22   A sequence of scaled and smoothed random textures.

To produce the image on the right side of Figure 5.21, replace this line of code with the following.

```
float r = smoothRandom(UV, 6);
```

To produce a grayscale noise texture similar to that in Figure 5.17, you will combine a sequence of images similar to those shown on the right side of Figure 5.21; such a sequence is illustrated in Figure 5.22. The scale of the UV coordinates in each image in the sequence are doubled, resulting in square regions whose dimensions are half those from the previous image. The randomly generated values will be scaled by half at each stage as well, so that the finer details will contribute a proportional amount to the accumulated total. As this process is reminiscent of fractals – shapes that contain the same pattern at different scales – this function for generating random values will be called **fractalRandom**. The final texture generated by this function is illustrated in Figure 5.23.

To produce the image in Figure 5.23, first add the following function to the code in the fragment shader:

```
// add smooth random values at different scales
//    weighted (amplitudes) so that sum is approximately 1.0
float fractalRandom(vec2 UV, float scale)
{
    float value = 0.0;
    float amplitude = 0.5;
    for (int i = 0; i < 6; i++)
```

FIGURE 5.23   Fractal noise produced from combining images from Figure 5.22.

```
    {
        value += amplitude * smoothRandom(UV, scale);
        scale *= 2.0;
        amplitude *= 0.5;
    }
    return value;
}
```

Then, in the **main** function in the fragment shader, replace the line of code where the variable **r** is declared with the following.

```
float r = fractalRandom(UV, 4);
```

While many other methods exist for producing random values, such as the Perlin noise and cellular noise algorithms, the functions here will be sufficient for our purposes. The next step will be to use these functions to produce random images simulating textures found in nature, such as those illustrated in Figure 5.24, which are meant to resemble clouds, lava, marble, and wood.

All of the examples from Figure 5.24 are generated by mixing two different colors, where the amount of interpolation is determined in part or in whole by the **fractalRandom** function. To create the cloud image, replace the code in the fragment shader with the following.

```
// clouds
float r = fractalRandom(UV, 5);
vec4 color1 = vec4(0.5, 0.5, 1, 1);
vec4 color2 = vec4(1, 1, 1, 1);
fragColor = mix( color1, color2, r );
```

To create the lava image, replace the code in the fragment shader with the following. Notice that the finer level of detail is created by using a larger scale value in the **fractalRandom** function.

```
// lava
float r = fractalRandom(UV, 40);
vec4 color1 = vec4(1, 0.8, 0, 1);
vec4 color2 = vec4(0.8, 0, 0, 1);
fragColor = mix( color1, color2, r );
```

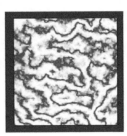

FIGURE 5.24   Procedurally generated textures: clouds, lava, marble, wood.

To create the marble image, replace the code in the fragment shader with the following. As you will see, this code differs by the scaling of the random value and the application of the **abs** and **sin** functions, which creates a greater contrast between the differently colored regions of the image.

```
// marble
float t = fractalRandom(UV, 4);
float r = abs(sin(20 * t));
vec4 color1 = vec4(0.0, 0.2, 0.0, 1.0);
vec4 color2 = vec4(1.0, 1.0, 1.0, 1.0);
fragColor = mix( color1, color2, r );
```

Finally, to create the wood image, replace the code in the fragment shader with the following. In this code, the addition of the **UV.y** component in the calculation produces horizontal lines that are then randomly distorted. In addition, the modifications in the calculation of the **r** variable result in lines that are more sharply defined in the image.

```
// wood grain
float t = 80 * UV.y + 20 * fractalRandom(UV, 2);
float r = clamp( 2 * abs(sin(t)), 0, 1 );
vec4 color1 = vec4(0.3, 0.2, 0.0, 1.0);
vec4 color2 = vec4(0.6, 0.4, 0.2, 1.0);
fragColor = mix( color1, color2, r );
```

## 5.7 USING TEXT IN SCENES

In this section, you will explore a way in which images of text can be added to three-dimensional scenes. Many of these approaches will naturally lead to additions to the graphics framework, such as a sprite material and an orthogonal camera that may be useful in other contexts as well.

### 5.7.1 Billboarding

One major use of text is to convey information to the viewer, as in a label. One way to incorporate a label in a scene is to apply it to an in-scene object, such as a sign or a marquee. The approach has the drawback that the viewer might not be able to read the label from all angles and inadvertently miss some useful information. One remedy for this issue is *billboarding*: orienting an object so that it always faces the camera, as illustrated in Figure 5.25. Two methods for implementing billboarding are using a special matrix transformation and using a custom material, each of which are discussed in detail and implemented in what follows.

One method for accomplishing billboarding is using a transformation called a *look-at matrix*, which as the name implies, orients one object towards another object called the *target*. The *look direction* or *forward direction* of a 3D object is its local negative z-axis, just as is the case when working with camera objects. Similarly, in this context, the positive

FIGURE 5.25   Billboarding a label above a crate.

local *x* axis and *y* axis are sometimes referred to as the *right direction* and the *up direction* of the object, respectively. The look direction is aligned with the vector from the position of the object to the position of the target. To avoid ambiguity, an up direction must be specified when calculating this matrix, as there are many ways to look along the look direction: the object could be tilted (rotated) to the left or the right by any amount with respect to this direction.

To determine the rotation components of a look-at matrix (the upper three-by-three submatrix), you can apply the same mathematical approach used in Chapter 3 to derive the matrices representing rotation around each of the coordinate axes: determine the results of applying the look-at transformation to the standard basis vectors $i$, $j$, and $k$. If $F$ represents this transformation, then in line with the vocabulary introduced above, $F(i)$ will equal the right direction, $F(j)$ will equal the up direction, and $-F(k)$ will equal the forward direction. These results will be the columns for the rotational component of the transformation matrix. The fourth column of the transformation matrix corresponds to the position of the object, which should not be changed in this matrix.

Before proceeding with the necessary calculations, a new vector operation must be introduced: the cross product. The *cross product* $v \times w$ of two vectors $v$ and $w$ in three-dimensional space produces a third vector $u$ which is perpendicular to both $v$ and $w$. The orientation of $u$ is given by the right-hand convention discussed in Chapter 3. For example, if $v$ and $w$ align with the $x$ and $y$ axes, respectively, then $u$ will align with the $z$ axis. The cross product operation is not commutative: switching the order in the product will reverse the orientation of the result; symbolically, $v \times w = -(w \times v)$. If $v$ and $w$ are parallel – aligned along the same direction – then the calculation of a perpendicular vector is ambiguous and the cross product returns the zero vector. The cross product will be used in calculating the right, up, and forward vectors, as they all must be perpendicular to each other. The actual formula for the cross product will not be discussed here, as it can be easily looked up in any vector algebra text. You will need to implement some changes to the vector class in order for these functions to be available for use. Inside the **Vector** class, add the following methods:

```java
public void multiplyScalar(double s)
{
    for (int i = 0; i < values.length; i++)
        values[i] *= s;
}
public static Vector multiplyScalar(double s, Vector v)
{
    Vector n = new Vector( v.values.length );
    for (int i = 0; i < v.values.length; i++)
        n.values[i] = s * v.values[i];
    return n;
}


public double getLength()
{
    double length = 0;
    for (int i = 0; i < values.length; i++)
        length += values[i] * values[i];
    return Math.sqrt(length);
}


public void setLength(double length)
{
    multiplyScalar( length / getLength() );
}


public static Vector add(Vector v, Vector w)
{
    Vector n = new Vector( v.values.length );
    for (int i = 0; i < v.values.length; i++)
        n.values[i] = v.values[i] + w.values[i];
    return n;
}


public static Vector subtract(Vector v, Vector w)
{
    Vector n = new Vector( v.values.length );
    for (int i = 0; i < v.values.length; i++)
        n.values[i] = v.values[i] - w.values[i];
    return n;
}
```

```
public static Vector cross(Vector v, Vector w)
{
    return new Vector(
        v.values[1] * w.values[2] - v.values[2] * w.values[1],
        v.values[2] * w.values[0] - v.values[0] * w.values[2],
        v.values[0] * w.values[1] - v.values[1] * w.values[0]   );
}
```

Since the forward vector points from the object position to the target position, this vector can be calculated by subtracting these positions. The object's up vector should lie in the plane spanned by the world up vector $\langle 0, 1, 0 \rangle$ and the object forward vector, and therefore the right vector will be perpendicular to these vectors. Thus, the right vector can be calculated from the cross product of the world up vector and the forward vector. (If the world up vector and the forward vector are pointing in the same direction, then the world up vector can be perturbed by a small offset to avoid a zero vector as the result.) Finally, the object's up vector can be calculated from the cross product of the right vector and the forward vector. Finally, all these vectors should have length 1, so each vector can be scaled by dividing it by its length. The natural place to implement these calculations is in the Matrix class. In the **Matrix** class in the **core** package, add the following method, which will be used to generate the look-at matrix:

```
public static Matrix makeLookAt(Vector position,
    Vector target)
{
    Vector worldUp = new Vector(0, 1, 0);
    Vector forward = Vector.subtract( target, position );
    Vector right = Vector.cross( forward, worldUp );

    // if forward and worldUp vectors are parallel,
    //     right vector is zero;
    //     fix by perturbing worldUp vector a bit
    if (right.getLength() < 0.001)
    {
        Vector offset = new Vector(0.001, 0, 0);
        right = Vector.cross( forward,
                    Vector.add(worldUp, offset) );
    }

    Vector up = Vector.cross( right, forward );
    // all vectors should have length 1
    forward.setLength(1);
    right.setLength(1);
    up.setLength(1);

    // the vectors are shorter than the matrix dimensions,
    //     so the last matrix column entry has default value 0;
```

```
//    only needs to be adjusted in the last matrix column.
Matrix m = new Matrix(4,4);
m.setCol(0, right);
m.setCol(1, up);
forward.multiplyScalar(-1);
m.setCol(2, forward);
m.setCol(3, position);
m.values[3][3] = 1;
return m;
}
```

Finally, in the **Object3D** class in the **core** package, add the following method, which will be used to apply the look-at matrix to an object, retaining the object's position while replacing its orientation so that the object faces the target.

```
public void lookAt(Vector targetPosition)
{
    transform = Matrix.makeLookAt(
        this.getWorldPosition(), targetPosition );
}
```

With these additions to the graphics framework, you can now recreate the scene illustrated in Figure 5.25. Since the side of the rectangle that faces forward (the local negative z direction) is the side on which the image is rendered backwards, a 180° rotation is applied to the geometry before creating the mesh so that the image will appear correctly when the look-at matrix is applied to the mesh. The scene will include a movement rig so that you can see the orientation of the label change in response to the movement of the camera. In the main project folder, create a copy of the file **Test_Template** and name it **Test_5_8**. In this file, inside the **initialize** method, replace the code starting from the line where the camera position is set, with the following code:

```
rig = new MovementRig();
rig.attach( camera );
rig.setPosition( new Vector(0, 1.5, 5) );
scene.add( rig );

Geometry boxGeometry = new BoxGeometry();
Material boxMaterial = new TextureMaterial(
    new Texture("images/crate.png") );
Mesh box = new Mesh( boxGeometry, boxMaterial );
box.setPosition( new Vector(0,0.5,0) );
scene.add( box );

Mesh grid = new GridHelper(10, 10,
    new Vector(1,1,1), new Vector(1,0.5,0.5), 2);
```

```
grid.rotateX(-Math.PI/2, true);
scene.add( grid );
Texture labelTexture = new Texture("images/crate-label.png");
Material labelMaterial = new TextureMaterial(labelTexture);
Geometry labelGeometry = new RectangleGeometry(1, 0.5);
labelGeometry.applyMatrix( Matrix.makeRotationY(3.14) );
label = new Mesh(labelGeometry, labelMaterial);
label.setPosition( new Vector(0, 1.5, 0) );
scene.add(label);
```

Finally, in the **update** method, add the following lines of code:

```
label.lookAt( camera.getWorldPosition() );

rig.update(input, deltaTime);
renderer.render(scene, camera);
```

With these additions, this new example is complete. When you run the application, you should be able to recreate the images from the perspectives illustrated in Figure 5.25.

Another approach to billboarding is by using a customized vertex shader that discards any rotation information from the model and view matrices (only retaining position related data) before applying the projection matrix. In computer graphics, a two-dimensional image used in a three-dimensional scene in this way is often referred to as a *sprite*, and accordingly the class material you will create to implement this shader will be called **SpriteMaterial**.

Such a material is also a natural place to build in support for tilesets. A *tileset* (sometimes also called a *spritesheet*) is a grid of rectangular images (called *tiles*) combined into a single image for convenience and efficiency. When rendering the scene, the UV coordinates of the object can be transformed so the desired tile is displayed from the tileset image. One situation where tilesets are useful is *texture packing*: combining multiple images into a single image for the purpose of reducing the number of textures required by an application. This may be particularly useful in an application where the text or image displayed on a particular surface will change periodically. The left side of Figure 5.26 shows an example of such an image. Another application is *spritesheet animation*: displaying a sequence of images in rapid succession to create the illusion of motion or continuous change. The right side of Figure 5.26 contains a four-by-four tileset; when the images are displayed in the order indicated, a small circle will appear to be rolling around within a larger circle.

The shaders you will create alongside the **SpriteMaterial** class will contain the same uniform matrices and attribute variables as previous materials. One new addition will be a boolean variable named **billboard**; if set to true, it will enable a billboard effect as previously described by replacing the rotation component of the combined model and view matrices with the identity matrix. In addition, to support tilesets, there will be a variable named **tileNumber**. If **tileNumber** is set to a number greater than –1,

 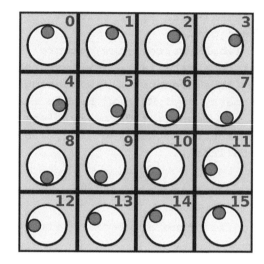

FIGURE 5.26    Tilesets used for texture packing (left) and spritesheet animation (right).

then the vertex shader will use the information stored in **tileCount** (the number of columns and rows in the tileset) to transform the UV coordinates so that the desired tile is rendered on the object.

To implement this material, in the **material** package, create a new Java class called **SpriteMaterial** with the following code:

```java
package material;

import math.Vector;
import core.Texture;

public class SpriteMaterial extends Material
{
    public SpriteMaterial(Texture texture)
    {
        super(
            "./src/material/SpriteMaterial.vert",
            "./src/material/SpriteMaterial.frag" );

        addUniform("vec3", "baseColor", new Vector(1,1,1) );
        addUniform("sampler2D", "tex",
            new Vector(texture.textureRef, 1));
        addUniform("bool", "billboard", 0);
        addUniform("float", "tileNumber", -1);
        addUniform("vec2", "tileCount", new Vector(1, 1));
        locateUniforms();
        addRenderSetting( "doubleSide", true );
    }
}
```

Next, you will create two additional files named **SpriteMaterial.frag** and **SpriteMaterial.vert**. Inside the fragment shader file, insert the following code:

```
uniform vec3 baseColor;
uniform sampler2D tex;
in vec2 UV;
out vec4 fragColor;

void main()
{
    vec4 color = vec4(baseColor, 1.0) * texture(tex, UV);

    if (color.a < 0.1)
        discard;

    fragColor = color;
}
```

And in the vertex shader file, insert the following code:

```
uniform mat4 projectionMatrix;
uniform mat4 viewMatrix;
uniform mat4 modelMatrix;
uniform bool billboard;
uniform float tileNumber;
uniform vec2 tileCount;

in vec3 vertexPosition;
in vec2 vertexUV;
out vec2 UV;

void main()
{
    mat4 mvMatrix = viewMatrix * modelMatrix;
    if ( billboard )
    {
        mvMatrix[0][0] = 1;
        mvMatrix[0][1] = 0;
        mvMatrix[0][2] = 0;
        mvMatrix[1][0] = 0;
        mvMatrix[1][1] = 1;
        mvMatrix[1][2] = 0;
        mvMatrix[2][0] = 0;
        mvMatrix[2][1] = 0;
        mvMatrix[2][2] = 1;
    }
    gl_Position = projectionMatrix * mvMatrix *
        vec4(vertexPosition, 1.0);
```

```
    UV = vertexUV;
    if (tileNumber > -1.0)
    {
        vec2 tileSize = 1.0 / tileCount;
        float columnIndex = mod(tileNumber, tileCount[0]);
        float rowIndex = floor(tileNumber / tileCount[0]);
        vec2 tileOffset = vec2( columnIndex/tileCount[0],
                1.0 - (rowIndex + 1.0)/tileCount[1] );
        UV = UV * tileSize + tileOffset;
    }
}
```

Lastly, you will make an application to test this material, using both the billboarding and spritesheet animation features. You will also include a movement rig to move the camera around the scene, and a grid for a fixed plane of reference as you move around the scene. To begin, create a copy of the file **Test_Template** named **Test_5_9**. In the **initialize** method, replace the code, starting from the line where the camera position is set, with the following code:

```
rig = new MovementRig();
rig.attach( camera );
rig.setPosition( new Vector(0, 1.5, 5) );
scene.add( rig );

Geometry geometry = new RectangleGeometry();
Material material = new SpriteMaterial(
    new Texture("images/rolling-ball.png") );
material.uniforms.get("billboard").data = 1;
material.uniforms.get("tileCount").data = new Vector(4,4);
material.uniforms.get("tileNumber").data = 0;
sprite = new Mesh( geometry, material );
sprite.setPosition( new Vector(0, 0.5, 0) );
scene.add( sprite );

Mesh grid = new GridHelper(10,10, new Vector(1,1,1),
    new Vector(1, 0.5, 0.5), 2);
grid.rotateX(-Math.PI/2, true);
scene.add( grid );
```

Finally, in the **update** method, add the following lines of code:

```
int tilesPerSecond = 8;
float tileNumber = (float)Math.floor(time * tilesPerSecond);
sprite.material.uniforms.get("tileNumber").data = tileNumber;

rig.update(input, deltaTime);
renderer.render(scene, camera);
```

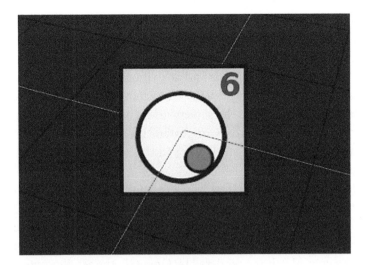

FIGURE 5.27    A frame from a spritesheet animation in a scene.

When you run this application, using the spritesheet on the right side of Figure 5.26, you should see the animation of the small circle rolling around the large circle, in a scene similar to that in Figure 5.27. Furthermore, as you move around the scene, the rectangle should always be facing the camera.

### 5.7.2  Heads-Up Displays and Orthogonal Cameras

The methods for viewing text implemented in the previous section are useful when the text only needs to be visible in a particular area in the scene. For text or graphics that should be visible to the viewer at all times, the most common approach is to use a *heads-up display* (HUD): a transparent layer containing these elements, rendered after the scene, and therefore appearing on top, as illustrated in Figure 5.28. Implementing this functionality will involve additions or modifications to multiple classes: **Matrix**, **Camera**, **Renderer**, and **Rectangle**.

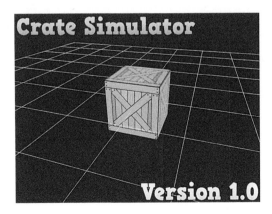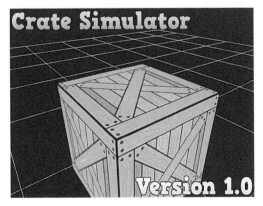

FIGURE 5.28    A heads-up display containing fixed text.

The objects to be included in the heads-up display will be added to a second scene, sometimes called the *HUD layer*. In contrast to the primary three-dimensional scene, where the scale is somewhat arbitrary and a perspective projection is used, the natural unit of measurement in the HUD layer is pixels and an orthographic projection is used. The viewable region of space in the HUD layer will be a rectangular box, whose width and height will be equal to the dimensions of the screen, and whose depth is arbitrary. In general, z coordinates in the HUD layer are only important if one object should be rendered above another. When used to determine stack order in this way, the z coordinate of an object is also called its *z-index*.

The viewable region can be specified by six constants: *left, right, bottom, top, near,* and *far,* denoted by the variables $l$, $r$, $b$, $t$, $n$, and $f$, respectively; the points $(x, y, z)$ in the region satisfy the conditions $l \le x \le r$, $b \le y \le t$, and $n \le -z \le f$ (the negation of $z$ due to the reversal of the $z$ direction in clip space, discussed in Chapter 3). This region in turn must be projected into the cubical volume rendered by OpenGL, the set of points $(x, y, z)$ where all components are bounded by –1 and +1. The necessary transformations in each coordinate are affine transformations, involving both scaling and translation. For example, the transformation of the $x$ coordinate is a function of the form $F(x) = p \cdot x + q$, and given that $F(l) = -1$ and $F(r) = +1$, it is possible to algebraically solve for the values of $p$ and $q$ in terms of $l$ and $r$. In particular, $p = 2/(r - l)$ and $q = -(r + l)/(r - l)$. Similar calculations can be used to derive the transformation needed for the y coordinate and the z coordinate. Since homogeneous coordinates are used throughout this graphics framework, these transformations can be combined into the following matrix:

$$
\begin{bmatrix}
\dfrac{2}{r-l} & 0 & 0 & -\dfrac{r+l}{r-l} \\
0 & \dfrac{2}{t-b} & 0 & -\dfrac{t+b}{t-b} \\
0 & 0 & -\dfrac{2}{f-n} & -\dfrac{f+n}{f-n} \\
0 & 0 & 0 & 1
\end{bmatrix}
$$

The next step is to add a method to the **Matrix** class that generates this matrix. To implement this, in the **Matrix** class in the **math** package, add the following methods:

```
public static Matrix makeOrthographic(
     double left, double right,
     double bottom, double top,
     double near, double far)
{
    Matrix m = new Matrix(4,4);
    m.setValues(2/(right-left), 0, 0,
                -(right+left)/(right-left),
            0, 2/(top-bottom), 0, -(top+bottom)/(top-bottom),
```

```
            0, 0, -2/(far-near), -(far+near)/(far-near),
            0, 0, 0, 1);
    return m;
}

public static Matrix makeOrthographic()
{
    return makeOrthographic(-1,1, -1,1, -1,1);
}
```

Next, the **Camera** class needs to be updated so that an orthographic matrix can be used as the projection matrix. This will be accomplished by adding a **setOrthographic** method containing the necessary parameters. For symmetry, a **setPerspective** method will be added as well. To implement these, in the **Camera** class in the **core** package, add the following methods:

```
public void setPerspective(double angleOfView,
        double aspectRatio, double near, double far)
{
    projectionMatrix = Matrix.makePerspective(angleOfView,
        aspectRatio, near, far);
}

public void setPerspective()
{
    projectionMatrix = Matrix.makePerspective();
}

public void setOrthographic(double left, double right,
        double bottom, double top, double near, double far)
{
    projectionMatrix = Matrix.makeOrthographic(left, right,
        bottom, top, near, far);
}

public void setOrthographic()
{
    projectionMatrix = Matrix.makeOrthographic();
}
```

At present, whenever a scene is rendered by the **Renderer** class, the color and depth buffers are cleared. In order for the HUD layer to be rendered on top of the main three-dimensional scene and have the main scene still be visible, the color buffer needs to not be cleared between these two renders. However, the depth buffer should still be cleared, because otherwise fragments from the HUD layer might not be rendered due to residual depth values from rendering the main scene.

First, in the **renderer** class in the **core** package, add two public boolean class properties named **clearColorBuffer** and **clearDepthBuffer**. Initialize them both to true in the constructor. Then, replace the line of code containing the **glClear** function with the following block of code:

```
// clear color and/or depth buffers
if (clearColorBuffer)
    glClear(GL_COLOR_BUFFER_BIT);
if (clearDepthBuffer)
    glClear(GL_DEPTH_BUFFER_BIT);
```

Finally, to simplify aligning these objects within the HUD layer, a few changes will be made to the **Rectangle** class, enabling any point to be assigned to any location within the rectangle. As the **Rectangle** class was originally written, the origin (0, 0) corresponds to the center of the rectangle. You will add two parameters, **position** and **alignment** (each a list of two numbers) that will affect the way the vertex position data is generated. The **alignment** components should be thought of as percentages (values between 0.00 and 1.00), corresponding to offsets along the width and height, used to indicate which point in the rectangle will correspond to **position**. For example, if **alignment[0]** has a value of 0.00, 0.50, or 1.00, then the rectangle will be left-aligned, centered, or right-aligned, respectively, with respect to the $x$ component of **position**. If **alignment[1]** has a value of 0.00, 0.50, or 1.00, then the rectangle will be bottom-aligned, centered, or top-aligned, respectively, with respect to the y component of position.

To implement the changes, in the **RectangleGeometry** class in the **geometry** package, change the declaration of the constructors to the following:

```
public RectangleGeometry(double width, double height)
{
    this( width, height, new Vector(0,0), new Vector(0.5,0.5) );
}

public RectangleGeometry(double width, double height,
            Vector position, Vector alignment)
{
    // leave method code as is
}
```

Then, change the block of code that assigns values to **P0**, **P1**, **P2**, and **P3**, to the following:

```
double x = position.values[0];
double y = position.values[1];
double a = alignment.values[0];
double b = alignment.values[1];
```

```
Vector P0 = new Vector(x +   (-a)*width, y +   (-b)*height, 0);
Vector P1 = new Vector(x + (1-a)*width, y +   (-b)*height, 0);
Vector P2 = new Vector(x +   (-a)*width, y + (1-b)*height, 0);
Vector P3 = new Vector(x + (1-a)*width, y + (1-b)*height, 0);
```

This completes all the changes necessary to be able to render the scene shown in Figure 5.24. To create the application, in the main src folder, make a copy of the file **Test_Template** and name it **Test_5_10**.

In the **initialize** method, replace the code starting from the line where the camera object is created, with the following code, which will set up the main scene.

```
// for non-square windows, adjust aspect ratio size
camera    = new Camera(60, 800/600f, 0.1, 1000);
rig = new MovementRig();
rig.attach( camera );
rig.setPosition( new Vector(0, 1.5, 5) );
scene.add( rig );

// main scene
Geometry boxGeometry = new BoxGeometry();
Material boxMaterial = new TextureMaterial(
    new Texture("images/crate.png") );
Mesh box = new Mesh( boxGeometry, boxMaterial );
box.setPosition( new Vector(0,0.5,0) );
scene.add( box );

Mesh grid = new GridHelper(10, 10,
    new Vector(1,1,1), new Vector(1,0.5,0.5), 2);
grid.rotateX(-Math.PI/2, true);
scene.add( grid );
```

The next step is to set up the HUD layer. When creating a rectangle to display an image in the HUD, the width and height of the rectangle should be set to the width and height of the image (although these values may also be scaled proportionally if desired). The HUD layer illustrated in Figure 5.28 contains two labels; the code that follows will create these two objects. The **position** and **alignment** parameter values for the first label are chosen to align the top-left corner of the rectangle with the point in the top-left of the screen, while the parameters for the second label align its bottom-right corner with the bottom-right of the screen. To continue, add the following code at the end of the **initialize** method:

```
// HUD scene
hudScene = new Scene();
hudCamera = new Camera();
hudCamera.setOrthographic(0,800, 0,600, 1,-1);
Geometry labelGeo1 = new RectangleGeometry(600, 80,
    new Vector(0,600), new Vector(0,1));
```

```
Material labelMat1 = new TextureMaterial(
        new Texture("images/crate-sim.png"));
Mesh label1 = new Mesh(labelGeo1, labelMat1);
hudScene.add( label1 );
Geometry labelGeo2 = new RectangleGeometry(400, 80, new
Vector(800,0), new Vector(1,0));
Material labelMat2 = new TextureMaterial(
    new Texture("images/version-1.png"));
Mesh label2 = new Mesh(labelGeo2, labelMat2);
hudScene.add( label2 );
```

Next, replace the code in the **update** method with the following code, which renders the scenes in the correct order and prevents the color buffer from being cleared as needed so that the content from each scene is visible.

```
rig.update(input, deltaTime);
renderer.clearColorBuffer = true;
renderer.render(scene, camera);
renderer.clearColorBuffer = false;
renderer.render(hudScene, hudCamera);
```

Finally, change the end of the program to the following, which increases the size of the graphics window so that it is better able to fit the HUD layer content.

```
new Test_5_10().run(800, 600);
```

At this point, when you run the application, you will be able to move the camera around the scene using the standard movement rig controls and produce images such as those illustrated in Figure 5.28.

## 5.8 RENDERING SCENES TO TEXTURES

The next goal is to render scenes to textures, which can be used for a variety of purposes. Figure 5.29 illustrates a scene based on the skysphere example shown in Figure 5.14, which also includes a sphere with a grid texture applied, and a dark box with a rectangle

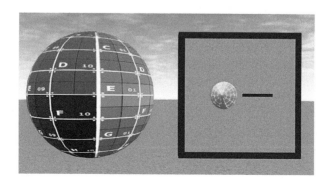

FIGURE 5.29   Rendering a scene to a texture within the scene.

positioned in front, representing a television screen. The texture used for the rectangle is a rendering of the scene from a second camera positioned above these objects and oriented downward. As you will see when you implement this scene, the sphere is also rotating, and the image in the rectangle constantly updates and shows this.

*Framebuffers*, introduced in Chapter 1, are of key importance when rendering to a texture. When OpenGL is initialized, a frame buffer is automatically generated, containing a color buffer and a depth buffer, and is attached to the window that displays graphics. When a scene is rendered, the image seen in the window corresponds to the data in the color buffer. To render an image to a texture, you will need to manually set up a framebuffer and configure the attached buffers (color and depth). These tasks will require the use of many OpenGL functions, which are discussed in what follows.

The first steps in working with framebuffers are to generate a reference and bind it to a target, analogous to the first steps when working with vertex buffers or textures. In the case of framebuffers, this is accomplished with the following two OpenGL functions:

**glGenFramebuffers(** *bufferCount* **)**
>    Returns a set of nonzero integers representing available framebuffer references. The number of references returned is specified by the integer parameter *bufferCount*.

**glBindFramebuffer(** *bindTarget, framebufferRef* **)**
>    The framebuffer referred to by the parameter *framebufferRef* is bound to the target specified by the parameter *bindTarget*, whose value is an OpenGL constant such as GL_FRAMEBUFFER or GL_DRAW_FRAMEBUFFER. Future OpenGL operations affecting the same *bindTarget* will be applied to the referenced framebuffer.
>
>    Next, the buffers used by the framebuffer need to be configured. To use a texture for a buffer (as you will for the color buffer), you use the following function:

**glFramebufferTexture(** *bindTarget, attachment, textureRef, level* **)**
>    Attaches a texture object specified by *textureRef* as the type of buffer specified by *attachment* to the framebuffer currently bound to *bindTarget*. The parameter *attachment* is an OpenGL constant such as GL_COLOR_ATTACHMENT*n* (for an integer *n*), GL_DEPTH_ATTACHMENT, or GL_STENCIL_ATTACHMENT. The parameter *level* is usually zero, indicating this is the base image level in the associated mipmap image.

Similar to textures, *renderbuffers* are OpenGL objects that store image data, but specifically used with and optimized for framebuffers. As usual, the first steps in working with these objects are to generate a reference and bind it to a target, which uses the following OpenGL functions:

**glGenRenderbuffers(** *bufferCount* **)**
>    Returns a set of nonzero integers representing available renderbuffer references. The number of references returned is specified by the integer parameter *bufferCount*.

**glBindRenderbuffer**( *bindTarget, renderbufferRef* )

The renderbuffer referred to by the parameter *renderbufferRef* is bound to the target specified by the parameter *bindTarget*, whose value must be the OpenGL constant GL_RENDERBUFFER. Future OpenGL operations affecting the same *bindTarget* will be applied to the referenced renderbuffer.

Once a render buffer is bound, storage is allocated with the following function:

**glRenderbufferStorage**( *bindTarget, format, width, height* )

Allocate storage for the renderbuffer currently bound to the target *bindTarget*, whose value must be the OpenGL constant GL_RENDERBUFFER. The data stored in the renderbuffer will have the type specified by the parameter *format*, whose value is an OpenGL constant such as GL_RGB, GL_RGBA, GL_DEPTH_COMPONENT, or GL_STENCIL. The dimensions of the buffer are specified by *width* and *height*.

The next OpenGL function is analogous in purpose to glFramebufferTexture, but is used instead when a renderbuffer will be used to store data instead of a texture.

**glFramebufferRenderbuffer**( *framebufferTarget, attachment, renderbufferTarget, renderbufferRef* )

Attaches a renderbuffer object specified by *renderbufferRef* as the type of buffer specified by *attachment* to the framebuffer currently bound to *framebufferTarget*. The parameter *attachment* is an OpenGL constant such as GL_COLOR_ATTACHMENT*n* (for an integer *n*), GL_DEPTH_ATTACHMENT, or GL_STENCIL_ATTACHMENT. The parameter *renderbufferTarget* must be the OpenGL constant GL_RENDERBUFFER.

Finally, to verify that the framebuffer has been configured correctly, you can use the following function:

**glCheckFramebufferStatus**( *bindTarget* )

Check if the framebuffer currently bound to *bindTarget* is complete: at least one color attachment has been added and all attachments have been correctly initialized.

With the knowledge of these OpenGL functions, you are now prepared to create the **RenderTarget** class. In the **core** package, create a new Java class named **RenderTarget** containing the following code. Note that if a texture is not supplied as a parameter, an empty texture is automatically generated.

```
package core;

import static org.lwjgl.opengl.GL40.*;
import math.Vector;
```

```java
public class RenderTarget
{
    // store associated texture dimensions
    public int width;
    public int height;
    public Texture texture;
    public int framebufferRef;

    public RenderTarget(Vector resolution)
    {
        width = (int)resolution.values[0];
        height = (int)resolution.values[1];
        // generate an empty texture
        texture = new Texture(width, height);
        // create a framebuffer
        framebufferRef = glGenFramebuffers();
        glBindFramebuffer(GL_FRAMEBUFFER, framebufferRef);

        // configure color buffer to use this texture
        glFramebufferTexture(GL_FRAMEBUFFER,
            GL_COLOR_ATTACHMENT0, texture.textureRef, 0);
        // generate a buffer to store depth information
        int depthBufferRef = glGenRenderbuffers();
        glBindRenderbuffer(GL_RENDERBUFFER, depthBufferRef);
        glRenderbufferStorage(GL_RENDERBUFFER,
            GL_DEPTH_COMPONENT, width, height);
        glFramebufferRenderbuffer(GL_FRAMEBUFFER,
            GL_DEPTH_ATTACHMENT, GL_RENDERBUFFER, depthBufferRef);

        // check framebuffer status
        int status = glCheckFramebufferStatus(GL_FRAMEBUFFER);
        if (status != GL_FRAMEBUFFER_COMPLETE)
            System.out.println("Framebuffer status error: "
                + status);
    }
}
```

In order to use a manually created framebuffer as the target when rendering (rather than the framebuffer attached to the window), you must also make a few additions to the **Renderer** class. First, because the texture to which you will be rendering may not be the same size as the window, you need to be able to specify how clip space coordinates map to window coordinates. In particular, you need to specify the size and location of the *viewport*: the rectangular area in the window used to display the color data from the currently active framebuffer. This rectangular area is specified by the coordinates of the lower-left corner and its width and height, which is set by the following OpenGL function:

**glViewport(** *x, y, width, height* **)**
> Specify the coordinates (*x, y*) of the lower-left corner and the *width* and *height* of the viewport rectangle. When a GL context is first created, (*x, y*) is initialized to (0, 0) and the *width* and *height* are initialized to the dimensions of the window.

To begin, in the **Renderer** class in the **core** package, at the very beginning of the **render** method, add the following code, which binds the correct framebuffer (the value zero indicating the framebuffer attached to the window is the render target), and sets the viewport size accordingly.

```
// activate render target
if (renderTarget == null)
{
    // set render target to window
    glBindFramebuffer(GL_FRAMEBUFFER, 0);
    glViewport(0,0, Base.windowWidth, Base.windowHeight);
}
else
{
    // set render target properties
    glBindFramebuffer(GL_FRAMEBUFFER,
        renderTarget.framebufferRef);
    glViewport(0,0, renderTarget.width, renderTarget.height);
}
```

At this point, you are ready to begin creating this example. Start by making a copy of the file **Test_5_2** (the skysphere example) and rename it to **Test_5_11**. To demonstrate that viewports work as expected, you will use an 800 by 600 size window, and a 512 by 512 size texture. To change the size of the window from the default, change the last line of the code in the application to the following:

```
new Test_5_11().run(800, 600);
```

So that the scene does not appear stretched, you need to set the aspect ratio of the camera accordingly. Thus, add this line of code after the camera object is created:

```
camera.setPerspective(60, 800/600f, 0.1, 1000);
```

Next, in the **initialize** method, add the following code to add new meshes to the scene.

```
Geometry sphereGeometry = new SphereGeometry();
Material sphereMaterial = new TextureMaterial(
    new Texture("images/grid.png") );
```

```
sphere = new Mesh( sphereGeometry, sphereMaterial );
sphere.setPosition( new Vector(-1.2, 1, 0) );
scene.add( sphere );

Geometry boxGeometry = new BoxGeometry(2, 2, 0.2);
Material boxMaterial = new SurfaceMaterial();
boxMaterial.uniforms.get("baseColor").data =
    new Vector(0.2, 0.2, 0.2);
Mesh box = new Mesh( boxGeometry, boxMaterial );
box.setPosition( new Vector(1.2, 1, 0) );
scene.add( box );
```

To create the "television screen" – the rectangular mesh whose material will use the texture from a render target – also add the following code to the **initialize** method.

```
renderTarget = new RenderTarget( new Vector(512,512) );

Geometry screenGeometry = new RectangleGeometry(1.8, 1.8);
Material screenMaterial = new TextureMaterial(
    renderTarget.texture );
Mesh screen = new Mesh( screenGeometry, screenMaterial );
screen.setPosition( new Vector(1.2, 1, 0.11) );
scene.add( screen );
```

To create the second camera that will be used when rendering to the texture, also add the following code to the **initialize** method. Note that the aspect ratio of the sky camera is derived from the dimensions of the previously created render target, and that the recently introduced look-at functionality is used to orient the sky camera in the desired direction.

```
// camera aspectRatio=1 by default, as needed
skyCamera = new Camera();
skyCamera.setPosition( new Vector(0, 10, 0.1) );
scene.add( skyCamera );
skyCamera.lookAt( new Vector(0, 0, 0) );
```

Finally, change the code in the **update** method to the following, which causes the sphere to spin, updates the movement rig, renders the scene to the render target (using the new sky camera), and then renders the scene to the window (using the original camera).

```
rig.update(input, deltaTime);
sphere.rotateY( 0.01337, true );

renderer.renderTarget = renderTarget;
renderer.render(scene, skyCamera);
renderer.renderTarget = null;
renderer.render(scene, camera);
```

With these additions, the example is complete. When you run the example, you should see a scene similar to that in Figure 5.29. Another application of rendering to a texture is to help orient a player moving a character around a large, complex environment by creating a "minimap": a texture similar to the one created in example in this section, but the sky camera moves in sync with the player's character and stays oriented toward the character at all times, and the result is rendered to a small rectangle in a HUD layer so that it stays fixed on screen and is visible to the player at all times.

A frequently used technique in computer graphics enabled by rendering to textures is postprocessing, which is described in detail and implemented in the next section.

## 5.9 POSTPROCESSING

In computer graphics, postprocessing is the application of additional visual effects to the image of a rendered scene. Figure 5.30 illustrates three such effects applied separately to a scene: *vignette* (reduced brightness toward the edges of an image), color inversion, and pixelation.

In addition, it is also desirable in many situations to chain these effects – apply them one after the other in sequence – to create a compound effect. For example, to replicate the appearance of older handheld video game system graphics, one could take the same base scene used in Figure 5.30 and apply a green tint effect followed by a pixelation effect, resulting in the image illustrated in Figure 5.31.

With the addition of the **RenderTarget** class from the previous section, incorporating postprocessing into the graphics framework is a straightforward task. Each effect will be implemented with a simple shader incorporated into a material. There will be a sequence of render passes, starting with the base scene, each of which is applied to a render target. The texture in each render target in the sequence will be used in a material implementing an effect for the next render pass in the sequence. The last render pass in the sequence will use a specified final render target; if none is specified, the window will be the target and the final result of the postprocessing effect sequence will be displayed.

To implement postprocessing functionality, a **Postprocessor** class will be created. This class will maintain lists of **Scene**, **Camera**, and **RenderTarget** objects. The original scene and camera will be the first elements in their respective lists. All subsequent scenes will consist of a single rectangle; its vertices will be aligned with clip space to eliminate the need for any matrix transformations in the vertex shader. In order to use the

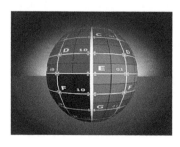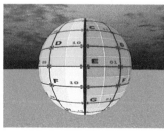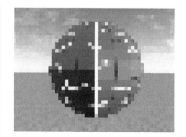

FIGURE 5.30 Postprocessing effects: vignette, color inversion, pixilation.

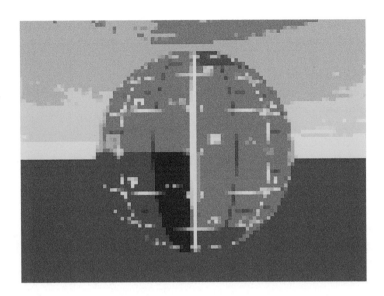

FIGURE 5.31   A compound postprocessing effect to simulate older video game system graphics.

**Renderer** class, a camera must be supplied, and so a camera using the default orthographic projection (aligned to clip space) will be reused for the additional render passes. To begin, in the **extras** package, create a new Java class named **Postprocessor** with the following code:

```java
package extras;

import static org.lwjgl.opengl.GL40.*;
import java.util.Arrays;
import java.util.List;
import java.util.ArrayList;
import math.Vector;
import core.*;
import geometry.Geometry;
import material.Material;

public class Postprocessor
{
    public Renderer renderer;
    public List<Scene> sceneList;
    public List<Camera> cameraList;
    public List<RenderTarget> renderTargetList;
    public RenderTarget finalRenderTarget;

    // reusable elements for added effects
    public Camera orthoCamera;
    public Geometry rectangleGeom;
```

```java
public Postprocessor(Renderer renderer, Scene scene,
    Camera camera, RenderTarget finalRenderTarget)
{
    this.renderer = renderer;
    sceneList = new ArrayList<Scene>();
    sceneList.add( scene );
    cameraList = new ArrayList<Camera>();
    cameraList.add( camera );
    renderTargetList = new ArrayList<RenderTarget>();
    renderTargetList.add( finalRenderTarget );

    this.finalRenderTarget = finalRenderTarget;

    orthoCamera = new Camera();
    // camera aligned with clip space by default
    orthoCamera.setOrthographic(-1,1, -1,1, 1,-1);

    // generate a rectangle already aligned with clip space;
    // no matrix transformations will be applied
    rectangleGeom = new Geometry();
    Vector P0 = new Vector(-1, -1);
    Vector P1 = new Vector( 1, -1);
    Vector P2 = new Vector(-1,  1);
    Vector P3 = new Vector( 1,  1);

    Vector T0 = new Vector(0, 0);
    Vector T1 = new Vector(1, 0);
    Vector T2 = new Vector(0, 1);
    Vector T3 = new Vector(1, 1);

    List positionList = Arrays.asList(P0,P1,P3, P0,P3,P2);
    float[] positionData = Vector.flattenList(positionList);

    List uvList = Arrays.asList(T0,T1,T3, T0,T3,T2);
    float[] uvData = Vector.flattenList(uvList);

    rectangleGeom.addAttribute("vec2", "vertexPosition",
        positionData);
    rectangleGeom.addAttribute("vec2", "vertexUV", uvData);
    rectangleGeom.vertexCount = 6;
}

public void addEffect(Material effect)
{
    Scene postScene = new Scene();
    Vector resolution = new Vector(800,600);
    RenderTarget target = new RenderTarget( resolution );
```

```
        // change the previous entry in the render target list
        //    to this newly created render target
        int size = renderTargetList.size();
        renderTargetList.set( size-1, target );
        // the effect in this render pass will use
        //    the texture that was written to
        // in the previous render pass
        effect.uniforms.get("tex").data =
            new Vector(target.texture.textureRef, 1);
        Mesh mesh = new Mesh( rectangleGeom, effect );
        postScene.add( mesh );

        sceneList.add( postScene );
        cameraList.add( orthoCamera );
        renderTargetList.add( finalRenderTarget );
    }

    public void render()
    {
        int passes = sceneList.size();
        for (int n = 0; n < passes; n++)
        {
            renderer.renderTarget = renderTargetList.get(n);
            renderer.render( sceneList.get(n),
                             cameraList.get(n) );

        }
    }
}
```

As previously mentioned, the postprocessing effects (the parameter in the **addEffect** method) are materials containing simple shaders, designed to work with the geometric object created by the **Postprocessor** class. Next, you will create a template material that only incorporates the data needed for postprocessing effects. To begin, in your src directory, create a new package called **effects**. Within that package, create a new Java class called **Effect** that contains the following code.

```
package effects;

import material.Material;
import math.Vector;

public class Effect extends Material
{
    public Effect()
    {
        super(
```

```
                 "./src/effects/Effect.vert",
                 "./src/effects/Effect.frag"  );

        // the actual texture reference is not 0;
        //   set from rendertarget by postprocessor class
        addUniform("sampler2D", "tex", new Vector(0, 1));
        locateUniforms();
    }
}
```

Next, create vertex shader and the fragment shader files named **Effect.vert** and **Effect.frag**, respectively. Inside the vertex shader, insert the following code:

```
in vec2 vertexPosition;
in vec2 vertexUV;
out vec2 UV;

void main()
{
    gl_Position = vec4(vertexPosition, 0.0, 1.0);
    UV = vertexUV;
}
```

And in the fragment shader, insert the following code:

```
in vec2 UV;
uniform sampler2D tex;
out vec4 fragColor;

void main()
{
    vec4 color = texture(tex, UV);
    fragColor = color;
}
```

Observe that, in the **Effect** class, the texture is rendered without any change; this is sometimes called a *pass-through* shader. The texture data stored in the **Uniform** object is set within the **addEffect** method in the **Postprocessor** class.

The next step is to create some basic effects. Each will involve some modifications to the fragment shader code in the template class created above. You will begin by creating one of the simplest postprocessing effects: color tinting, illustrated with a red tint applied in Figure 5.32.

This effect is accomplished by averaging the red, green, and blue components of each pixel, and then multiplying it by the tint color. You will add the tint color as a parameter in the class constructor, and create a corresponding uniform variable in the shader and uniform object in the class. To implement this, in the **effects** package, make a copy

FIGURE 5.32   Color tint postprocessing effect.

of the **Effect** class, **Effect.frag** and name them **TintEffect** and **TintEffect. frag** respectively. Inside the class named **TintEffect**, change the name of the class to **TintEffect**, and change the initialization method declaration to the following:

```
public TintEffect(Vector tintColor)
```

Change the fragment shader file path to the newly created **TintEffect.frag** and lastly add the following line of code near the end of the class, before the **locateUniforms** method is called.

```
addUniform("vec3", "tintColor", tintColor);
```

Inside the fragment shader, replace the code to the following:

```
in vec2 UV;
uniform vec3 tintColor;
uniform sampler2D tex;
out vec4 fragColor;

void main()
{
    vec4 color = texture(tex, UV);
    float gray = (color.r + color.g + color.b) / 3.0;
    fragColor = vec4(gray * tintColor, 1.0);
}
```

Now that you have a basic effect to work with, you can create an application that uses it together with the **Postprocessor** class. In your main folder, start by making a copy of the class **Test_5_2** (the skysphere example) and rename it to **Test_5_12**. Add the following import statement:

```
import effects.*;
```

Optionally, in the **initialize** method, you may add the following code to include a textured sphere, so that the resulting scene more closely resembles those in this section:

```
Geometry sphereGeometry = new SphereGeometry();
Material sphereMaterial = new TextureMaterial(
    new Texture("images/grid.png") );
sphere = new Mesh( sphereGeometry, sphereMaterial );
sphere.setPosition( new Vector(0,1,0) );
scene.add( sphere );
```

Next, in the **initialize** method, add the following code to set up postprocessing:

```
// set up postprocessing
postprocessor = new Postprocessor(renderer, scene,
    camera, null);
postprocessor.addEffect( new TintEffect( new Vector(1,0,0) ) );
```

Finally, replace the line of code in the **update** method referencing the **renderer** object to the following:

```
postprocessor.render();
```

When you run this example, you will see a scene similar to Figure 5.32. In the remainder of this section, you will create the effects illustrated earlier. After writing the code for each one, you can test it using the class **Test_5_12** by changing the effect that is added to the postprocessor.

To create the color inversion effect from Figure 5.30, make a copy of the **Effect** class, **Effect.frag** and name them **InvertEffect** and **InvertEffect.frag**, respectively. In the new class, change the name of the class to **InvertEffect** as well as the fragment shader path. Inside the fragment shader, replace the code with the following:

```
in vec2 UV;
uniform sampler2D tex;
out vec4 fragColor;

void main()
{
    vec4 color = texture(tex, UV);
    vec4 invert = vec4(1.0 - color.r, 1.0 - color.g,
                       1.0 - color.b, 1.0);
    fragColor = invert;
}
```

To create the pixelation effect from Figure 5.30, when determining the color of each fragment, you will round the UV coordinates to a level of precision determined by the dimensions of the texture (indicated by the parameter **resolution**) and the desired size of each of the constant colored boxes in the pixelation (indicated by the variable **pixelSize**). To implement this, make a copy of the **Effect** class, **Effect.frag** and name them **PixelateEffect** and **PixelateEffect.frag**, respectively. In the new class, change the name of the class to **PixelateEffect** as well as the fragment shader file path. Next, change the initialization method declaration to the following.

```
public PixelateEffect(float pixelSize, Vector resolution)
```

Next, add the following code near the end of the class, before the **locateUniforms** method is called.

```
addUniform("float", "pixelSize", pixelSize);
addUniform("vec2", "resolution", resolution);
```

Finally, inside the fragment shader, replace the code with the following:

```
in vec2 UV;
uniform sampler2D tex;
uniform float pixelSize;
uniform vec2 resolution;
out vec4 fragColor;

void main()
{
    vec2 factor = resolution / pixelSize;
    vec2 newUV = floor( UV * factor ) / factor;
    vec4 color = texture(tex, newUV);
    fragColor = color;
}
```

To create the vignette effect from Figure 5.30, you will use the UV coordinates to recalculate the clip space coordinates, which are (0, 0) at the center and extend between −1 and 1 on each axis. The color of each fragment will be interpolated between the texture color and a specified dimming color; the color is typically black (which is the reason for the "dimming" terminology) but other colors may be used just as well. The amount of interpolation will depend on the distance between the fragment position and the origin. The distance at which dimming begins is specified by the parameter **dimStart**, while the distance at which the pixel matches the dimming color is specified by the parameter **dimEnd**. To implement this, make a copy of the **Effect** class, **Effect.frag** and name them **VignetteEffect** and **VignetteEffect.frag**, respectively. In the new class, change the name of the class to **VignetteEffect**, the fragment shader file path and the initialization method declaration to the following.

```
public VignetteEffect(float dimStart, float dimEnd,
                    Vector dimColor)
```

Next, add the following code near the end of the class, before the **locateUniforms** method is called.

```
addUniform("float", "dimStart", dimStart);
addUniform("float", "dimEnd", dimEnd);
addUniform("vec3", "dimColor", dimColor);
```

Finally, replace the code in the fragment shader to the following:

```
in vec2 UV;
uniform sampler2D tex;
uniform float dimStart;
uniform float dimEnd;
uniform vec3 dimColor;
out vec4 fragColor;

void main()
{
    vec4 color = texture(tex, UV);

    // calculate position in clip space from UV coordinates
    vec2 position = 2 * UV - vec2(1,1);
    // calculate distance (d) from center,
    //    which affects brightness
    float d = length(position);
    // calculate brightness (b) factor:
    //    at d=dimStart, b=1; at d=dimEnd, b=0.
    float b = (d - dimEnd)/(dimStart - dimEnd);
    // prevent oversaturation
    b = clamp(b, 0, 1);
    // mix the texture color and dim color
    fragColor = vec4( b * color.rgb + (1-b) * dimColor, 1 );
}
```

The last effect that will be introduced will be reducing the color precision in an image, illustrated in Figure 5.33, which was used to produce the composite effect illustrated in Figure 5.31.

The method for creating this effect is similar to that from the pixelation effect. In this case, the texture colors are rounded to a particular level of precision determined by the parameter **levels**. To implement this, make a copy of the **Effect** class, **Effect.frag**

FIGURE 5.33   Color reduction postprocessing effect.

and name them **ColorReduceEffect** and **ColorReduceEffect.frag**, respectively. In the new class, change the name of the class to **ColorReduceEffect**, the fragment shader file path and the initialization method declaration to the following:

```
public ColorReduceEffect(float levels)
```

Next, add the following line of code before the **locateUniforms** method is called:

```
addUniform("float", "levels", levels);
```

Finally inside the fragment shader file, replace the code with the following,

```
in vec2 UV;
uniform sampler2D tex;
uniform float levels;
out vec4 fragColor;

void main()
{
    vec4 color = texture(tex, UV);
    vec4 reduced = round(color * levels) / levels;
    reduced.a = 1.0;
    fragColor = reduced;
}
```

With all these effects at your disposal, you can also experiment with different parameter settings and combinations of effects. In particular, to recreate the compound effect shown in Figure 5.31, in your application, replace the code involving the **addEffect** method with the following code, to set up a chain of postprocessing effects.

```
postprocessor.addEffect(
    new TintEffect(new Vector(0,1,0)) );
postprocessor.addEffect( new ColorReduceEffect(5) );
postprocessor.addEffect(
    new PixelateEffect(8, new Vector(800,600)) );
```

## 5.10 SUMMARY AND NEXT STEPS

In this chapter you extended the graphics framework, adding the ability to apply textures to the surfaces of geometric shapes. You created multiple animated effects, used algorithms to generate textures involving randomness and inspired by natural phenomena, generated textures involving text, and set up a postprocessing render system with a collection of special effects. This required additions to many of the geometry classes, modifications of multiple core classes (including **Uniform**, **Matrix**, **Object3D**, **Camera**, and **Renderer**), and the introduction of new material classes.

In the next chapter, you will add even more realism and sophistication to your three-dimensional scenes by learning how to add lights, shading, and shadows to the graphics framework.

# CHAPTER 6

# Light and Shadow

Lighting effects can greatly enhance the three-dimensional (3D) nature of a scene, as illustrated in Figure 6.1, which illustrates a light source and shaded objects, specular highlights, bump map textures that simulate surface detail, a postprocessing effect to simulate a glowing sun, and shadows cast from objects onto other objects.

When using lights, the colors on a surface may be brighter or dimmer, depending on the angle at which the light rays meet the surface. This effect is called shading, and enables viewers to observe the 3D nature of a shape in a rendered image, without the need for vertex colors or textures, as illustrated in Figure 6.2.

In this chapter, you will learn how to calculate the effects of different types of light, such as ambient, diffuse, and specular, as well as how to simulate different light sources such as directional lights and point lights. Then you will create new types of Light objects to store this data, update various geometric classes to store additional related data, create a set of materials to process this data, and incorporate all these elements into the rendering process. Finally, you will learn about and implement the advanced topics illustrated by Figure 6.1, including bump mapping to simulate surface details, additional postprocessing techniques to generate light bloom and glow effects, and shadow mapping, which enables objects to cast shadows on other objects.

## 6.1 INTRODUCTION TO LIGHTING

There are many different types of lighting that may be used when rendering an object. *Ambient lighting* affects all points on all geometric surfaces in a scene by the same amount. Ambient light simulates light that has been reflected from other surfaces, and ensures that objects or regions not directly lit by other types of lights remain at least partially visible. *Diffuse lighting* represents light that has been scattered and thus will appear lighter or darker in various regions, depending on the angle of the incoming light. *Specular lighting* creates bright spots and highlights on a surface to simulate *shininess*: the tendency of a surface to reflect light. These three types of lighting applied to a torus-shaped surface are illustrated in Figure 6.3. (A fourth type of lighting is *emissive lighting*, which is light emitted by an object that can be used to create a glow-like effect, but this will not be covered here.)

DOI: 10.1201/9781003153375-6

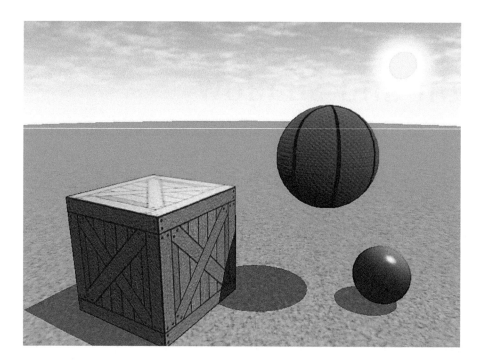

FIGURE 6.1    Rendered scene with lighting effects.

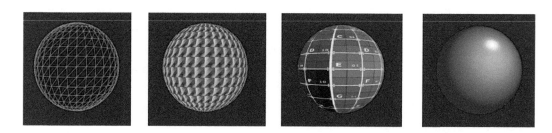

FIGURE 6.2    Four techniques to visualize a sphere: wireframe, vertex colors, texture, and shading.

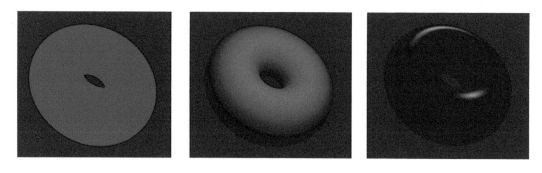

FIGURE 6.3    Ambient, diffuse, and specular lighting on a torus-shaped surface.

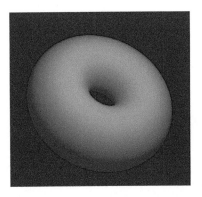

FIGURE 6.4    The Lambert and Phong illumination models on a torus-shaped surface.

An *illumination model* is a combination of lighting types used to determine the color at each point on a surface. Two of the most commonly used illumination models are the Lambert model and the Phong model, illustrated in Figure 6.4. The *Lambert model* uses a combination of ambient and diffuse lighting, particularly appropriate for simulating the appearance of matte or rough surfaces, where most of the light rays meeting the surface are scattered. The *Phong model* uses ambient, diffuse, and specular lighting, and is particularly appropriate for reflective or shiny surfaces. Due to the additional lighting data and calculations required, the Phong model is more computationally intensive than the Lambert model. The strength or sharpness of the shine in the Phong model can be adjusted by parameters stored in the corresponding material, and if the strength of the shine is set to zero, the Phong model generates results identical to the Lambert model.

The magnitude of the effect of a light source at a point depends on the angle at which a ray of light meets a surface. This angle is calculated as the angle between two vectors: the direction vector of the light ray, and a *normal vector*: a vector perpendicular to the surface. Figure 6.5 illustrates normal vectors for multiple surfaces as short line segments. When calculating normal vectors to a surface, one has the option of using either vertex normal vectors or face normal vectors. *Face normal vectors* are perpendicular to the triangles in the mesh used to represent the surface. *Vertex normal vectors* are perpendicular to the

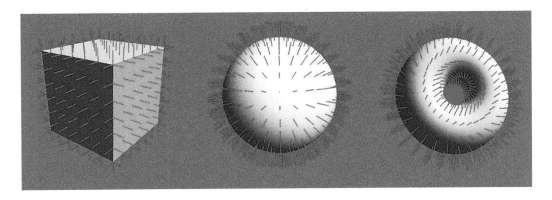

FIGURE 6.5    Normal vectors to a box, a sphere, and a torus.

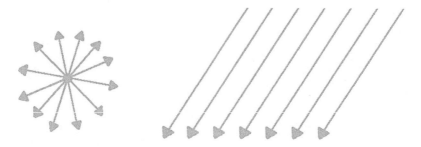

FIGURE 6.6    Directions of emitted light rays for point light (left) and directional light (right).

geometric surface being approximated; the values of these vectors do not depend on the triangulation of the surface, and can be calculated precisely when the parametric function defining the surface is known. For a surface defined by flat sides (such as a box or pyramid), there is no difference between vertex normals and face normals.

Different types of light objects will be used to simulate different sources of light, each of which emits light rays in different patterns. A *Point Light* simulates rays of light being emitted from a single point in all directions, similar to a lightbulb, and incorporates *attenuation*: a decrease in intensity as the distance between the light source and the surface increases. A *Directional Light* simulates a distant light source such as the sun, in which all the light rays are oriented along the same direction and there is no attenuation. (As a result, the position of a directional light has no effect on surfaces that it lights.) These light ray direction patterns are illustrated in Figure 6.6. For simplicity, in this framework, point lights and directional lights will only affect diffuse and specular values, and ambient light contributions will be handled by a separate *Ambient Light* structure, although there is no physical analog for this object.

The choice of using face normal vectors or vertex normal vectors, and the part of the shader program in which light-related calculations appear, define different *shading models*. The original and simplest is the *flat shading model*, in which face normal vectors are used, calculations take place in the vertex shader, and light contribution values are passed along to the fragment shader. The result is a faceted appearance, even on a smooth surface such as a sphere, as illustrated in Figure 6.7. The *Gouraud shading model* uses vertex normal

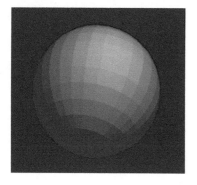

FIGURE 6.7    Rendering a sphere using flat shading (left) and Phong shading (right).

vectors and calculates the effect of light at each vertex in the vertex shader; these values are passed through the graphics pipeline to the fragment shader, leading to interpolated values for each fragment, and resulting in a smoother overall appearance (although there may be visual artifacts along the edges of some triangles). The most computationally intensive example that will be implemented in this framework, and the one that provides the smoothest and most realistic results, is the *Phong shading model* (not to be confused with the Phong illumination model), also illustrated in Figure 6.7. In this shading model, the normal vector data is passed from the vertex shader to the fragment shader, normal vectors are interpolated for each fragment, and the light calculations are performed at that stage.

## 6.2 LIGHT CLASSES

To incorporate lighting effects into the graphics framework, the first step is to create a series of light objects that store the associated data. For simplicity, a base **Light** class will be created that stores data that could be needed by any type of light, including a constant that specifies the type of light (ambient, directional or point). Some lights will require position or direction data, but since the **Light** class will extend the **Object3D** class, this information can be stored in and retrieved from the associated transformation matrix. Extensions of the **Light** class will represent the different types of lights, and their constructors will store values in the relevant fields defined by the base class.

To begin, in the main source folder, create a new package named **light**. In this package, create a new Java class named **Light** with the following code:

```
package light;

import core.Object3D;
import math.Vector;

public class Light extends Object3D
{
    public static int AMBIENT = 1;
    public static int DIRECTIONAL = 2;
    public static int POINT = 3;

    public int lightType;
    public Vector color;
    public Vector attenuation;

    public Light()
    {
        lightType = 0;
        color = new Vector(1, 1, 1);
        attenuation = new Vector(1, 0, 0);
    }
}
```

As previously mentioned and alluded to by the constant values in the **Light** class, there will be three extensions of the class that represent different types of lights: ambient light, directional light, and point light. To implement the class representing ambient light, the simplest of the three as it only uses the color data, in the **light** package create a new Java class named **AmbientLight** with the following code:

```
package light;

import math.Vector;

public class AmbientLight extends Light
{
    public AmbientLight(Vector color)
    {
        lightType = Light.AMBIENT;
        this.color = color;
    }
}
```

Next, you will implement the directional light class. However, you first need to add some functionality to the **Object3D** class that enables you to get and set the direction an object is facing, also called the *forward* direction, which is defined by the orientation of its local negative *z* axis. This concept was originally introduced in the discussion of the look-at matrix in Chapter 5. The **setDirection** method is effectively a local version of the **lookAt** method. To calculate the direction an object is facing, the **getDirection** method requires the rotation component of the mesh's transformation matrix, which is the top-left three-by-three submatrix; this functionality will be provided by a new method called **getRotationMatrix**. To proceed, in the **Object3D** class in the **core** package add the following three methods to the class.

```
// returns 3x3 upper-left submatrix with rotation data
public Matrix getRotationMatrix()
{
    return transform.minor(3,3);
}
public Vector getDirection()
{
    Vector forward = new Vector(0,0,-1);
    return getRotationMatrix().multiplyVector( forward );
}
public void setDirection(Vector direction)
{
    Vector position = getPosition();
    Vector targetPosition = Vector.add(position, direction);
    lookAt( targetPosition );
}
```

With these additions, you are ready to implement the class that represents directional lights. In the **light** package, create a new Java class named **DirectionalLight** with the following code:

```java
package light;

import math.Vector;

public class DirectionalLight extends Light
{
    public DirectionalLight(Vector color, Vector direction)
    {
        lightType = Light.DIRECTIONAL;
        this.color = color;
        setDirection(direction);
    }
}
```

Finally, you will implement the class that represents point lights. The variable **attenuation** stores a list of parameters that will be used when calculating the decrease in light intensity due to increased distance, which will be discussed in more detail later. In the **light** package, create a new Java class named **PointLight** with the following code:

```java
package light;

import math.Vector;

public class PointLight extends Light
{
    public PointLight(Vector color, Vector position,
        Vector attenuation)
    {
        lightType = Light.POINT;
        this.color = color;
        setPosition(position);
        this.attenuation = attenuation;
    }

    // sets default attenuation coefficients
    public PointLight(Vector color, Vector position)
    {
        this(color, position, new Vector(1, 0, 0.1));
    }
}
```

## 6.3 NORMAL VECTORS

Just as working with textures required the addition of a new attribute (representing UV coordinates) to geometry classes, working with lights also requires new attributes, as discussed in the beginning of this chapter, representing vertex normal vectors and face normal vectors. The next step will be to add new attributes containing these two types of vectors to the previously created geometry classes: rectangles, boxes, polygons, and parametric surfaces. The shader code that will be created later in this chapter will access this data through shader variables named **vertexNormal** and **faceNormal**. In the case of rectangles, boxes, and polygons, since the sides of these shapes are flat, these two types of normal vectors are the same. Curved surfaces defined by parametric functions will require slightly more effort to calculate these two types of normal vectors.

### 6.3.1 Rectangles

Since a rectangle is a flat shape aligned with the $xy$-plane, the normal vectors at each vertex all point in the same direction: $\langle 0, 0, 1 \rangle$, aligned with the positive $z$-axis, as illustrated in Figure 6.8.

To implement normal vectors for rectangles, in the **RectangleGeometry** class in the **geometry** package, add the following code under each of the UV components to maintain cohesion:

```
// normal vector
Vector N0 = new Vector(0,0,1);
List normalList = Arrays.asList(N0,N0,N0, N0,N0,N0);
float[] normalData = Vector.flattenList(normalList);
addAttribute("vec3", "vertexNormal", normalData);
addAttribute("vec3", "faceNormal", normalData);
```

### 6.3.2 Boxes

To begin, recall the alignment of the vertices in a box geometry, illustrated in Figure 6.9.

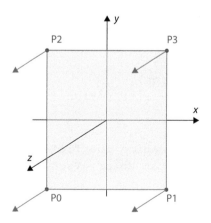

FIGURE 6.8  Normal vectors for a rectangle.

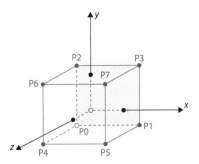

FIGURE 6.9   Vertices in a box geometry.

Since a box has six flat sides, there will be six different normal vectors required for this shape. The right and left sides, as they are perpendicular to the $x$-axis, will have normal vectors $\langle 1, 0, 0\rangle$ and $\langle -1, 0, 0\rangle$. The top and bottom sides, perpendicular to the $y$-axis, will have normal vectors $\langle 0, 1, 0\rangle$ and $\langle 0, -1, 0\rangle$. The front and back sides, perpendicular to the $z$-axis, will have normal vectors $\langle 0, 0, 1\rangle$ and $\langle 0, 0, -1\rangle$. Observe that each corner point is part of three different sides; for example, point P6 is part of the left, top, and front sides. Thus, each corner of the cube may correspond to one of three normal vectors, depending on the triangle being generated in the rendering process. To add normal vector data for this shape, in the **BoxGeometry** class in the **geometry** package, add the following code like you did with the previous class:

```
// normal vectors for x+, x-, y+, y-, z+, z-
Vector N1 = new Vector( 1,   0,   0);
Vector N2 = new Vector(-1,   0,   0);
Vector N3 = new Vector( 0,   1,   0);
Vector N4 = new Vector( 0,  -1,   0);
Vector N5 = new Vector( 0,   0,   1);
Vector N6 = new Vector( 0,   0,  -1);

List normalList = Arrays.asList(
        N1,N1,N1,N1,N1,N1, N2,N2,N2,N2,N2,N2,
        N3,N3,N3,N3,N3,N3, N4,N4,N4,N4,N4,N4,
        N5,N5,N5,N5,N5,N5, N6,N6,N6,N6,N6,N6   );
float[] normalData = Vector.flattenList(normalList);
addAttribute("vec3", "vertexNormal", normalData);
addAttribute("vec3", "faceNormal", normalData);
```

### 6.3.3 Polygons

Just as was the case for rectangles, since polygons are flat shapes aligned with the $xy$-plane, the normal vectors at each vertex are $\langle 0, 0, 1\rangle$. To add normal vector data for polygons, in the **PolygonGeometry** class in the **geometry** package, you will need to add code in three different parts. First, before the **for** loop, add the following code:

```
ArrayList<Vector> normalList   = new ArrayList<Vector>();
Vector normalVector = new Vector(0,0,1);
```

Within the **for** loop, the same line of code is repeated three times because each triangle has three vertices; as with the other attributes, three vectors are appended to the corresponding data array.

```
normalList.add( normalVector );
normalList.add( normalVector );
normalList.add( normalVector );
```

After the **for** loop, add the following code:

```
float[] normalData = Vector.flattenList(normalList);
addAttribute("vec3", "vertexNormal", normalData);
addAttribute("vec3", "faceNormal", normalData);
```

This completes the necessary additions to the **Polygon** class.

### 6.3.4 Parametric Surfaces

Finally, you will add normal vector data for parametric surfaces. Unlike the previous cases, this will involve some calculations. To calculate the face normal vectors for each triangle, you will use the cross product operation, which takes two vectors as input and produces a vector perpendicular to both of the input vectors. Since each triangle is defined by three points P0, P1, P2, one can subtract these points in pairs to create two vectors $v = P1 - P0$ and $w = P2 - P0$ aligned with the edges of the triangle. Then the cross product of $v$ and $w$ results in the desired face normal vector $n$. This calculation is illustrated in Figure 6.10.

To calculate the vertex normal vector at a point P0 on the surface involves the same process, except that the points P1 and P2 used for this calculation are chosen to be very close to P0 in order to more precisely approximate the exact normal to the surface. In particular, assume that the surface is defined by the parametric function S, and that $P0 = S(u, v)$. Let $h$ be a small number, such as $h = 0.0001$. Then define two additional points $P1 = S(u+h, v)$

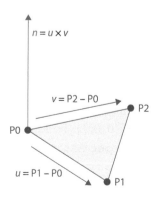

FIGURE 6.10   Calculating the normal vector for a triangle.

and P2 = S(*u*, *v+h*). With the three points P0, P1, and P2, one may then proceed exactly as before to obtain the desired vertex normal vector.

To implement these calculations, you will need to add some methods to the **Vertex** class and the **Surface** class. First, in the **Vertex** class, add the following method under the **unflattenList** method:

```
public static Vector calcNormal(Vector P0, Vector P1, Vector P2)
{
    Vector v1 = Vector.subtract(P1, P0);
    Vector v2 = Vector.subtract(P2, P0);
    Vector normal = Vector.cross(v1, v2);
    normal.setLength(1);
    return normal;
}
```

Next, in the **Surface** class, add the following method under the **getUVs** method:

```
// calculate normal vectors to surface (vertex normals)
public Vector[][] getNormals(
        double uStart, double uEnd, int uResolution,
        double vStart, double vEnd, int vResolution)
{

    Vector[][] normals =
        new Vector[uResolution+1][vResolution+1];
    double deltaU = (uEnd - uStart) / uResolution;
    double deltaV = (vEnd - vStart) / vResolution;
    for (int uIndex = 0; uIndex < uResolution+1; uIndex++)
    {
        for (int vIndex = 0; vIndex < vResolution+1; vIndex++)
        {
            double u = uStart + uIndex * deltaU;
            double v = vStart + vIndex * deltaV;
            double h = 0.0001;
            Vector P0 = function.apply(u, v);
            Vector P1 = function.apply(u+h, v);
            Vector P2 = function.apply(u, v+h);
            normals[uIndex][vIndex] =
                Vector.calcNormal(P0, P1, P2);
        }
    }
    return normals;
}
```

Finally, in the **SurfaceGeometry** class in the **geometry** package, after the method that calculates the contents of the **uvs** list, add the following code, which uses the method to calculate a normal vector from three points as previously described, and populates a list with vertex normal vectors at the position of each vertex.

```
Vector[][] vertexNormals = surface.getNormals(
        uStart, uEnd, uResolution, vStart, vEnd, vResolution);
```

Then, immediately before the nested **for** loop that groups the vertex data into triangles, add the following code:

```
ArrayList<Vector> vertexNormalList =
    new ArrayList<Vector>();
ArrayList<Vector> faceNormalList = new ArrayList<Vector>();
```

Within the nested **for** loop, after data is appended to the **uvList**, add the following code:

```
// vertex normal vectors
Vector nA = vertexNormals[uIndex+0][vIndex+0];
Vector nB = vertexNormals[uIndex+1][vIndex+0];
Vector nD = vertexNormals[uIndex+0][vIndex+1];
Vector nC = vertexNormals[uIndex+1][vIndex+1];
vertexNormalList.addAll( Arrays.asList(nA,nB,nC, nA,nC,nD) );

// face normal vectors
Vector fn0 = Vector.calcNormal(pA, pB, pC);
Vector fn1 = Vector.calcNormal(pA, pC, pD);
faceNormalList.addAll(
    Arrays.asList(fn0,fn0,fn0, fn1,fn1,fn1) );
```

Finally, after the nested **for** loop, add the following lines of code before the vertices are totaled:

```
float[] vertexNormalData =
    Vector.flattenList(vertexNormalList);
float[] faceNormalData = Vector.flattenList(faceNormalList);
addAttribute("vec3", "vertexNormal", vertexNormalData);
addAttribute("vec3", "faceNormal", faceNormalData);
```

Another related change that needs to be made is in the **Geometry** class' **applyMatrix** method, which currently transforms only the position-related data stored in an attribute of a geometry. When transforming a geometry, the normal vector data should also be updated, but only by the rotational part of the transformation (as normal vectors are assumed to be in standard position, with initial point at the origin). This functionality is especially important for cylinder-based shapes, as they include both a surface geometry component and one or two transformed polygon geometry components. To implement this, in the **Geometry** class in the **geometry** package, in the **applyMatrix** method, add the following code directly after the **uploadData** method is called on the vertex positions.

```
// extract the rotation submatrix
Matrix rotationMatrix = matrix.minor(3,3);

// update vertex normal data
float[] oldVertexNormalData =
    attributes.get("vertexNormal").dataArray;
List<Vector> oldVertexNormalList =
    Vector.unflattenList(oldVertexNormalData, 3);
List<Vector> newVertexNormalList =
    new ArrayList<Vector>();
for (Vector oldNormal : oldVertexNormalList)
{
    Vector newNormal = matrix.multiplyVector(oldNormal);
    newVertexNormalList.add( newNormal );
}
float[] newVertexNormalData =
    Vector.flattenList(newVertexNormalList);
attributes.get("vertexNormal").dataArray = newVertexNormalData;
attributes.get("vertexNormal").uploadData();

// update face normal data
float[] oldFaceNormalData =
    attributes.get("faceNormal").dataArray;
List<Vector> oldFaceNormalList =
    Vector.unflattenList(oldFaceNormalData, 3);
List<Vector> newFaceNormalList = new ArrayList<Vector>();
for (Vector oldNormal : oldFaceNormalList)
{
    Vector newNormal = matrix.multiplyVector(oldNormal);
    newFaceNormalList.add( newNormal );
}
float[] newFaceNormalData =
    Vector.flattenList(newFaceNormalList);
attributes.get("faceNormal").dataArray = newFaceNormalData;
attributes.get("faceNormal").uploadData();
```

With these additions to the graphics framework, all geometric objects now include the vertex data that will be needed for lighting-based calculations.

## 6.4 USING LIGHTS IN SHADERS

The next major step in implementing lighting effects is to write a shader to perform the necessary calculations, which will require the data stored in the previously created **Light** class. Since scenes may feature multiple light objects, a natural way to proceed is to create a data structure within the shader to group this information together, analogous to the **Light** class itself. After learning how data is uploaded to a GLSL structure and updating the **Uniform** class as needed, the details of the light calculations will be explained. You will then implement three shaders: the flat shading model, the Lambert illumination model, and the Phong illumination model. While the first of these models uses face normal data in the vertex shader, the latter two models will use Phong shading, where vertex normal data will be interpolated and used in the fragment shader.

## 6.4.1 Structs and Uniforms

In GLSL, data structures are used to group together related data variables as a single unit, thus defining new types. These are created using the keyword **struct**, followed by a list of member variable types and names. For example, a structure to store light-related data will be defined as follows:

```
struct Light
{
    int lightType;
    vec3 color;
    vec3 direction;
    vec3 position;
    vec3 attenuation;
};
```

Following the definition of a struct, variables of this type may be defined in the shader. Fields within a struct are accessed using dot notation; for example, given a **Light** variable named **sun**, the information stored in the **direction** field can be accessed as **sun.direction**. The data for a uniform struct variable cannot be uploaded by a single OpenGL function, so there will be a significant addition to the **Uniform** class corresponding to light-type objects. When storing such an object, the **Uniform** class variable **variableRef** will not store a single uniform variable reference, but rather a collection whose keys are the names of the struct fields and whose values are the corresponding variable references. When uploading data to the GPU, multiple **glUniform**-type functions will be called.

To add this functionality, in the **Uniform** class in the **core** package, add the following import statements:

```
import java.util.HashMap;
import light.*;
```

Add the following line of code after the **variableRef** is declared:

```
// reference for multiple variable locations in program
private HashMap<String, Integer> variableRefMap;
```

Then, modify the **locateVariable** method to the following block of code:

```
// get and store reference for program variable with given name
public void locateVariable(int programRef, String variableName)
{
    if (dataType.equals("Light"))
    {
        variableRefMap = new HashMap<String, Integer>();
        variableRefMap.put("lightType",
            glGetUniformLocation(programRef,
                variableName + ".lightType") );
        variableRefMap.put("color",
            glGetUniformLocation(programRef,
                variableName + ".color") );
        variableRefMap.put("direction",
            glGetUniformLocation(programRef,
                variableName + ".direction") );
        variableRefMap.put("position",
            glGetUniformLocation(programRef,
                variableName + ".position") );
        variableRefMap.put("attenuation",
            glGetUniformLocation(programRef,
                variableName + ".attenuation") );
    }
    else
        variableRef = glGetUniformLocation(programRef,
            variableName);
```

Also in the **Uniform** class, in the **uploadData** method **if-else** block, add the following code:

```
else if (dataType.equals("Light"))
{
    Light L = (Light)data;
    glUniform1i( variableRefMap.get("lightType"),
        (int)L.lightType );
    Vector col = L.color;
    glUniform3f( variableRefMap.get("color"),
        (float)col.values[0], (float)col.values[1],
        (float)col.values[2] );

    Vector dir = L.getDirection();
    glUniform3f( variableRefMap.get("direction"),
        (float)dir.values[0], (float)dir.values[1],
        (float)dir.values[2] );
```

```
    Vector pos = L.getPosition();
    glUniform3f( variableRefMap.get("position"),
        (float)pos.values[0], (float)pos.values[1],
        (float)pos.values[2] );

    Vector att = L.attenuation;
    glUniform3f( variableRefMap.get("attenuation"),
        (float)att.values[0], (float)att.values[1],
        (float)att.values[2] );
}
```

## 6.4.2 Light-Based Materials

In each of the three materials that will be created in this section, key features will be the **Light** struct previously discussed, the declaration of four uniform **Light** variables (this will be the maximum supported by this graphics framework), and a function (named **lightCalc**) to calculate the effect of light sources at a point. In the flat shading material, these elements will be added to the vertex shader, while in the Lambert and Phong materials, these elements will be added to the fragment shader instead.

To begin, you will create the flat shader material. In the **material** package, create a new Java class called **FlatMaterial** containing the following code; the code for the vertex and fragment shaders and for adding uniform objects will be added later.

```
package material;

import math.Vector;
import core.Texture;

public class FlatMaterial extends Material
{
    public FlatMaterial(Texture texture)
    {
        super(
            "./src/material/FlatMaterial.vert",
            "./src/material/FlatMaterial.frag" );
    if (texture == null)
        addUniform("bool", "useTexture", 0);
    else
    {
        addUniform("bool", "useTexture", 1);
        addUniform("sampler2D", "tex",
            new Vector(texture.textureRef, 1));
    }
    locateUniforms();
    addRenderSetting( "doubleSide", true );
    addRenderSetting( "wireframe", false );
    addRenderSetting( "lineWidth", 1 );}
}
```

In the flat shading model, lights are processed in the vertex shader. Thus, create a file named **FlatMaterial.vert** and add the following code:

```
struct Light
{
    // 1 = AMBIENT, 2 = DIRECTIONAL, 3 = POINT
    int lightType;
    // used by all lights
    vec3 color;
    // used by directional lights
    vec3 direction;
    // used by point lights
    vec3 position;
    vec3 attenuation;
};

uniform Light light0;
uniform Light light1;
uniform Light light2;
uniform Light light3;
```

Next, you will implement the **lightCalc** function. The function will be designed so that it may calculate the contributions from a combination of ambient, diffuse, and specular light. In the flat shading and Lambert materials, only ambient and diffuse light contributions are considered, and thus the only parameters required by the **lightCalc** function are the light source itself, and the position and normal vector for a point on the surface. Values for the contributions from each type of light are stored in the variables **ambient**, **diffuse**, and **specular**, each of which is initially set to zero, and then modified as necessary according to the light type.

The calculations for the diffuse component of a directional light and a point light are quite similar. One difference is in the calculation of the light direction vector: for a directional light, this is constant, but for a point light, this is dependent on the position of the light and the position of the point on the surface. Once the light direction vector is known, the contribution of the light source at a point can be calculated. The value of the contribution depends on the angle between the light direction vector and the normal vector to the surface. When this angle is small (close to zero), the contribution of the light source is close to 100%. As the angle approaches 90°, the contribution of the light source approaches 0%. This models the observation that light rays meeting a surface at large angles are scattered, which reduces the intensity of the reflected light. Fortunately, this mathematical relationship is easily captured by the cosine function, as $\cos(0°) = 1$ and $\cos(90°) = 0$. Furthermore, it can be proven that the cosine of the angle between two unit vectors (vectors with length one) is equal to the dot product of the vectors, which can be calculated with the GLSL function **dot**. If the value of the cosine is negative, this indicates that the surface is inclined at an angle away from the light source, in which case the contribution should be set to zero; this will be accomplished with the GLSL function **max**, as you will see.

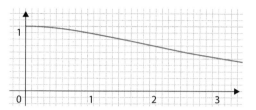

FIGURE 6.11    Attenuation of a light source as a function of distance.

Finally, point lights also incorporate attenuation effects: the intensity of the light should decrease as the distance $d$ between the light source and the surface increases. This effect is modeled mathematically by multiplying the diffuse component by the factor $1/(a + b \cdot d + c \cdot d^2)$, where the coefficients $a$, $b$, $c$ are used to adjust the rate at which the light effect decreases. Figure 6.11 displays a graph of this function for the default attenuation coefficients $a = 1$, $b = 0$, $c = 0.1$, which results in the function $1/(1 + 0 \cdot d + 0.1 \cdot d^2)$. Observe that in the graph, when the distance is at a minimum ($d = 0$) the attenuation factor is 1, and the attenuation is 50% approximately when $d = 3.2$.

To implement the **lightCalc** function, in the vertex shader code, add the following after the declaration of the uniform light variables:

```
vec3 lightCalc(Light light, vec3 pointPosition, vec3 pointNormal)
{
    float ambient = 0;
    float diffuse = 0;
    float specular = 0;
    float attenuation = 1;
    vec3 lightDirection = vec3(0,0,0);

    if ( light.lightType == 1 ) // ambient light
    {
        ambient = 1;
    }
    else if ( light.lightType == 2 ) // directional light
    {
        lightDirection = normalize(light.direction);
    }
    else if ( light.lightType == 3 ) // point light
    {
        lightDirection = normalize(
            pointPosition - light.position);
        float distance = length(light.position - pointPosition);
        attenuation = 1.0 / (light.attenuation[0] +
            light.attenuation[1] * distance +
            light.attenuation[2] * distance * distance);
    }
```

```
if ( light.lightType > 1 ) // directional or point light
{
    pointNormal = normalize(pointNormal);
    diffuse = max( dot(pointNormal, -lightDirection), 0.0 );
    diffuse *= attenuation;
}

return light.color * (ambient + diffuse + specular);
}
```

With these additions in place, you are ready to complete the vertex shader for the flat shading material. In addition to the standard calculations involving the vertex position and UV coordinates, you also need to calculate the total contribution from all of the lights. If data for a light variable has not been set, then the light's **lightType** variable defaults to zero, in which case the value returned by **lightCalc** is also zero. Before being used in the **lightCalc** function, the model matrix needs to be applied to the position data, and the rotational part of the model matrix needs to be applied to the normal data. The total light contribution is passed from the vertex shader to the fragment shader for use in determining the final color of each fragment. In the vertex shader code, add the following code after the body of the **lightCalc** function.

```
uniform mat4 projectionMatrix;
uniform mat4 viewMatrix;
uniform mat4 modelMatrix;
in vec3 vertexPosition;
in vec2 vertexUV;
in vec3 faceNormal;
out vec2 UV;
out vec3 light;

void main()
{
    gl_Position = projectionMatrix * viewMatrix * modelMatrix
                    * vec4(vertexPosition, 1);
    UV = vertexUV;
    // calculate total effect of lights on color
    vec3 position = vec3(
        modelMatrix * vec4(vertexPosition, 1) );
    vec3 normal = normalize( mat3(modelMatrix) * faceNormal );
    light = vec3(0,0,0);
    light += lightCalc( light0, position, normal );
    light += lightCalc( light1, position, normal );
    light += lightCalc( light2, position, normal );
    light += lightCalc( light3, position, normal );
}
```

Next, you need to add the code for the flat material fragment shader. In addition to the standard elements of past fragment shaders, this new shader also uses the light value calculated in the vertex shader when determining the final color of a fragment. This material (as well as the two that follow) will include an optional texture parameter. If this parameter is not **null**, it will cause a shader variable **useTexture** to be set to true, in which case a color sampled from the supplied texture will be combined with the material's base color. To implement this, create a new file named **FlatMaterial.frag** with the following code:

```
uniform vec3 baseColor;
uniform bool useTexture;
uniform sampler2D tex;
in vec2 UV;
in vec3 light;
out vec4 fragColor;
void main()
{
    vec4 color = vec4(baseColor, 1.0);
    if ( useTexture )
        color *= texture( tex, UV );
    color *= vec4( light, 1 );
    fragColor = color;
}
```

Finally, you must add the necessary uniform objects to the material using the **addUniform** method. To proceed, before the method **locateUniforms** is called, add the following code. (The data for the light objects will be supplied by the **Renderer** class, handled similarly to the model, view, and projection matrix data.)

```
addUniform( "vec3", "baseColor", new Vector(1,1,1) );
addUniform( "Light", "light0", null );
addUniform( "Light", "light1", null );
addUniform( "Light", "light2", null );
addUniform( "Light", "light3", null );
```

Next, add the following code that sets the remaining uniform variables, depending on whether or not a texture is being utilized.

```
if (texture == null)
    addUniform("bool", "useTexture", 0);
else
{
    addUniform("bool", "useTexture", 1);
    addUniform("sampler2D", "tex",
        new Vector(texture.textureRef, 1));
}
```

This completes the code required for the **FlatMaterial** class.

Next, to create the Lambert material, make a copy of the **FlatMaterial** class and name the copy **LambertMaterial**. Within this file, change the name of the class **LambertMaterial** as well as the shader file paths. Since the Phong shading model will be used in this material (as opposed to the Gouraud shading model), the light-based calculations will occur in the fragment shader. Therefore, create two additional files named **LambertMaterial.frag** and **LambertMaterial.vert**. Move the code inside **FlatMaterial.vert** involving the definition of the **Light** struct, the declaration of the four **Light** variables, and the function **lightCalc** from the vertex shader to the beginning of the fragment shader. Then, since vertex normals will be used instead of face normals, and since the position and normal data must be transmitted to the fragment shader for use in the **lightCalc** function there, change the code for the vertex shader to the following:

```
uniform mat4 projectionMatrix;
uniform mat4 viewMatrix;
uniform mat4 modelMatrix;
in vec3 vertexPosition;
in vec2 vertexUV;
in vec3 vertexNormal;
out vec3 position;
out vec2 UV;
out vec3 normal;
void main()
{
    gl_Position = projectionMatrix * viewMatrix * modelMatrix
                    * vec4(vertexPosition, 1);
    position = vec3( modelMatrix * vec4(vertexPosition, 1) );
    UV = vertexUV;
    normal = normalize( mat3(modelMatrix) * vertexNormal );
}
```

In the Lambert material fragment shader, the light calculations will take place and be combined with the base color (and optionally, texture color data). Replace the fragment shader code following the declaration of the **lightCalc** function with the following:

```
uniform vec3 baseColor;
uniform bool useTexture;
uniform sampler2D tex;
in vec3 position;
in vec2 UV;
in vec3 normal;
out vec4 fragColor;

void main()
{
    vec4 color = vec4(baseColor, 1.0);
    if ( useTexture )
        color *= texture( tex, UV );
```

```
    // calculate total effect of lights on color
    vec3 total = vec3(0,0,0);
    total += lightCalc( light0, position, normal );
    total += lightCalc( light1, position, normal );
    total += lightCalc( light2, position, normal );
    total += lightCalc( light3, position, normal );
    color *= vec4( total, 1 );
    fragColor = color;
}
```

This completes the required code for the **LambertMaterial** class.

Finally, you will create the Phong material, which includes specular light contributions. This calculation is similar to the diffuse light calculation, involving the angle between two vectors (which can be calculated using a dot product), but in this case, the vectors of interest are the reflection of the light direction vector and the vector from the viewer or virtual camera to the surface point. These elements are illustrated in Figure 6.12. First, the light direction vector *d* impacts the surface at a point. Then the vector *d* is reflected around the normal vector *n*, producing the reflection vector *r*. The vector from the virtual camera to the surface is indicated by *v*. The angle of interest is indicated by *a*; it is the angle between the vector *r* and the vector *v*.

The impact of specular light on an object is typically adjusted by two parameters: *strength*, a multiplicative factor which can be used to make the overall specular light effect appear brighter or dimmer, and *shininess*, which causes the highlighted region to be more blurry or more sharply defined, which corresponds to how reflective the surface will be perceived. Figure 6.13 illustrates the effects of increasing the shininess value by a factor of 4 in each image from the left to the right.

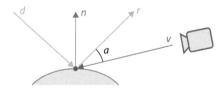

FIGURE 6.12    The vectors used in the calculation of specular highlights.

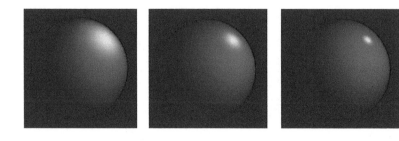

FIGURE 6.13    The effect of increasing shininess in specular lighting.

To implement these changes, make a copy of the file **LambertMaterial** and name the copy **PhongMaterial**. Within this file, change the name of the class to **PhongMaterial**. Afterwards, create the required shader file copies to be supplied; named, **PhongMaterial.vert** and **PhongMaterial.frag**. To perform the necessary calculations in the **lightCalc** function, it must take in additional data. Before the declaration of the **lightCalc** function inside the **PhongMaterial.frag** file add the following uniform declarations (so that this function can access the associated values):

```
uniform vec3 viewPosition;
uniform float specularStrength;
uniform float shininess;
```

Then, within the **lightCalc** function, in the block of code corresponding to the condition **light.lightType > 1**, after the diffuse value is calculated, add the following code that will calculate the specular component when needed (when there is also a nonzero diffuse component):

```
if (diffuse > 0)
{
    vec3 viewDirection =
        normalize(viewPosition - pointPosition);
    vec3 reflectDirection =
        reflect(lightDirection, pointNormal);
    specular = max( dot(viewDirection, reflectDirection), 0.0 );
    specular = specularStrength * pow(specular, shininess);
}
```

Finally, in the section of the **PhongMaterial** class code where the uniform data is added, add the following lines of code, which supplies default values for the specular lighting parameters.

```
addUniform("vec3", "viewPosition", new Vector(0,0,0) );
addUniform("float", "specularStrength", 1.0f);
addUniform("float", "shininess", 32.0f);
```

This completes the required code for the **PhongMaterial** class.

## 6.5 RENDERING SCENES WITH LIGHTS

In this section, you will update the **Renderer** class to extract the list of **Light** objects that have been added to a scene, and supply that information to the corresponding uniforms. Following that, you will create a scene featuring all three types of lights and all three types of materials. To begin, in the **Renderer** class in the **core** package, add the following import statement:

```
import light.*;
```

Next, during the rendering process, a list of lights must be extracted from the scene graph structure. This will be accomplished in the same way that the list of mesh objects is extracted: by filtering the list of descendents of the root of the scene graph. Furthermore, since data for four lights is expected by the shader, if less than four lights are present, then default **Light** objects will be created (which result in no contribution to the overall lighting of the scene) and added to the list. To proceed, in the **render** method, after the **meshList** variable is created, add the following code:

```java
// extract list of all Light objects in scene
ArrayList<Light> lightList = new ArrayList<Light>();
for (Object3D obj : descendentList)
    if (obj instanceof Light)
        lightList.add( (Light)obj );
// scenes support 4 lights; precisely 4 must be present
while ( lightList.size() < 4 )
    lightList.add( new Light() );
```

Next, for all light-based materials, you must set the data for the four uniform objects referencing lights; these materials can be identified during the rendering stage by checking if there is a uniform object stored with the key "light0." Additionally, for the Phong material, you must set the data for the camera position; this case can be identified by checking for a uniform under the key "viewPosition." This can be implemented by adding the following code in the **for** loop that iterates over **meshList**, directly after the matrix uniform data is set.

```java
// if material uses light data, add lights from list
if ( mesh.material.uniforms.containsKey("light0") )
{
    for (int lightNumber = 0; lightNumber < 4; lightNumber++)
    {
        String lightName = "light" + lightNumber;
        Light lightObject = lightList.get(lightNumber);
        mesh.material.uniforms.get(lightName).data
            = lightObject;
    }
}
// add camera position if needed (specular lighting)
if ( mesh.material.uniforms.containsKey("viewPosition") )
    mesh.material.uniforms.get("viewPosition").data =
        camera.getWorldPosition();
```

With these additions to the graphics framework, you are ready to create an example. To fully test all the classes you have created so far in this chapter, you will create a scene that includes all the light types (ambient, directional, and point), as well as all the material types (flat, Lambert, and Phong). When you are finished, you will see a scene containing three

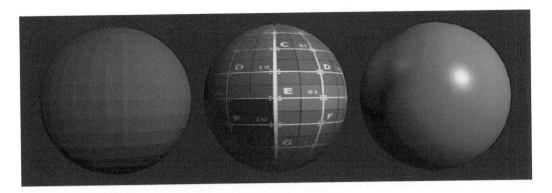

FIGURE 6.14    Rendered scene with all light types and material types.

spheres, similar to that in Figure 6.14. From left to right is a sphere with a red flat-shaded material, a sphere with a textured Lambert material, and a sphere with a blue-gray Phong material. The scene also includes a dark gray ambient light, a white directional light, and a red point light. The latter two light types and their colors may be guessed by the specular light colors on the third sphere and the amount of the sphere that is lit by each of the lights; the point light illuminates less of the sphere due to its nearness to the sphere.

To begin, you will first make some additions to the **Test_Template** class for future convenience. In this file, add the following import statement:

```
import light.*;
```

Next, make a copy of the template file and name it **Test_6_1**. In this new class, in the **initialize** method, replace the code starting from the line where the camera object is created, with the following code, which will set up the main scene.

```
camera.setPerspective(60, 800/600f, 0.1, 1000 );

rig = new MovementRig();
rig.attach( camera );
rig.setPosition( new Vector(0.5, 1, 4) );
scene.add( rig );

Mesh grid = new GridHelper(10,10, new Vector(1,1,0), new
Vector(1,1,1), 2);
grid.rotateX(-Math.PI/2, true);
scene.add( grid );

Mesh axes = new AxesHelper(2, 8);
axes.translate(0, 0.01, 0, true);
scene.add( axes );

Light ambient = new AmbientLight( new Vector(0.1, 0.1, 0.1) );
scene.add( ambient );
```

```
Light directionalLight = new DirectionalLight(
        new Vector(0.8, 0.8, 0.8), new Vector(-1, -1, -2) );
scene.add( directionalLight );

Light pointLight = new PointLight(
        new Vector(0.9, 0, 0), new Vector(1, 1, 0.8) );
scene.add( pointLight );

directionalLight.setPosition( new Vector(3,2,0) );

Geometry sphereGeometry = new SphereGeometry();

Material flatMaterial = new FlatMaterial(null);
flatMaterial.uniforms.get("baseColor").data =
        new Vector(0.6, 0.2, 0.2);
Mesh sphere1 = new Mesh(sphereGeometry, flatMaterial);
sphere1.setPosition( new Vector(-2.2, 0, 0) );
scene.add( sphere1 );

Material lambertMaterial = new LambertMaterial(
        new Texture("images/grid.png") );
Mesh sphere2 = new Mesh(sphereGeometry, lambertMaterial);
sphere2.setPosition( new Vector(0, 0, 0) );
scene.add( sphere2 );

Material phongMaterial = new PhongMaterial(null);
phongMaterial.uniforms.get("baseColor").data =
        new Vector(0.5, 0.5, 1);
Mesh sphere3 = new Mesh(sphereGeometry, phongMaterial);
sphere3.setPosition( new Vector(2.2, 0, 0) );
scene.add( sphere3 );
```

Finally, change the last line of code in the file to the following, to make the window large enough to easily see all three spheres simultaneously:

```
new Test_6_1().run(1600,1200);
```

When you run this program, you should see an image similar to that in Figure 6.14.

## 6.6 EXTRA COMPONENTS

In Chapter 4, the **AxesHelper** and **GridHelper** classes were introduced to help provide a sense of orientation and scale within a scene by creating simple meshes. In the same spirit, in this section you will create two additional classes, **PointLightHelper** and **DirectionalLightHelper**, to visualize the position of point lights and the direction of directional lights, respectively. Figure 6.15 illustrates the two helpers added to the scene from the previous test example. Note that a wireframe diamond shape is present at the

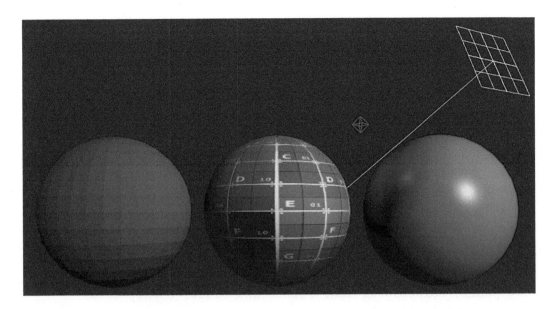

FIGURE 6.15   Objects illustrating the properties of point lights and directional lights.

location of the point light, and a small wireframe grid with a perpendicular ray illustrates the direction of the directional light. Furthermore, in both cases, the color of the helper objects is equal to the color of the associated lights.

First you will implement the directional light helper, which is a grid helper object with an additional line segment added. To proceed, in the **extras** package, create a new Java class named **DirectionalLightHelper** containing the following code:

```java
package extras;

import light.DirectionalLight;
import geometry.Geometry;
import math.Vector;

public class DirectionalLightHelper extends GridHelper
{
    public DirectionalLightHelper(DirectionalLight light)
    {
        super(1, 4, light.color, new Vector(1,1,1), 1);

        Geometry line = new Geometry();
        float[] posData = new float[] {0,0,0, 0,0,-10};
        line.addAttribute("vec3", "vertexPosition", posData);
        float[] colData = new float[] {1,1,0, 0,0,0};
        line.addAttribute("vec3", "vertexColor", colData);
        line.vertexCount = 2;
        this.geometry.merge(line);
    }
}
```

Next, you will implement the point light helper, which is a wireframe sphere geometry whose resolution parameters are small enough that the sphere becomes an octahedron. To proceed, in the **extras** package, create a new Java class named **PointLightHelper** containing the following code:

```java
package extras;

import core.Mesh;
import light.PointLight;
import geometry.SphereGeometry;
import material.SurfaceMaterial;
import math.Vector;

public class PointLightHelper extends Mesh
{
    public PointLightHelper(PointLight light, double size,
        int lineWidth)
    {
        super( new SphereGeometry(size, 4, 2),
            new SurfaceMaterial() );

        this.material.uniforms.get("baseColor").data =
            light.color;
        this.material.renderSettings.get("wireframe").data =
            true;
        this.material.renderSettings.get("doubleSide").data =
            true;
        this.material.renderSettings.get("lineWidth").data =
            lineWidth;
    }

    public PointLightHelper(PointLight light)
    {
        this(light, 0.1, 1);
    }
}
```

Next, you will test these helper objects out by adding them to the previous test example. As an extra feature, you will also illustrate the dynamic lighting effects of the graphics framework and learn how to keep the light source and helper objects in sync. In the **Test_6_1** class, add the following the variable declarations at the class level so that the lights can be accessed in the **update** method later.

```java
public DirectionalLight directionalLight;
public PointLight pointLight;
```

Next, change the code where the directional and point lights are created to the following:

```
directionalLight = new DirectionalLight(
        new Vector(0.8, 0.8, 0.8), new Vector(-1, -1, -2) );
scene.add( directionalLight );

pointLight = new PointLight(
        new Vector(0.9, 0, 0), new Vector(1, 1, 0.8) );
scene.add( pointLight );
```

Then, also in the **initialize** method after the code that you just modified, add the following. Note that the helper objects are added to their corresponding lights rather than directly to the scene. This approach takes advantage of the scene graph structure and guarantees that the transformations of each pair will stay synchronized. In addition, the position of the directional light has been set. This causes no change in the effects of the directional light; it has been included to position the directional light helper object at a convenient location that does not obscure the other objects in the scene.

```
Mesh directionalHelper =
    new DirectionalLightHelper(directionalLight);
directionalLight.setPosition( new Vector(3,2,0) );
directionalLight.add( directionalHelper );

Mesh pointHelper =
    new PointLightHelper( pointLight );
pointLight.add( pointHelper );
```

Finally, you will add some code that makes the point light move up and down while the directional light tilts from left to right. In the **update** method, add the following code:

```
directionalLight.setDirection(
    new Vector(-1, Math.sin(0.7*time), -2) );
pointLight.setPosition(
    new Vector(1, Math.sin(time), 0.8) );
```

When you run the program, you should see the helper objects move as described, and the lighting on the spheres in the scene will also change accordingly.

## 6.7 BUMP MAPPING

Another effect that can be accomplished with the addition of lights is *bump mapping*: a technique for simulating details on the surface of an object by altering the normal vectors and using the adjusted vectors in lighting calculations. This additional normal vector detail is stored in a texture called a *bump map* or a *normal map*, in which the $(r, g, b)$ values at each point correspond to the $(x, y, z)$ values of a normal vector. This concept is illustrated in Figure 6.16. The left image in the figure shows a colored texture of a brick wall. The middle image in the figure shows the associated grayscale *height map*, in which light colors

FIGURE 6.16   A color texture, height map texture, and normal map texture for a brick wall.

represent a large amount of displacement in the perpendicular direction, while dark colors represent a small amount. In this example, the white regions correspond to the bricks, which extrude slightly from the wall, while the darker regions correspond to the mortar between the bricks, which here appears pressed into the wall to a greater extent. The right image in the figure represents the normal map. Points that are shades of red represent normal vectors mainly oriented toward the positive x-axis, while green and blue amounts correspond to the y-axis and z-axis directions, respectively. Observe that in the normal map for this example, the top edge of each brick appears to be light green, while the right edge appears to be pink.

When normal map data is combined with pre-existing normal data in the fragment shader, and the result is used in light calculations, the object in the resulting scene will appear to have geometric features that are not actually present in the vertex data. This is illustrated in Figure 6.17, where the bump map from Figure 6.16 has been applied to a rectangle geometry, and is lit by a point light from two different positions. The light and dark regions surrounding each brick create an illusion of depth even though the mesh itself is perfectly flat.

When a color texture and a bump map are used in combination, the results are subtle but significantly increase the realism of the scene. This is particularly evident in an interactive scene with dynamic lighting – a scene containing lights whose position, direction, or other properties change.

FIGURE 6.17   A normal map applied to a rectangle, with point light source on the upper-left (left) and upper right (right).

To implement bump mapping is fairly straightforward. The following modifications should be carried out for both the files **LambertMaterial**, **PhongMaterial** and both of their respective shader files in the **material** package.

In the fragment shader inside both files, before the **main** function, add the following uniform variable declarations.

```
uniform bool useBumpTexture;
uniform sampler2D bumpTexture;
uniform float bumpStrength;
```

If **useBumpTexture** is set to **true**, then the normal data encoded within the bump texture will be multiplied by the strength parameter and added to the normal vector to produce a new normal vector. To implement this, in the **main** function in the fragment shader, change the lines of code involving the variable **total** (used for calculating the total light contribution) to the following:

```
vec3 bNormal = normal;
if (useBumpTexture)
    bNormal += bumpStrength *
        vec3(texture( bumpTexture, UV ));
vec3 total = vec3(0,0,0);
total += lightCalc( light0, position, bNormal );
total += lightCalc( light1, position, bNormal );
total += lightCalc( light2, position, bNormal );
total += lightCalc( light3, position, bNormal );
color *= vec4( total, 1 );
```

Finally, you need to add the corresponding uniform data. Since texture slot 1 is already in use by the shader, texture slot 2 will be reserved for the bump texture. In the main files before the function **locateUniforms** is called, add the following line of code (which indicates that by default, texture materials do not use bump mapping textures).

```
addUniform("bool", "useBumpTexture", 0);
```

Next, add the following method, which can be used for adding bump mapping data to a material:

```
public void addBumpData(Texture bumpTexture, float bumpStrength)
{
    uniforms.get("useBumpTexture").data = 1;
    addUniform("sampler2D", "bumpTexture",
        new Vector(bumpTexture.textureRef, 2));
    addUniform("float", "bumpStrength", bumpStrength);
    locateUniforms();
}
```

With these additions, the graphics framework can now support bump mapping. To create an example, you can use the color and normal map image files provided with this library;

alternatively, bump maps or normal maps may be easily found with an image-based internet search, or produced from height maps using graphics editing software such as The GNU Image Manipulation Program (GIMP), freely available at http://gimp.org.

To proceed, make a copy of the **Test_Template** class and name it **Test_6_2**. In this new file, in the **initialize** method, replace the code after the line where the camera object is created, with the following code:

```
camera.setPerspective(60, 800/600f, 0.1, 1000 );

rig = new MovementRig();
rig.attach( camera );
rig.setPosition( new Vector(0,0,2.5) );
scene.add( rig );

Light ambientLight = new AmbientLight(
    new Vector(0.1, 0.1, 0.1) );
scene.add( ambientLight );

Light pointLight = new PointLight(
    new Vector(1,1,1), new Vector(1.2, 1.2, 0.3) );
scene.add( pointLight );

Geometry geometry = new RectangleGeometry(2,2);
LambertMaterial bumpMaterial = new LambertMaterial(
    new Texture("images/brick-color.png") );
bumpMaterial.addBumpData(
    new Texture("images/brick-bump.png"), 1.0f );

mesh = new Mesh(geometry, bumpMaterial);
scene.add(mesh);
```

When you run the application, you should see a scene similar to that in Figure 6.18. To fully explore the effects of bump mapping, you may want to add a movement rig, animate the position of the light along a path (similar to the previous example), or apply the material to a different geometric surface, such as a sphere.

FIGURE 6.18   Combining color texture with normal map texture.

## 6.8 BLOOM AND GLOW EFFECTS

In this section, you will learn how to implement light-inspired postprocessing effects. The first of these is called *light bloom*, or just *bloom*, which simulates the effect of an extremely bright light overloading the sensors in a real-world camera, causing the edges of bright regions to blur beyond their natural borders. Figure 6.19 illustrates a scene containing a number of crates in front of a simulated light source. The left side of the figure shows the scene without a bloom effect, and the right side shows the scene with the bloom effect, creating the illusion of very bright lights.

A similar combination of postprocessing filters can be used to create a glow effect, in which objects appear to radiate a given color. Figure 6.20 illustrates a scene similar to Figure 6.19, but with the background light source removed, and each of the three crates

FIGURE 6.19   **Light bloom postprocessing effect.**

FIGURE 6.20   **Glow postprocessing effect.**

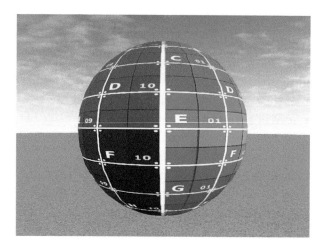

FIGURE 6.21 Default scene with no postprocessing effects.

appears to be glowing a different color. Most notably, in contrast to the bloom effect, the colors used for glow do not need to appear in the original scene.

These techniques require three new postprocessing effects: brightness filtering, blurring, and additive blending. These effects will be created in the same style used in the section on postprocessing in Chapter 5, starting from the template effect file. To prepare for testing these effects, make a copy of the file **Test_5_12** and name it **Test_6_3**. After writing the code for each effect, you can test it in the application by adding the import statement corresponding to the effect and changing the effect that is added to the postprocessor. Recall that if no effects are added to the postprocessor, then the original scene is rendered, illustrated in Figure 6.21; this will serve as a baseline for visual comparison with the postprocessing effects that follow.

First you will create the brightness filter effect, which only renders the pixels with a certain brightness, as illustrated in Figure 6.22.

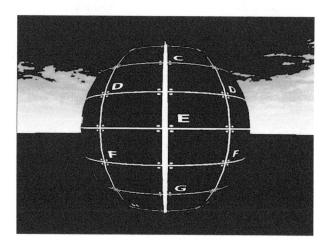

FIGURE 6.22 Brightness filter postprocessing effect.

This effect is accomplished by only rendering a fragment if the sum of the red, green, and blue components is greater than a given threshold value; otherwise, the fragment is discarded. You will add the threshold value as a parameter in the class constructor, and create a corresponding uniform variable in the shader and uniform object in the class. To implement this, in the **effects** package, make a copy of the **Effect** class as well as the fragment shader file and name them **BrightFilterEffect** and **BrightFilterEffect. frag**. In the new Java class, change the name of the class to **BrightFilterEffect**, change the path to the fragment shader and change the initialization method declaration to the following:

```
public BrightFilterEffect(float threshold)
```

Next, change the fragment shader code to the following:

```
in vec2 UV;
uniform sampler2D tex;
uniform float threshold;
out vec4 fragColor;

void main()
{
    vec4 color = texture(tex, UV);
    if (color.r + color.g + color.b < threshold)
        fragColor = vec4(0,0,0,1);
    else
        fragColor = color;
}
```

Finally, add the following line of code near the end of the Java class file, before the **locateUniforms** method is called.

```
addUniform("float", "threshold", threshold);
```

This completes the code for the brightness filter effect; recall that you may use the file **Test_6_3** to test this effect, in which case you should see a result similar to Figure 6.22. Note to make sure to change the instantiation at the very bottom of the class to Test_6_3.

The next effect you will create is a blur effect, which blends the colors of adjacent pixels within a given radius. For computational efficiency, this is typically performed in two passes: first, a weighted average of pixel colors is performed along the horizontal direction (called a *horizontal blur*), and then these results are passed into a second shader where a weighted average of pixel colors is performed along the vertical direction (called a *vertical blur*). Figure 6.23 shows the results of applying the horizontal and vertical blur effects separately to the base scene, while Figure 6.24 shows the results of applying these effects in sequence, resulting in blur in all directions.

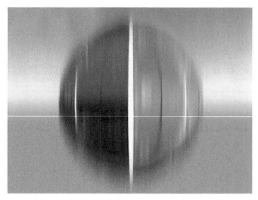

FIGURE 6.23 Horizontal blur (left) and vertical blur (right).

To create the horizontal blur effect, you will sample the pixels within the bounds specified by a parameter named **blurRadius**. Since textures are sampled using UV coordinates, the shader will also need the dimensions of the rendered image (a parameter named **textureSize**) to calculate the pixel-to-UV coordinate conversion factor (which is **1/textureSize**). Then, within the fragment shader, a **for** loop will calculate a weighted average of colors along this line, with the greatest weight applied to the pixel at the original UV coordinates, and the weights decreasing linearly toward the ends of the sample region. The sum of these colors is normalized by dividing by the sum of the weights, which is equal to the alpha component of the sum (since the original alpha component at each point equals to one). To implement this, in the **effects** package, make a copy of the **Effect** class, **Effect.frag** and name them **HorizontalBlurEffect** and **HorizontalBlurEffect.frag**. In the new class, change the name of the class to

FIGURE 6.24 A combined two-pass blur postprocessing effect.

**HorizontalBlurEffect** as well as the fragment shader file path, and change the initialization function declaration to the following:

```
public HorizontalBlurEffect(Vector textureSize, int blurRadius)
```

Next, add these two lines of code before the **locateUniforms** method is called:

```
addUniform("vec2", "textureSize", textureSize);
addUniform("int", "blurRadius", blurRadius);
```

Finally, change the fragment shader code to the following:

```
in vec2 UV;
uniform sampler2D tex;
uniform vec2 textureSize;
uniform int blurRadius;
out vec4 fragColor;
void main()
{
    vec2 pixelToTextureCoords = 1 / textureSize;
    vec4 averageColor = vec4(0,0,0,0);
    for (int offsetX = -blurRadius; offsetX <= blurRadius;
            offsetX++)
    {
        float weight = blurRadius - abs(offsetX) + 1;
        vec2 offsetUV = vec2(offsetX, 0) * pixelToTextureCoords;
        averageColor += texture(tex, UV + offsetUV)
            * weight;
    }
    averageColor /= averageColor.a;
    fragColor = averageColor;
}
```

This completes the code for the horizontal blur effect. The vertical blur effect works in the same way, except that the texture is sampled along vertical lines. To create this effect, make a copy of the **HorizontalBlurEffect** class and its fragment shader, name them **VerticalBlurEffect** and **VerticalBlurEffect.frag**, respectively. In the new Java class, change the name of the class to **VerticalBlurEffect** as well as the fragment shader file path. The only other change that needs to be made is the for loop in the fragment shader, which should be changed to the following:

```
for (int offsetY = -blurRadius; offsetY <= blurRadius; offsetY++)
{
    float weight = blurRadius - abs(offsetY) + 1;
    vec2 offsetUV = vec2(0, offsetY) * pixelToTextureCoords;
    averageColor += texture(tex, UV + offsetUV) * weight;
}
```

At this point, the blur shader effects are complete, and can be applied individually or in sequence to create images with effects similar to those seen in Figures 6.23 and 6.24.

The next effect you will create is an additive blend effect, where an additional texture is overlaid on a rendered scene, using a weighted sum of the individual pixel colors. In some applications, color values are multiplied together; this is particularly useful for shading, as the component values of a color are between zero and one, and multiplying by values in this range decreases values and darkens the associated colors. Alternatively, adding color components increases values and brightens the associated colors, which is particularly appropriate when simulating light-based effects. This effect is illustrated in Figure 6.25, where the original scene is additively blended with the grid texture.

To implement this, in the **effects** package, make a copy of the **Effect** class and fragment shader and name them **AdditiveBlendEffect** and **AdditiveBlendEffect.frag**, respectively. In the new Java class, change the name of the class to **AdditiveBlendEffect** as change the fragment shader file path accordingly. Next, change the initialization method declaration to the following:

```
public AdditiveBlendEffect(Texture blendTexture,
    float originalStrength, float blendStrength)
```

Next, add the following three lines of code right before **locateUniforms** is called:

```
addUniform("sampler2D", "blendTexture",
    new Vector(blendTexture.textureRef, 2));
addUniform("float", "originalStrength", originalStrength);
addUniform("float", "blendStrength", blendStrength);
```

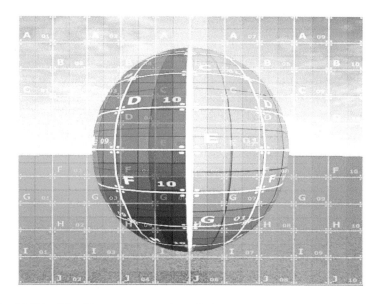

FIGURE 6.25   Additive blending postprocessing effect.

Note that since texture slot 1 is used for the original texture, texture slot two will be reserved for the blended texture. Lastly, in the fragment shader file, replace the code with the following block:

```
in vec2 UV;
uniform sampler2D tex;
uniform sampler2D blendTexture;
uniform float originalStrength;
uniform float blendStrength;
out vec4 fragColor;
void main()
{
    vec4 originalColor = texture(tex, UV);
    vec4 blendColor = texture(blendTexture, UV);
    vec4 color = originalStrength * originalColor +
                 blendStrength * blendColor;
    fragColor = color;
}
```

With these additions, the additive blend shader effect is complete.

To combine these effects to create a light bloom effect, assuming that all the necessary imports have been added to **Test_6_3**, add effects to the postprocessor object as follows:

```
postprocessor.addEffect( new BrightFilterEffect(2.4f) );
postprocessor.addEffect( new HorizontalBlurEffect(
    new Vector(800,600), 30 ) );
postprocessor.addEffect( new VerticalBlurEffect(
    new Vector(800,600), 30 ) );
// access results of first render pass (original scene)
Texture mainSceneTex =
    postprocessor.renderTargetList.get(0).texture;
postprocessor.addEffect( new AdditiveBlendEffect(
    mainSceneTex, 2, 1) );
```

Note that the results of the first render pass (the original scene) are accessed through the postprocessor object and blended with the results of the bright filtered light after the light has been blurred. Running this application will result in an image similar to that shown in Figure 6.26.

Next, you will use these shaders to create a glow effect. One method to implement glow is to use a second scene, referred to here as the glow scene, containing only the objects that should glow. (This is analogous to the brightness filter step used in creating the light bloom effect.) The objects in the glow scene should use the same geometry data and transform matrices as their counterparts in the original scene, but in the glow scene they will be rendered with a solid-colored material corresponding to the desired glow color.

FIGURE 6.26   Light bloom postprocessing effect.

Two postprocessing objects are then used to accomplish the glow effect. The first renders the glow scene, applies a blur filter, and stores the result in a render target (accomplished by setting the **finalRenderTarget** parameter). The second renders the original scene, and then applies an additive blend effect using the results from the first postprocessor. Creating a red glow effect applied to the sphere in the main scene in this section will produce an image similar to Figure 6.27.

To implement this example, make a copy of the file **Test_6_3** and name it **Test_6_4**. In the class level, add the two following properties so they may be accessed in the update method:

```
public Postprocessor glowPass, comboPass;
```

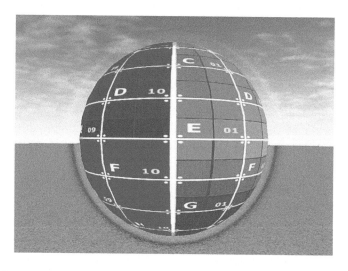

FIGURE 6.27   Glow postprocessing effect.

In the **initialize** method replace all of the code involving postprocessing with the following code:

```
// glow scene
Scene glowScene = new Scene();
Material redMaterial = new SurfaceMaterial();
redMaterial.uniforms.get("baseColor").data = new Vector(1,0,0);
Mesh glowSphere = new Mesh(sphereGeometry, redMaterial);
glowSphere.transform = sphere.transform;
glowScene.add( glowSphere );

// glow postprocessing
Vector size = new Vector(800, 600);
RenderTarget glowTarget = new RenderTarget( size );
glowPass = new Postprocessor(renderer, glowScene,
    camera, glowTarget);
glowPass.addEffect( new HorizontalBlurEffect(size, 50) );
glowPass.addEffect( new VerticalBlurEffect(size, 50) );

// combining results of glow effect with main scene
comboPass = new Postprocessor(renderer, scene, camera, null);
comboPass.addEffect( new AdditiveBlendEffect(
    glowTarget.texture, 1, 3) );
```

Finally, replace the code in the update method with the following:

```
glowPass.render();
comboPass.render();
```

Running this application should produce a result similar to Figure 6.27. If desired, the intensity of the glow can be changed by altering the value of the **blendStrength** parameter in the additive blend effect.

## 6.9 SHADOWS

In this section, you will add shadow rendering functionality to the graphics framework. In addition to adding further realism to a scene, shadows can also be fundamental for estimating relative positions between objects. For example, the left side of Figure 6.28 shows a scene containing a ground and a number of crates; it is difficult to determine whether the crates are resting on the ground. The right side of Figure 6.28 adds shadow effects, which provide visual cues to the viewer so that they may gain a better understanding of the arrangement of the objects in the scene.

### 6.9.1 Theoretical Background

In this graphics framework, shadows will be based on a single directional light. By definition, the light rays emitted by directional light have a constant direction and are not

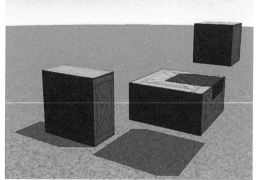

FIGURE 6.28    A scene without shadows (left) and with shadows (right).

affected by distance; these qualities will also be present in the corresponding shadows. A point will be considered to be "in shadow" (or more precisely, in the shadow of another object) when there is another point along the direction of the light ray that is closer to the light source. In this case, the closer point is also said to have "cast a shadow" on the more distant point. The colors corresponding to a point in shadow will be darkened during the rendering process, which simulates a reduced amount of light impacting the surface at that point.

The data required for creating shadows will be gathered in a rendering pass called a *shadow pass*, performed before the main scene is rendered. The purpose of the shadow pass is to render the scene from the position and direction of the light source to determine what points are "visible" to the light. The visible points are considered to be illuminated by light rays, and no further shading will be applied. The points that are not visible from the light are considered to be in shadow and will be darkened.

Recall that during the pixel processing stage of the graphics pipeline, for each pixel in the rendered image, the depth buffer stores the distance from the viewer to the corresponding point in the scene. This information is used during the rendering process when a fragment would correspond to the same pixel as a previously processed fragment, in order to determine whether the new fragment is closer to the viewer, in which case the new fragment's data overwrites the data currently stored in the color and depth buffers. In the final rendered image of a scene, each pixel corresponds to a fragment that is the shortest distance from the camera, as compared to all other fragments that would correspond to the same pixel. This "shortest distance" information from the depth buffer can be used to generate shadows according to the following algorithm (called *shadow mapping*):

- Render the scene from the point of view of the directional light and store the depth buffer values.

- When rendering the main scene, calculate the distance from each fragment to the light source. If this distance is greater than the corresponding stored depth value, then the fragment is not closest to the light source, and therefore it is in shadow.

FIGURE 6.29  A scene including a directional light and shadows.

The depth buffer values that are generated during the shadow pass will be stored in a texture called the *depth texture*, which will contain grayscale colors at each pixel based on the corresponding depth value. Due to the default configuration of the depth test function, depth values near zero (corresponding to dark colors) represent nearby points. Conversely, depth values near zero (corresponding to light colors) represent more distant points. To help visualize these concepts, Figure 6.29 depicts a scene, including shadows cast by a directional light, rendered from the point of view of a perspective camera. The position and direction of the directional light are indicated by a directional light helper object. On the left side of Figure 6.30 we see the same scene, rendered by a camera using an orthographic projection, from the point of view of the directional light. For convenience, this secondary

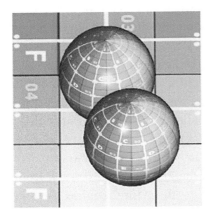 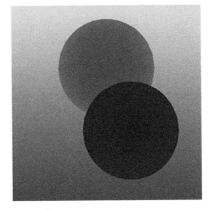

FIGURE 6.30  A scene viewed from a directional light (left) and the corresponding depth texture (right).

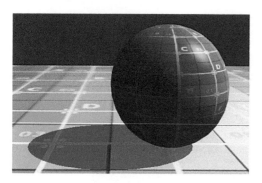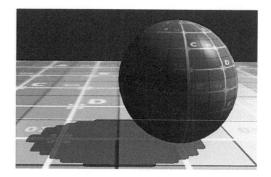

FIGURE 6.31    Shadow pixelation artifacts.

camera will be referred to as the *shadow camera*. Note that no shadows are visible from this point of view; indeed, the defining characteristic of shadows is that they are exactly the set of points *not* visible from the shadow camera. The right side of Figure 6.30 shows the corresponding grayscale depth texture that will be produced during the shadow pass.

When rendering shadows with this approach, there are some limitations and constraints that should be kept in mind when setting up a scene. First, the appearance of the shadows is affected by the resolution of the depth texture; low resolutions will lead to shadows that appear pixelated, as illustrated in Figure 6.31. Second, the points in the scene that may cast shadows or be in shadow are precisely those points contained in the volume rendered by the shadow camera. One could increase the viewing bounds of the shadow camera to encompass a larger area, but unless the resolution of the depth texture is increased proportionally, there will be fewer pixels corresponding to each unit of world space, and the pixelation of the shadows will increase. To reduce shadow pixelation, one typically adjusts the shadow camera bounding parameters to closely fit the region of the scene involving shadows.

A point will be considered to be in shadow when two conditions are true: the surface must be facing the light at the point in question, and the distance from the point to the light must be greater than the value stored in the depth texture (indicating that a closer point exists and is casting a shadow on this point). The first of these conditions can be checked by examining the angle between the light direction and the normal vector to the surface at that point. If the cosine of that angle is greater than zero, then the angle is less than 90°, indicating that the surface is indeed facing the light at that point. (Since this calculation requires interpolated normal vectors for each fragment, the shadow calculations will only be implemented for the Lambert and Phong materials in this framework.)

To check the second condition, depth information must be extracted from the depth texture. Selecting the correct point from the depth texture requires us to know where a particular fragment would appear if it were being rendered during the shadow pass. Calculating this information during the normal rendering pass requires access to the information stored by the shadow camera object (its projection matrix and view matrix). Position calculations are most efficiently handled in a vertex shader, where the standard model/view/projection matrix multiplications are typically performed. The result will be in clip space coordinates, where the coordinates of points in the visible region are each in the range from –1 to 1. Once this calculation is performed on the vertex position, this value (which will be called the *shadow position*, as it is derived from shadow camera data) will be transmitted to the fragment shader and interpolated for each fragment.

In the fragment shader, the coordinates of the shadow position variable can be used to calculate and recover the required depth values. The x and y coordinates can be used to derive the coordinates of the corresponding pixel in the rendered image (as viewed from the shadow camera), or more importantly, the UV coordinates corresponding to that pixel, which are needed to retrieve a value stored in the depth texture. Since clip space coordinates range from –1 to 1, while UV coordinates range from zero to one, the shadow position coordinates need to be transformed accordingly before sampling the texture. Recall that the value retrieved from the depth texture represents the distance to the closest point (relative to the shadow camera frame of reference), and is in the range from zero to one. The distance from the fragment being processed to the shadow camera is stored in the z component of the shadow position variable. After converting this value to the range from zero to one, you can compare the distance from the fragment to the shadow camera with the closest stored distance to the shadow camera. If the fragment distance is greater, then a different point is closer to the shadow camera along this direction, in which case the fragment is considered to be in shadow and its color will be adjusted accordingly.

With this knowledge, you are now prepared to add shadow effects to the graphics framework.

## 6.9.2 Adding Shadows to the Framework

The steps involved in adding shadow casting functionality to the graphics framework are similar to the steps involved in adding the lighting effects at the beginning of this chapter. First, a special material called **DepthMaterial** will be created to generate the depth texture during the shadow pass. Then a **Shadow** class will be created to store the objects necessary for shadow calculations (including a reference to the directional light, the shadow camera, and a render target to be used during the shadow pass). In the **LambertMaterial** and **PhongMaterial** classes, a shadow struct will be defined to group related variables used in the shadow calculations. Then the vertex and fragment shaders of both these materials will be updated with additional uniform objects and code. The **Uniform** class will be extended to store **Shadow** objects and upload data to the corresponding fields in a uniform shadow variable in the shaders. Finally, the **Renderer** class will be updated with a new enableShadows method, which will generate a **Shadow** object and cause a shadow pass to be performed by the **render** method before the main scene is rendered. As usual, after the framework classes have been updated, you will create an interactive scene to verify that everything works as expected.

To begin, you will first create the **DepthMaterial** class. In the **material** package, create a new Java class named **DepthMaterial**, and two new shader files named **DepthMaterial.frag** and **depthMaterial.vert**. Inside the newly created class, insert the following code:

```java
package material;

public class DepthMaterial extends Material
{
    public DepthMaterial()
    {
        super(
            "./src/material/DepthMaterial.vert",
            "./src/material/DepthMaterial.frag" );
        locateUniforms();
    }
}
```

Next, insert the following block of code inside the fragment shader file:

```glsl
out vec4 fragColor;
void main()
{
    float z = gl_FragCoord.z;
    fragColor = vec4(z, z, z, 1);
}
```

Note the use of the built-in GLSL variable **gl_FragCoord**, whose z coordinate stores the depth value. Since the fragment shader is using grayscale colors to encode depth values in the texture, any component of the texture color may be used later on to retrieve this "closest distance to light" information.

Finally, insert the following code into the vertex shader file:

```glsl
in vec3 vertexPosition;
uniform mat4 projectionMatrix;
uniform mat4 viewMatrix;
uniform mat4 modelMatrix;

void main()
{
    gl_Position = projectionMatrix * viewMatrix * modelMatrix
        * vec4(vertexPosition, 1.0);
}
```

Next, you will create a **Shadow** class to store the objects necessary for the shadow mapping algorithm previously described. For points in the scene that do not map to pixels within the depth texture, the pixel should be colored white, which will prevent shadows from being generated at that point. For this reason, it is important to use the texture parameter wrap setting CLAMP_TO_BORDER; the default texture border color was already set to white in the **Texture** class, however, there needs to be two minor adjustments to the **Texture** class and the **RenderTarget** class.

In the **Texture** class in the **core** package, replace the code where the empty texture constructor is defined with the following:

```
// generate an empty texture - used by RenderTarget class
public Texture(int width, int height, int magFilter,
               int minFilter, int wrap)
{
    this.width = width;
    this.height = height;
    this.magFilter = magFilter;
    this.minFilter = minFilter;
    this.wrap = wrap;
    uploadData();
}

public Texture(int width, int height)
{
    this(width, height, GL_LINEAR, GL_LINEAR, GL_CLAMP_TO_EDGE);
}
```

Next, in the **RenderTarget** class, replace the constructor definition with the following:

```
public RenderTarget(Vector resolution, int magFilter,
                    int minFilter, int wrap)
```

Also replace the code where the empty texture is generated to be consistent with the modified texture constructor:

```
// generate an empty texture
texture = new Texture(width, height,
    magFilter, minFilter, wrap);
```

Finally, include the following code directly below the first constructor:

```
public RenderTarget(Vector resolution)
{
    this(resolution, GL_NEAREST, GL_NEAREST, GL_CLAMP_TO_EDGE);
}
```

This concludes the modifications necessary to proceed with the **Shadow** class definition.

Now, to proceed, in the **light** package, create a Java class named **Shadow** with the following code:

```java
package light;

import static org.lwjgl.opengl.GL40.*;
import light.DirectionalLight;
import core.*;
import material.DepthMaterial;
import math.Vector;

public class Shadow
{
    public DirectionalLight lightSource;
    // camera used to render scene from perspective of light
    public Camera camera;
    // target used during the shadow pass,
    //    contains depth texture
    public RenderTarget renderTarget;
    // render only depth data to target texture
    public DepthMaterial material;
    // controls darkness of shadow
    public float strength;
    // used to avoid visual artifacts
    //    due to rounding/sampling precision issues
    public float bias;
    // constructor
    public Shadow(DirectionalLight lightSource,
        float strength, Vector resolution, float bias)
    {
        this.lightSource = lightSource;
        this.camera = new Camera();
        setCameraBounds(-5,5, -5,5, 0,20);
        this.lightSource.add( this.camera );

        this.renderTarget = new RenderTarget( resolution,
            GL_NEAREST, GL_NEAREST, GL_CLAMP_TO_BORDER );
        this.material = new DepthMaterial();
        this.strength = strength;
        this.bias = bias;
    }

    public Shadow(DirectionalLight lightSource)
    {
        this(lightSource, 0.5f, new Vector(512,512), 0.01f);
    }
```

```
public void setCameraBounds(double left, double right,
        double bottom, double top, double near, double far)
{
    camera.setOrthographic(left, right,
        bottom, top, near, far);
}

public void updateInternal()
{
    camera.updateViewMatrix();
    material.uniforms.get("viewMatrix").data =
        camera.viewMatrix;
    material.uniforms.get("projectionMatrix").data =
        camera.projectionMatrix;
}
}
```

Next, you will need to update both the Lambert and Phong materials to support shadow effects. The following modifications should be made to both the **LambertMaterial** and **PhongMaterial** classes in the **material** package.

In the initialize methods, add the following uniform object before **locateUniforms** is called:

```
addUniform("bool", "useShadow", 0);
```

Next, add the following method to both classes:

```
public void enableShadow()
{
    uniforms.get("useShadow").data = 1;
    addUniform("Shadow", "shadow0", null);
    locateUniforms();
}
```

Since shadow-related calculations will take place in both the vertex and fragment shader, in the code for each, add the following struct definition before the **main** function:

```
struct Shadow
{
    // direction of light that casts shadow
    vec3 lightDirection;

    // data from camera that produces depth texture
    mat4 projectionMatrix;
    mat4 viewMatrix;
```

```
    // texture that stores depth values from shadow camera
    sampler2D depthTexture;

    // regions in shadow multiplied by (1-strength)
    float strength;

    // reduces unwanted visual artifacts
    float bias;
};
```

After the Shadow struct definition in the vertex shader, add the following variables:

```
uniform bool useShadow;
uniform Shadow shadow0;
out vec3 shadowPosition0;
```

In the vertex shader **main** function, add the following code, which calculates the position of the vertex relative to the shadow camera.

```
if (useShadow)
{
    vec4 temp0 = shadow0.projectionMatrix * shadow0.viewMatrix *
        modelMatrix * vec4(vertexPosition, 1);
    shadowPosition0 = vec3( temp0 );
}
```

After the Shadow struct definition in the fragment shader, add the following variables:

```
uniform bool useShadow;
uniform Shadow shadow0;
in vec3 shadowPosition0;
```

In the fragment shader **main** function, before the value of **fragColor** is set, add the following code, which determines if the surface is facing toward the light direction, and determines if the fragment is in the shadow of another object. When both of these conditions are true, the fragment color is darkened by multiplying the **color** variable by a value based on the shadow strength parameter.

```
if (useShadow)
{
    // determine if surface is facing towards light direction
    float cosAngle = dot( normalize(normal),
                          -normalize(shadow0.lightDirection) );
    bool facingLight = (cosAngle > 0.01);
```

```
// convert range [-1, 1] to range [0, 1]
//   for UV coordinate and depth information
vec3 shadowCoord = ( shadowPosition0.xyz + 1.0 ) / 2.0;
float closestDistanceToLight = texture2D(
            shadow0.depthTexture, shadowCoord.xy).r;
float fragmentDistanceToLight = clamp(shadowCoord.z, 0, 1);
// determine if fragment lies in shadow of another object
bool inShadow = ( fragmentDistanceToLight >
                closestDistanceToLight + shadow0.bias );

if (facingLight && inShadow)
{
    float s = 1.0 - shadow0.strength;
    color *= vec4(s, s, s, 1);
}
}
```

Now that the contents of the **Shadow** class and the related struct are understood, you will update the **Uniform** class to upload this data as needed. In the **Uniform** class in the **core** package, in the **locateVariable** method, add the following code as a new case within the **if-else** block:

```
else if (dataType.equals("Shadow"))
{
    variableRefMap = new HashMap<String, Integer>();
    variableRefMap.put("lightDirection",
        glGetUniformLocation(programRef,
            variableName + ".lightDirection") );
    variableRefMap.put("projectionMatrix",
        glGetUniformLocation(programRef,
            variableName + ".projectionMatrix") );
    variableRefMap.put("viewMatrix",
        glGetUniformLocation(programRef,
            variableName + ".viewMatrix") );
    variableRefMap.put("depthTexture",
        glGetUniformLocation(programRef,
            variableName + ".depthTexture") );
    variableRefMap.put("strength",
        glGetUniformLocation(programRef,
            variableName + ".strength") );
    variableRefMap.put("bias",
        glGetUniformLocation(programRef,
            variableName + ".bias") );
}
```

Then, in the **Uniform** class **uploadData** method, add the following code as a new case within the **if-else** block. (The texture unit reference value was chosen to be a value not typically used by other textures.)

```
else if (dataType.equals("Shadow"))
{
    Shadow S = (Shadow)data;
    Vector dir = S.lightSource.getDirection();

    glUniform3f( variableRefMap.get("lightDirection"),
        (float)dir.values[0], (float)dir.values[1],
        (float)dir.values[2] );

    glUniformMatrix4fv( variableRefMap.get("projectionMatrix"),
            true, S.camera.projectionMatrix.flatten() );

    glUniformMatrix4fv( variableRefMap.get("viewMatrix"),
            true, S.camera.viewMatrix.flatten() );

    // configure depth texture
    int textureObjectRef = S.renderTarget.texture.textureRef;
    int textureUnitRef = 15;
    glActiveTexture( GL_TEXTURE0 + textureUnitRef );
    glBindTexture( GL_TEXTURE_2D, textureObjectRef );
    glUniform1i( variableRefMap.get("depthTexture"),
        textureUnitRef );

    glUniform1f( variableRefMap.get("strength"), S.strength );
    glUniform1f( variableRefMap.get("bias"), S.bias );
}
```

The final set of changes and additions involve the **Renderer** class. To begin, add the two following properties to the class level:

```
public boolean shadowsEnabled;
public Shadow shadowObject;
```

Add the two following methods which will enable the shadow pass that will soon be added to the **render** method:

```
public void enableShadows(DirectionalLight shadowLight,
    float strength, Vector resolution, float bias)
{
    shadowsEnabled = true;
    shadowObject = new Shadow(shadowLight,
        strength, resolution, bias);
}
```

```
public void enableShadows(DirectionalLight shadowLight)
{
    enableShadows(shadowLight, 0.5f, new Vector(512,512), 0.01f);
}
```

The main addition to the **Renderer** class is the shadow pass. The collection of mesh objects in the scene must be gathered into a list before the shadow pass; therefore, the corresponding block of code will be moved, as shown in what follows.

During the shadow pass, the framebuffer stored in the shadow render target will be used, and buffers cleared as normal. If there are no objects in the scene to generate a color for a particular pixel in the depth texture, then that pixel should be colored white, which will prevent a shadow from being generated at that location, and therefore this is used as the clear color for the shadow pass. Much of the remaining code that follows is a simplified version of a standard render pass, as only one material (the depth material) will be used, and only triangle-based meshes need to be included at this stage. To proceed, at the beginning of the **render** method, add the following code:

```
// shadow pass start -----------------------------
if (shadowsEnabled)
{
    // set render target properties
    glBindFramebuffer(GL_FRAMEBUFFER,
        shadowObject.renderTarget.framebufferRef);
    glViewport(0,0, shadowObject.renderTarget.width,
        shadowObject.renderTarget.height);

    // set default color to white,
    //    used when no objects present to cast shadows
    glClearColor(1,1,1,1);

    glClear(GL_COLOR_BUFFER_BIT);
    glClear(GL_DEPTH_BUFFER_BIT);

    // reset original clear color
    glClearColor(
        (float)clearColor.values[0], (float)clearColor.values[1],
        (float)clearColor.values[2], (float)clearColor.values[3] );

    // everything in the scene gets rendered with depthMaterial
    //    so only need to call glUseProgram & set matrices once
    glUseProgram( shadowObject.material.programRef );

    shadowObject.updateInternal();

    for (Mesh mesh : meshList)
    {
```

```
                // skip invisible meshes
                if (!mesh.visible)
                    continue;

                // only triangle-based meshes cast shadows
                if (mesh.material.drawStyle != GL_TRIANGLES)
                    continue;

                // bind VAO
                glBindVertexArray( mesh.vaoRef );

                // update transform data
                shadowObject.material.uniforms.get("modelMatrix").data =
                    mesh.getWorldMatrix();

                // update uniforms (matrix data) in shadow material
                for (Uniform uniform :
                        shadowObject.material.uniforms.values())
                    uniform.uploadData();

                // no render settings to update

                glDrawArrays( GL_TRIANGLES, 0,
                    mesh.geometry.vertexCount );
        }
    }
    // shadow pass end -----------------------------
```

Finally, in the standard rendering part of the **render** method, the **Shadow** object needs to be copied into the data variable of the corresponding **Uniform** object, when shadow rendering has been enabled and if such a uniform exists in the material of the mesh being drawn at that stage. To implement this, in the final **for** loop that iterates over **meshList**, in the section where mesh material uniform data is set and before the **uploadData** method is called, add the following code:

```
// add shadow data if enabled and used by shader
if ( shadowsEnabled &&
        mesh.material.uniforms.containsKey("shadow0") )
    mesh.material.uniforms.get("shadow0").data = shadowObject;
```

This completes the additions to the **Renderer** class in particular, and support for rendering shadows in the graphics framework in general. You are now ready to create an example to produce a scene similar to that illustrated in Figure 6.28.

In your main project directory, create a new class named **Test_6_5** containing the following code, presented here in its entirety for simplicity. Note the inclusion of commented out code, which can be used to illustrate the dynamic capabilities of shadow rendering, render the scene from the shadow camera perspective, or display the depth texture on a mesh within the scene.

```java
import core.*;
import math.*;
import geometry.*;
import material.*;
import extras.*;
import effects.*;
import light.*;

public class Test_6_5 extends Base
{
    public Renderer renderer;
    public Scene scene;
    public Camera camera;
    public MovementRig rig;

    public DirectionalLight dirLight;

    public void initialize()
    {
        renderer = new Renderer();
        renderer.setClearColor( new Vector(0.25, 0.25, 0.25, 1) );
        scene = new Scene();
        camera = new Camera();
        camera.setPerspective(60, 4/3f, 0.1, 1000);

        rig = new MovementRig();
        rig.attach( camera );
        rig.setPosition( new Vector(0, 2, 5) );
        scene.add( rig );

        AmbientLight ambLight = new AmbientLight(
            new Vector(0.2, 0.2, 0.2) );
        scene.add( ambLight );

        dirLight = new DirectionalLight(
            new Vector(1,1,1), new Vector(-1,-1,0) );
        dirLight.setPosition( new Vector(2,4,0) );
        scene.add( dirLight );
        Mesh directHelper = new DirectionalLightHelper(dirLight);
        dirLight.add( directHelper );

        Geometry sphereGeometry = new SphereGeometry();
        LambertMaterial shadowMaterial = new LambertMaterial(
            new Texture("images/grid.png") );
        shadowMaterial.enableShadow();
```

```java
        Mesh sphere1 = new Mesh(sphereGeometry, shadowMaterial);
        sphere1.setPosition( new Vector(-2, 1, 0) );
        scene.add( sphere1 );

        Mesh sphere2 = new Mesh(sphereGeometry, shadowMaterial);
        sphere2.setPosition( new Vector(1, 2.2, -0.5) );
        scene.add( sphere2 );

        renderer.enableShadows( dirLight );

        /*
        // optional: render depth texture to mesh in scene.
        //   note: this object may also cast a shadow in scene.
        Texture depthTexture =
            renderer.shadowObject.renderTarget.texture;
        Mesh shadowDisplay = new Mesh(
            new RectangleGeometry(),
            new TextureMaterial(depthTexture) );
        shadowDisplay.setPosition( new Vector(-1,3,0) );
        scene.add( shadowDisplay );
        */

        Mesh floor = new Mesh( new RectangleGeometry(20, 20),
            shadowMaterial );
        floor.rotateX(-3.14/2, true);
        scene.add(floor);
    }

    public void update()
    {
        // view dynamic shadows;
        //   need to increase shadow camera range
        Vector target = new Vector(-2, 0, 2*Math.sin(time));
        dirLight.lookAt(target);

        rig.update(input, deltaTime);
        renderer.render( scene, camera );

        /*
        // optional: render scene from shadow camera
        Camera shadowCam = renderer.shadowObject.camera;
        renderer.render( scene, shadowCam );
        */
    }

    // driver method
    public static void main(String[] args)
```

```
    {
        new Test_6_5().run(800, 600);
    }
}
```

At this point, you can now easily include shadows in your scenes. If desired, you can also include them together with the other lighting-based effects implemented throughout this chapter, to create scenes showcasing a variety of techniques as illustrated in Figure 6.1.

## 6.10 SUMMARY AND NEXT STEPS

In this chapter, you learned about different types of lighting, light sources, illumination models, and shading models. After creating ambient, directional, and point light objects, you added normal vector data to geometric objects, and used them in conjunction with light data to implement lighting with flat-shaded, Lambert, and Phong materials. You used normal vector data encoded in bump map textures to add the illusion of surface detail to geometric objects with light. Then you extended the set of postprocessing effects, enabling the creation of light bloom and glow effects. Finally, you added shadow rendering capabilities to the framework, which built on all the concepts you have learned throughout this chapter.

While this may be the end of this book, hopefully it is just the beginning of your journey into computer graphics. As you have seen, LWJGL and OpenGL can be used together to create a framework that enables you to rapidly build applications featuring interactive, animated 3D scenes with highly sophisticated graphics. The goal of this book has been to guide you through the creation of this framework, providing you with a complete understanding of the theoretical underpinnings and practical coding techniques involved, so that you can not only make use of this framework, but also further extend it to create any 3D scene you can imagine. Good luck to you in your future endeavors!

# Index